SEND THEM HERE

MCGILL-QUEEN'S REFUGEE AND FORCED MIGRATION STUDIES

Series editors: Megan Bradley and James Milner

Forced migration is a local, national, regional, and global challenge with profound political and social implications. Understanding the causes and consequences of, and possible responses to, forced migration requires careful analysis from a range of disciplinary perspectives, as well as interdisciplinary dialogue.

The purpose of the McGill-Queen's Refugee and Forced Migration Studies series is to advance in-depth examination of diverse forms, dimensions, and experiences of displacement, including in the context of conflict and violence, repression and persecution, and disasters and environmental change. The series will explore responses to refugees, internal displacement, and other forms of forced migration to illuminate the dynamics surrounding forced migration in global, national, and local contexts, including Canada, the perspectives of displaced individuals and communities, and the connections to broader patterns of human mobility. Featuring research from fields including politics, international relations, law, anthropology, sociology, geography, and history, the series highlights new and critical areas of enquiry within the field, especially conversations across disciplines and from the perspective of researchers in the global South, where the majority of forced migration unfolds. The series benefits from an international advisory board made up of leading scholars in refugee and forced migration studies.

1 The Criminalization of Migration
   Context and Consequences
   Edited by Idil Atak and James C. Simeon

2 A National Project
   Syrian Refugee Resettlement in Canada
   Edited by Leah K. Hamilton, Luisa Veronis, and Margaret Walton-Roberts

3 Strangers to Neighbours
   Refugee Sponsorship in Context
   Edited by Shauna Labman and Geoffrey Cameron

4 Send Them Here
   Religion, Politics, and Refugee Resettlement in North America
   Geoffrey Cameron

Send Them Here

Religion, Politics, and Refugee Resettlement in North America

GEOFFREY CAMERON

McGill-Queen's University Press
Montreal & Kingston · London · Chicago

© McGill-Queen's University Press 2021

ISBN 978-0-2280-0550-6 (cloth)
ISBN 978-0-2280-0551-3 (paper)
ISBN 978-0-2280-0599-5 (ePDF)
ISBN 978-0-2280-0600-8 (ePUB)

Legal deposit first quarter 2021
Bibliothèque nationale du Québec

Printed in Canada on acid-free paper that is 100% ancient forest free (100% post-consumer recycled), processed chlorine free

This book has been published with the help of a grant from the Canadian Federation for the Humanities and Social Sciences, through the Awards to Scholarly Publications Program, using funds provided by the Social Sciences and Humanities Research Council of Canada.

We acknowledge the support of the Canada Council for the Arts.

Nous remercions le Conseil des arts du Canada de son soutien.

Library and Archives Canada Cataloguing in Publication

Title: Send them here: religion, politics, and refugee resettlement in North America / Geoffrey Cameron.

Names: Cameron, Geoffrey, author.

Series: McGill-Queen's refugee and forced migration studies; 4.

Description: Series statement: McGill-Queen's refugee and forced migration studies; 4 | Includes bibliographical references and index.

Identifiers: Canadiana (print) 20200337483 | Canadiana (ebook) 20200337599 | ISBN 9780228005506 (cloth) | ISBN 9780228005513 (paper) | ISBN 9780228005995 (ePDF) | ISBN 9780228006008 (ePUB)

Subjects: LCSH: Refugees—Government policy—Canada—History—20th century. | LCSH: Canada—Emigration and immigration—Government policy—History—20th century. | LCSH: Refugees—Government policy—United States—History—20th century. | LCSH: United States—Emigration and immigration—Government policy—History—20th century.

Classification: LCC JV7233 .C27 2021 | DDC 325.71—dc23

This book was typeset by Marquis Interscript in 10.5/13 Sabon.

For Clara and Theodore

Contents

Acknowledgments ix

Abbreviations xiii

Introduction 3

1 A Moral Alternative to Power Politics: Why Religious Groups Mobilized for Refugee Resettlement 26

2 Overcoming Restriction: Religious Groups and the Post-War Refugee Policy Process 58

3 A Continuous Chain of Efforts: Issue Networks and Policy Communities 86

4 Shifting Alliances: Refugees, Human Rights, and Policy Reform 112

5 Coming Full Circle: Indochina, Legislative Reform, and the Post-War Legacy 138

Conclusion 163

Notes 171

Bibliography 213

Index 231

Acknowledgments

The seeds of this book were planted in June 2012, two days after our daughter took her first steps. I was invited to consult about writing an historical account of the Iranian Bahá'í refugee resettlement program in the 1980s. Douglas Martin helped to lead the Canadian program, which was not widely publicized at the time, and he was looking for someone to write about it. This meeting led to a magazine article in the *Literary Review of Canada* and then to an academic and policy symposium at the University of Ottawa. It sparked my interest in refugee-resettlement policy and led me deeper into questions about the origins and development of this policy. I wish to thank Gerald Filson for arranging that first meeting, and Douglas Martin, Alex Frame, and Mona Mojgani for helping with the research that led to the *Literary Review of Canada* article.

I undertook the research for this book as part of my doctoral dissertation in the Department of Political Science at the University of Toronto. The work was guided by my supervisor, Randall Hansen, who asked all of the right questions to advance my thinking and writing. I could not have asked for a better mentor along the way. Phil Triadafilopoulos has been a significant influence on my thinking since the beginning of my doctoral studies. I was able to try out early ideas in his seminars, and I was grateful to have his continuing advice as a member of my examination committee. I owe a special thanks to the brilliant Audrey Macklin, who stepped outside of her disciplinary home to advise and encourage my research. Rob Vipond and James Milner were other members of my examination committee, and I could not have been happier to discuss this research with these two generous and engaged scholars. I was also fortunate to study with a group of intelligent scholars whose vision of a better world continues to inspire me: Kiran Banerjee, Nathan Lemphers, Lama Mourad, Lior Scheffer, Emily Scott, and Craig Damien Smith.

Throughout this research, I benefited from conversations with a number of people who have been (and continue to be) actively engaged in refugee policy discourse. In the United States, this includes Shaina Ward of Refugee Council USA, Liza Lieberman of HIAS, Jen Smyers and Will Haney of Church World Service, and Todd Scribner of the United States Conference of Catholic Bishops. In Canada, Howard Adelman, Heather MacDonald, Brian Dyck, Martin Mark, Raphael Girard, Gordon Barnett, and Bill Janzen shared their thoughts and recollections with me. I owe a special debt of thanks to Mike Molloy, a former refugee policy mandarin-turned-historian, who encouraged me from the start, welcomed me to his home, shared boxes of documents, and read my dissertation from start to finish. Shauna Labman and Laura Madokoro blazed a trail of research I happily followed. My collaboration with Shauna on a parallel project on private refugee sponsorship in Canada inspired my thinking and helped to connect me to an impressive community of refugee-studies scholars across the country.

Throughout much of the research and writing process, I was associated with a migration research group of the Institute for Studies in Global Prosperity, and the work of that group shaped my thinking around many fundamental questions and concepts. Haleh Arbab, Keri Schewel, Ben Schewel, Katyana Melic, and others have been friends and compatriots along this journey. Naisohn Arfai, Julia Berger, Eric Farr, Nazila Ghanea, Holly Hanson, Michael Karlberg, and Todd Smith have also been steady influences and sources of advice.

Aspects of this book were presented to a number of workshops and seminars hosted by: Craig Damien Smith with the Global Migration Lab at the Munk School of Global Affairs and Public Policy; Sara Pavan with the Migration, Citizenship and Democratic Participation workshop at Queen's University; Megan Bradley with the McGill Refugee Research Group at McGill University; and Jack Lucas and Rob Vipond with the Toronto Political Development Workshop at the University of Toronto. At the latter workshop, Gene Zubovich made a number of especially helpful comments as a respondent to my paper.

On a more practical note, I owe particular thanks to the librarians who helped me navigate boxes upon boxes of archival material. In no particular order, thank you to: Maria Mazzenga (Catholic University of America), Mary Brown (Center for Migration Studies), Lisa Jacobsen (Presbyterian Historical Society), Albert King (Rutgers University), David Langbart (U.S. National Archives), Adam Berenbak (Center for Legislative Archives – U.S. National Archives), Joseph Jackson (Library of Congress), Jennifer S. Comins and Betty Bolden (Butler Library, Columbia University), Catherine Butler and Alexandra McEwen (Library and Archives Canada), and Janice Rosen (Canadian Jewish Congress).

At McGill-Queen's University Press, I have Kyla Madden to thank for her initial encouragement to submit the manuscript to the Press when I was still only a few chapters into my dissertation. She helped to steer the manuscript through its evolution into a book, and her astute comments and notes along the way were a profound source of encouragement. Thank you, also, to James Milner and Megan Bradley for including this book in the McGill-Queen's Refugee and Forced Migration Studies Series.

The research been supported by generous funding from the Social Sciences and Humanities Research Council and the Pierre Elliott Trudeau Foundation. My cohort of 2014 Trudeau Scholars inspired and sustained me over the challenging years of research and writing.

I am so grateful to the National Spiritual Assembly of the Baha'is of Canada for their unwavering support of my studies, allowing flexibility in my work with the Office of Public Affairs during the years I was researching and writing this book. To my current and former colleagues, Karen McKye, Gerald Filson, Corinne Box, Susie Tamas, Andrea Salguero, Kylych Kubatbekov, Cedric Gaber, Ashraf Rushdy, Delaram Erfanian, and Laura Friedmann – thank you for accepting the extra burdens this must have imposed from time to time.

And finally, my family – to whom this book is dedicated. To Mom and Dad, for providing the strong foundation upon which all of my pursuits have been built, and for continuing to help in so many ways to create the time and space for this work. To Lita, for never doubting this was a good idea and for having faith in my abilities during times of uncertainty. For Clara and Theodore: I hope this makes you proud.

Abbreviations

ACCR	American Christian Committee for Refugees
ACVA	American Council of Voluntary Agencies for Foreign Service
AFL	American Federation of Labor
AJC	American Jewish Committee
CCC	Canadian Council of Churches
CCCRR	Canadian Christian Council for Resettlement of Refugees
CCDP	Citizens Committee on Displaced Persons
CCIR	Citizens Commission on Indochinese Refugees
CCR	Catholic Committee for Refugees
CIO	Committee of Industrial Organization
CJC	Canadian Jewish Congress
CLWR	Canadian Lutheran World Relief
CRS	Catholic Relief Services
CWS	Church World Service
DP	Displaced Person
DPC	Displaced Persons Commission
FCC	Federal Council of Churches
HEW	Department of Health, Education and Welfare
HIAS	Hebrew Immigrant Aid Society
ICEM	Intergovernmental Committee for European Migration
ICMC	International Catholic Migration Commission
INA	Immigration and Nationality Act
IRC	International Rescue Committee
IRO	International Refugee Organization
JDC	Jewish Joint Distribution Committee
JIAS	Jewish Immigrant Aid Services
MCCC	Mennonite Central Committee of Canada

NCC	National Council of Churches
NCWC	National Catholic Welfare Conference
NSC	National Security Council
PCHRR	President's Committee for Hungarian Refugee Relief
RRA	Refugee Relief Act (1953)
RSS	Rural Settlement Society
UJRA	United Jewish Relief Agencies
UNHCR	United Nations High Commissioner for Refugees
USEP	United States Escapee Program
USNA	United Service for New Americans
WCC	World Council of Churches
WRS	War Relief Services
WRY	World Refugee Year

SEND THEM HERE

Introduction

As the Allied armies advanced across Germany and Austria in the spring of 1945, they were accompanied by millions of people. A U.S. State Department memo described the situation as "[one] of the greatest population movements in history taking place before our eyes."[1] These refugees included Jews who had been in hiding and those liberated from concentration camps, millions of forced labourers from Eastern Europe, Russian prisoners of war, and others who had fled the advance of the Soviet army. Most of them returned home or settled locally, but those who sought emigration elsewhere found the doors closed. Refugees who made it through the war had to survive the conditions of camps in Germany, Italy, and Austria until other states opened their borders. Overseas resettlement became the only viable solution.

Refugee advocates in North America soon championed the cause of resettlement, against the initial resistance of their governments. An influential editorial published in 1946 in *Life Magazine* captured a rallying cry for these advocates: "Send Them Here." In response to its publication, the ranking member of the House Judiciary Committee in the United States, Emanuel Celler (D-NY), wrote to the editor of the magazine: "Your plea, 'Send Them Here,' should be re-echoed throughout the land so that a strong, healthy public opinion may be developed to break down the bias, bigotry and ignorance which bar reform in our immigration statutes ... I stand ready and willing to cooperate with church and layman groups in a program of public education and Congressional action to open our doors in welcome to the oppressed and the homeless."[2] The call to "send them here" was echoed by American and Canadian refugee advocates who were often affiliated with religious groups. The interaction between these groups and policymakers in the period after the war, and during the subsequent decades, continued to shape the development of refugee law and policy.

This book is about the development of refugee-resettlement policy. Resettlement is an organized scheme to relocate refugees from a country of asylum to a more permanent place of residence. It contrasts with other policy responses to refugee crises, such as the provision of humanitarian aid, repatriation, temporary residence, or local integration. It also differs from the idea of orderly emigration for minorities living under hostile governments, which emerged during the interwar period.[3] The resettlement of displaced persons (DPs) after the Second World War marked the beginning of a policy that targeted refugees who had already moved from their country of origin and were in search of permanent status in a third country – the idea of resettlement as we know it today.

Resettlement has not received significant attention from political scientists, despite the fact that it is considered one of three durable solutions to refugee crises and a key element of global refugee policy. Although less than 1 per cent of the world's refugees are resettled each year – usually, fewer than 200,000 people – resettlement complements and reinforces measures to support local integration, refugee relief, and asylum processes around the globe.[4] Through resettlement, some of the world's most vulnerable refugees move in an orderly and managed process of immigration to a more secure future in more than two dozen countries. The two leading countries of resettlement have historically been the United States and Canada, which received 77 per cent of all resettled refugees between 2003 and 2017.[5] Both countries depend upon close cooperation with religious and voluntary groups in order to implement their programs. Although the coronavirus pandemic has virtually halted resettlement around the world, there is every reason to expect resettlement programs to restart along the path to recovery – whenever that may be.

This book is also about the role of religious groups in refugee policy. Religious and voluntary groups played a central role in humanitarian discourse, refugee relief, and immigrant aid long before the advent of refugee resettlement. Caroline Shaw's history of refugee relief in the "long-nineteenth century" shows how private organizations, often affiliated with religious communities, advanced a discourse of refugee aid that led to the institutionalization of this moral imperative.[6] As Andrew Thompson notes, the emergence of mid-twentieth-century

Christian internationalism promoted "the importance of nonstate, person-to-person international relations," which included a growing concern with refugee welfare.[7] During the interwar period, the refugee regime overseen by the League of Nations depended heavily upon the cooperation of private, voluntary organizations – many of which were engaged with helping co-religionists.[8] The contemporary involvement of religious groups in refugee resettlement, therefore, was preceded by a legacy of advocacy and practical action aimed at refugee protection. One of the objectives of this book is to explain the role and influence of religious groups on refugee policy as resettlement evolved in the decades after the Second World War.

More generally, this book presents new answers to two puzzles within the comparative study of immigration and refugee policy. The first is why the United States and Canada have been such positive outliers with regard to the number of refugees they accept for resettlement each year. The total numbers themselves appear relatively low in relation to the global need, and yet the American and Canadian numbers have historically been much higher than those of other countries of comparable size or prosperity. The geographic distance of both countries from refugee-producing states gives them an unusual degree of choice about whether to admit refugees. These choices are almost entirely at the discretion of elected leaders, who face significant political disincentives to accept large numbers of refugees. Foreign policy in the context of Cold War politics is part of the reason for the development of refugee resettlement after the Second World War. However, as the evidence in later chapters will reveal, it is insufficient as an explanation for the evolution of policy and structures when other aligned states remained relatively closed. Acquiring an understanding of why and how these countries developed their resettlement policies is relevant to current international efforts to expand resettlement in dozens of other states.

A second puzzle is why the United States and Canada developed different, counter-intuitive structures to implement refugee resettlement. Canada created a system of private sponsorship, where hundreds of organized groups – together with small groups of citizens – are permitted to select refugees to resettle and pay a portion of their resettlement costs. Private sponsors in Canada have resettled over 300,000 refugees since the late 1970s under this unique partnership between government and civil-society groups.[9] Private sponsorship is intended to complement a government-funded resettlement program by increasing resettlement numbers, controlling the burden on public expenditure, and stimulating favourable public opinion.[10]

It is surprising that this resettlement policy developed in more statist Canada and not in the more individualist and liberal United States. As Seymour Lipset wrote in his comparative study of the United States and Canada: "Canada has been and is more class-aware, elitist, law-abiding, statist, collectively-oriented, and particularistic (group-oriented) society than the United States."[11] Indeed, Canada's pluralist arrangement stands in contrast with the history of a Canadian government that has been more willing to take a corporatist approach to public policy in other areas, even when it has involved close cooperation with religious groups.[12]

In the United States, refugee policy developed as a more corporatist arrangement: a small handful of religious groups (and later, a few non-religious groups) were subsidized to implement the state's resettlement quotas. Something closely resembling this arrangement is still in place today: nine voluntary groups (six of which are religious groups) implement the entirety of the U.S. resettlement program. This is surprising because the United States is a more classical liberal state that does not typically favour such coordinated and managed approaches to policy implementation. As Lipset observes, the United States has long been "the extreme example of a classical liberal or Lockean society, one that rejected the assumptions of the alliance of throne and alter ... [and] of communitarianism."[13] Indeed, the United States has been especially reluctant to embrace corporatism that ties the state into close partnership with religious groups, particularly the Catholic Church.[14]

My central argument is that the interaction of domestic religious groups with policy processes in the United States and Canada provided the central dynamics driving the development of resettlement policy between 1945 and 1980. Religious groups intervened in contingent decision-making and implementation processes during a critical juncture after the Second World War, helping to forge new institutional arrangements for resettlement. They encountered different decision-making venues in each country. In the United States, immigration policy was created by Congress and the White House, and the cooperation of religious groups was instrumental to the process of passing the first legislation to admit European refugees. The promise of participation by religious groups – especially Christian groups – in the resettlement process helped to secure votes from restrictionist lawmakers. In Canada, immigration policymaking was concentrated in the bureaucracy. Bureaucrats managing immigration programs were looking for workers to contribute to the economy, while religious groups sought sponsorship of family members and humanitarian cases. Private sponsorship was created as a reluctant partnership between bureaucrats and religious groups, who were granted privileges of sponsorship in exchange for assuming some financial responsibility for settlement.

As Jewish, Protestant, and Catholic groups participated in policy implementation, they formed networks that connected their leaders to decision makers in government. And as new Cold War refugee crises exploded in Hungary and elsewhere, these networks produced feedback effects that led temporary structures – first developed to resolve the post-war crisis – to become more permanent and path dependent. These structures evolved in the context of emerging conditions, but the basic templates of cooperation between the state and religious groups remained in place. Canada had private sponsorship – or some early form of it – and the United States had a handful of approved voluntary groups implementing its resettlement program. The provisional arrangements forged in both countries were finally established in law by the 1980s, creating the domestic legal foundations for contemporary refugee-resettlement policy.

These legal foundations are the 1980 Refugee Act in the United States and the 1976 Immigration Act in Canada. The 1980 Refugee Act affirmed the United Nations definition of a refugee, raised the annual ceiling for refugee admissions, and created new structures of coordination and consultation between Congress and the president. Crucially, it also established a clear framework for cooperation with religious and voluntary groups in the implementation of resettlement, with "full and adequate federal support for [their] resettlement efforts."[15] Canada enshrined its own system of resettlement in its 1976 Immigration Act. The act recognized "humanitarian migrants" as a separate class from the family or economic classes of migrants, and outlined processes for their selection. Its most innovative feature was arguably its provision for private sponsorship of any recognized refugee by "any body corporate ... and any group of Canadian citizens or permanent residents." The act came into force in 1978 and was the basis for the creation of the first sponsorship framework agreements with religious groups – beginning with the Mennonite Central Committee of Canada (MCCC) – in 1979.

This book traces the long path of policy and institutional development leading to the passage of these pieces of landmark legislation, with features that entrenched different modes of cooperation with religious and voluntary groups. It illuminates how refugee resettlement developed in the two leading destination countries, and demonstrates the crucial role played by religious groups and coalitions in policy implementation. In doing so, it reveals how these groups helped to create the institutional capacity and political will to resettle relatively large numbers of refugees.

EXPLANATORY SCHEMES

The fact political scientists have not devoted concentrated attention to refugee resettlement means that we do not have a robust explanation for its development. Instead, scholars studying the sources of refugee-resettlement policy have advanced arguments that fit within a number of different – and, to some extent, overlapping – explanatory schemes. These schemes encompass sets of arguments that follow similar structures, themes, and variables. I discuss five of these explanatory schemes below: ad hoc policy development, Cold War politics, international burden sharing, labour demand, and changing norms and ideas. This discussion is not meant to be exhaustive, or to present each scheme as mutually exclusive. My purpose is to highlight how different explanatory schemes organize the primary variables shaping policy development. The arguments advanced offer significant insights into the politics of refugee policy, ultimately pointing to interlocking variables that lead states to consider refugee resettlement. Each of them, however, regards the state as a generally unitary actor that follows a clear strategic rationale in calibrating its response to refugee crises. Statism and methodological nationalism are the norm.[16] As I argue below, to develop a satisfactory explanation for the development of refugee resettlement in the United States and Canada, it is necessary to move beyond a focus on the unitary state. The incorporation of domestic groups into analysis of the policy process gives added analytical leverage to efforts to understand how states respond to refugee crises and the way in which they design institutional arrangements to manage refugee resettlement.

Resettlement as Ad Hoc Policy

Within the first explanatory scheme, scholars argue that both the United States and Canada repeatedly improvised a series of disconnected ad hoc responses to refugee crises abroad in the period between the Second World War and the passage of major refugee legislation. For example, Anastasia Brown and Todd Scribner write, "For nearly 40 years after the War, the US commitment to refugee resettlement played out in an ad hoc fashion as it responded to emerging crises in different ways."[17] In his history of U.S. Cold War refugee policy, Carl Bon Tempo claims that all such programs "were ad hoc responses to refugee crises."[18] In a similar vein, Norman Zucker asserts: "Federal refugee resettlement policies and programs, like admission policy, developed in an ad hoc, reactive way."[19]

The literature on Canadian refugee policy also features arguments about the ad hoc development of that policy before the 1976 Immigration Act. Freda Hawkins argues that a cluster of refugee programs in the 1970s "made it plain to Canadian ... politicians and officials that the old, *ad hoc*, case-by-case approach to refugee admission was now useless by itself; and that a clearly defined refugee policy was a necessity."[20] Ninette Kelley and Michael Trebilcock argue that in the 1960s "refugees were admitted on an ad hoc basis."[21] Shauna Labman claims that Canada and the United States "shifted from *ad hoc* responses to specific crises to formal resettlement policies mainly in response to the refugee flows out of Indochina in the 1970s."[22]

In one respect, these arguments are accurate: decisions about the total number of refugees to admit, and from which countries, were made on a case-by-case basis. Furthermore, certain features of refugee policy after the Second World War were indeed ad hoc in the sense that they were provisional decisions made during a period of contingency and policy innovation. However, the admission and resettlement procedure itself followed a template of cooperation with religious and voluntary groups. Further, the development of procedures and policies was not spontaneously improvised in response to each Cold War-era refugee crisis. These policies and programs were indeed reactive, as most refugee policy tends to be, but they were not simply designed from scratch in responses to each new refugee crisis. As I show in the following chapters, there was a significant degree of continuity in the evolution of the policy frameworks themselves. If we see refugee policy as simply an ad hoc response to global crises, then it becomes almost impossible to arrive at any kind of explanation for policy development. It is necessary to separate the political decisions to admit refugees – which can appear to be ad hoc and improvised – from the development of policy and institutional frameworks.

Resettlement as Cold War Politics

Another set of arguments contends that the development of resettlement policy is a product of geopolitics. This assumes that, where states identify refugee resettlement with their strategic interest, they are more likely to adopt an expansive policy.[23] In his landmark study of immigration policy in the United States, Aristide Zolberg writes, "Refugee policy has tended to be driven by strategic considerations arising quite directly from the dynamics of the international political system: providing asylum to the victims of one's enemies was consistent with the imperatives of realpolitik in that it demonstrated the antagonist's evil ways and undermined its legitimacy."[24] As Michael Teitelbaum similarly notes, "refugee admissions policies have been guided ... by the belief that refugee outflows serve to embarrass and discredit adversary nations."[25] Matthew Price calls this the "political conception" of asylum, where states use refugee policy to express disapproval of rival states – for example, by resettling large numbers of refugees in order to publicize the "exit" of so many citizens and reinforce the perception that rival states are failing.[26] In the words of Zolberg, this approach to refugee resettlement understands "statecraft and humanitarianism" as going "hand in hand."[27]

The genesis of refugee resettlement was, indeed, deeply intertwined with foreign policy.[28] Geopolitics were an essential catalyst in these early decision-making processes. At the end of the war, refugees repatriated to the Soviet Union faced violence and persecution upon return. In one of the opening salvos of the Cold War, the United States and its Western allies created the International Refugee Organization (IRO) in 1946 and gave it a mandate to coordinate international refugee resettlement of DPs who refused repatriation. This action was taken despite Soviet objections and the reticence of potential destination countries (including the United States and Canada) to accept refugees.[29] During the Cold War, the conception of refugee resettlement in Western countries was further marked by strategic considerations. Most refugees resettled in Canada and the United States during this period came from European Communist countries.

Yet, although strategic considerations exerted a significant influence on the refugee-admission decisions of the United States and Canada during the period under review, resettlement was not simply the handmaiden of realist international politics. Strategic interests were only one dimension of the policy process that generated refugee resettlement. As Matthew Gibney notes, U.S. refugee policy during the Cold War was the product of an "ordered tension" between a foreign policy that demanded openness to particular refugees and democratic responsiveness to public opinion that wanted restriction.[30] In post-war Canada, the Department of External Affairs sought larger admissions of refugees in order for the country to assume new international responsibilities, while the Department of Mines and Resources (responsible for immigration[31]) preferred restrictions to preserve labour-market conditions favourable to native-born workers. Furthermore, political resistance to Jewish immigration in Quebec exerted another pressure on governments that relied on votes from that region to maintain power.[32] As Laura Madokoro has noted, the exclusion of Chinese refugees in Hong Kong from emerging resettlement programs in the United States and Canada reflected the "race thinking" that marked the early development of refugee policy.[33] Since the late nineteenth century, race had become progressively incorporated into the immigration laws of both countries in order to limit or restrict mobility from large regions of the world.[34] The reality, then, is complex. Although strategic considerations have been imprinted on resettlement policy, scholarship that advances this narrative often assumes a mechanical relationship between the two – when in fact pressures arising from within and outside of the government play an influential role in decisions about when, how, and which refugees are to be resettled.

Furthermore, foreign policy itself has had little discernible influence on the institutional arrangements created to manage arrivals. The Cold War may have helped to mobilize political constituencies to favour the admission of certain populations, but this does not generate a sufficient explanation for the diverging trajectories of durable policy frameworks in the United States and Canada.

Resettlement as Burden Sharing

A third set of arguments presents resettlement policy within the context of "burden sharing" between states. It is seen as the resolution to a collective-action problem which arises when states share an interest in resolving a refugee crisis but require cooperation on a fair distribution of refugees in order to address the crisis. Resolving such a crisis is a "public good," meaning that it is non-rivalrous and non-excludable: all parties benefit, whether they contribute through refugee admissions or not. Actors, therefore, want the benefits of collective action without bearing the costs of contributing, and so, without enforcement or the provision of selective incentives, collective action can fail. Astri Suhrke describes the problem in the following way: "Since public good benefits are by definition indivisible, if one state admits refugees, others will benefit from the greater international order that ensues regardless of their own admissions. As a result, all will be tempted to cheat by letting 'the other' state do the job."[35] This approach views resettlement as an action undertaken by a state to accept its "fair share" of a collective burden, with the intention of inducing others to do the same.

According to this approach, the decision to resettle refugees is typically the outcome of coordination between some number of states. Suhrke argues that mass resettlement following the Indochina refugee crisis was primarily due to a "hegemonic scheme" whereby the United States "put pressure on other states, set the rules for collective action, and took its own 'fair share.'"[36] Alexander Betts points to Comprehensive Plans of Action in Central America and Indochina, whereby the United Nations High Commissioner for Refugees (UNHCR) successfully facilitated international burden sharing in the case of long-standing refugee situations.[37] The convening power of a multilateral institution and the negotiation skills of its senior leadership were complemented by the use of development assistance to incentivize agreement by participating states to resettle refugees. These kinds of cases, however, are more the exception than the rule. Most resettled refugees do not move as a result of major international agreements of the kind analyzed by Betts and Suhrke.

In the United States and Canada, the concept of burden sharing has been an important dimension of the policy discourse. One of the early U.S. laws admitting refugees was the Fair Share Law of 1960, which specified that the United States would admit 25 per cent of the number of European refugees under the mandate of the UNHCR that were accepted by other states.[38] Early Canadian resettlement efforts were also influenced by the desire to assume a proper share of responsibility for resettling refugees in order to take a position of international leadership in the post-war order.[39] During the Cold War, internal Canadian policy documents reveal that one of the rationales for Canadian resettlement efforts was the hope that "Canada's continuing participation in the resettlement of refugees ... will have a significant impact in encouraging other nations to share the burden."[40]

Conceptions of fairness and international burden sharing exert a powerful influence on refugee policy discourse, but it is hard to specify exactly how they shape decision-making processes or the management of resettlement. Calling attention to states' international responsibilities can be a rhetorical weapon wielded by refugee advocates; or, alternatively, restrictionists can point to the shirking of responsibilities by other states as a reason to reduce admissions. Another problem is specifying precisely what constitutes a "fair share." Although scholars like James Hathaway, Alexander Neve, and Peter Shuck have tried to elaborate a legal system of equitable burden sharing, such schemes have not been implemented.[41] Even where international burden sharing is institutionalized to a degree, such as in the case of the European Union, it has fallen short of its aspirations and produced unintended (and, at times, perverse) consequences.[42] Therefore, in many cases burden sharing is more an aspiration or rhetorical tool than it is an overarching explanation for why or how states resettle refugees.

Resettlement as Labour-Market Policy

A fourth set of arguments connects resettlement to labour-market policy. They presume that, when the economy is expanding, states will resettle more refugees to meet labour-market demand, and when it is in recession they will reduce or shut down these admissions. There are several distinct lines of argument advanced within this explanatory scheme. The first is that capitalist states will be more open to immigration in general when economic conditions demand additional labour inputs.[43] This was clearly apparent in post-Second World War Canada, where initial resistance to admitting displaced people was eventually overcome as the post-war economic boom took hold.[44] Julie Gilmour notes that the 1947 government decision to admit DPs was "a win-win situation from the perspective of the Department of Labour, woods operators, and most refugees; Canada's resource industries could be expanded, Canada could hold its head up in international circles, and those displaced persons seeking to get as far away from the Soviet Union as possible found work in the Canadian bush."[45] Howard Adelman adds that the post-war admission of refugees was initially blocked by discrimination and antisemitism among bureaucrats, but "the key that unlocked the door to Canada was self-interest, for labour was needed to feed a rapidly expanding and industrializing economy."[46]

A second line of argument is that public opinion and interest groups tend to be opposed to redistributive policy vis-à-vis outsiders during periods of economic hardship. It is more difficult to pass measures that admit refugees when the public is more responsive to the spending and perceived job competition associated with higher refugee admissions.[47] In the post-war period, U.S. labour unions and veterans groups initially were opposed to admitting refugees and displaced persons out of concern that they would compete for jobs with American workers. However, as unemployment decreased, unions were persuaded to join in advocating for larger refugee admissions on humanitarian grounds.[48] Nevertheless, labour unions have generally not been – in the United States and Canada, anyway – significant actors in refugee policy networks since the 1950s.

Economic conditions are clearly relevant to the context in which refugee-resettlement decisions are made, but there is not a consistent correlation between economic cycles and the number of refugee admissions or the institutional arrangements created to support them. The major refugee movements during the period under consideration occurred within the context of refugee "crises," not economic expansion; such crises created a window of opportunity for advocacy groups and political decision makers to deliberate on the parameters and scale of refugee admissions. Although jobs, public opinion, and the economy are often part of this deliberation and discourse, the opening for debate is usually created by contingent events and driven by the preferences of the actors involved – and not by labour-market conditions themselves. At best, labour demand has been a variable within the policy debate over the number of admissions and, at times, the criteria of selection.

Resettlement as International Norm

A fifth explanatory scheme presents resettlement policy as a consequence of evolving norms and ideas taking root in liberal-democratic countries in the mid- to late twentieth century. Scholars such as Yasemin Nuhoglu Soysal and David Jacobsen contend that human rights norms upholding "universal personhood" have superseded citizenship-based rights, leading states to admit more immigrants than they might otherwise prefer.[49] International human rights, as Jacobsen argues, "are becoming the vehicle that is transforming the nation-state system ... [and] the basis of state legitimacy is shifting from the principles of sovereignty and national self-determination to international human rights."[50] To extend the argument, states resettle refugees to signal their support for international human rights and enhance their legitimacy within the international community.

A modified version of this argument contends that changing global norms generate a context in which domestic and international deliberation on immigration policy proceeds. Normative contexts, according to Triadafilos Triadafilopoulos, "embody a particular era's moral foundations."[51] They comprise a set of global structures, processes, and beliefs that exert an influence on domestic politics by "authorizing" particular policies and practices while helping to discredit others.[52] In other words, domestic decision making and judicial processes are carried out with a reflexive awareness of shifting international norms, without being directly determined by them.[53] To think of resettlement in this way is to see it as a voluntary action taken by a state that is looking to "show leadership" to other democracies by signalling its commitment to liberal values through its acceptance of the costs of refugee admissions.

Resettlement policy is, indeed, embedded within the structure of international norms and institutions. Following the Second World War, Western states sought to build a liberal world order governed by shared norms and international institutions. These norms were encoded in international law, including the 1951 United Nations Convention Relating to the Status of Refugees and its 1967 Protocol, which extended the definition of the refugee (and corresponding protections) globally, beyond its initial European remit. They also became institutionalized within multilateral institutions, such as the UNHCR and other UN agencies with responsibilities for refugees.

Human rights and other liberal norms, which place primary value on the individual, significantly influence the way in which refugee resettlement is carried out. For instance, the definition of a refugee in the 1967 Protocol specifies individualized criteria to determine refugee status – a departure from historical practices of recognizing refugees on a group basis by identifying persecuted minorities. Furthermore, states primarily rely upon UNHCR refugee-status determination processes when accepting refugees for resettlement, processes that take into account individualized experiences of persecution.

Still, although liberal norms influence resettlement policy, states also exercise their discretion and sovereignty in a number of ways. First, they can choose which refugees to resettle in response to domestic pressures or strategic interests. They also run separate refugee-status determination processes to recognize individuals who are not refugees under the 1967 Protocol. They will recognize members of specific minority groups (such as Jews from Soviet Russia or Bahá'ís from Iran) as refugees without having to prove individual-based persecution. During the Cold War, many refugees were recognized and resettled simply by virtue of being from a Communist state. In short, despite the strong imprint of liberal norms on refugee resettlement, states still carve out exceptions and special measures in their policies reflective of domestic preferences.

Furthermore, ideas do not come to achieve their power and influence independent of social and political actors.[54] As this book demonstrates, ideas about the humanitarian conception of the refugee, responsibility for refugee protection, and social participation in resettlement and integration were taken up by religious groups in their advocacy. These groups themselves were often key vectors in the transmission of the ideas that came to embody what Triadafilopoulos calls the "moral foundations" of the post-war era.[55] In comparison, as we will see, politicians and other decision makers were relative laggards in adapting to ideas about refugee protection and resettlement.

This discussion of explanatory schemes related to refugee-resettlement policy is not intended to invalidate any one of them, but to note their respective contributions and limitations. Each of them contains and advances an explanation for refugee resettlement as a strategic decision taken by a state, pointing to the different ways in which these interests are structured. However, arguments advanced within these schemes ignore or underestimate the importance of domestic groups in processes of decision making and policy implementation. I do not discount the powerful role of strategic considerations in shaping the response of states to refugee crises, but the inclusion of organized groups adds more precision to the causal story of the development of refugee policy – particularly at the stage of institutional design and policy implementation. Next, therefore, I elaborate an approach that incorporates the role of domestic groups to explain the development of refugee policy.

ORGANIZED GROUPS, NETWORKS, AND POLICY CHANGE

Political scientists have long recognized the influential role of organized groups in democratic politics.[56] Early pluralists argued that a porous democratic political system helps mediate between the demands of different interest groups, fostering stability and incremental policy changes over time.[57] While pluralists were criticized for failing to attend to the role of bias, power, and collective-action problems within the interest-group system, their core insights about the important role of organized groups in different phases of the policy process have endured.[58] Governments often rely upon groups for expertise, public mobilization, and policy implementation, and a satisfactory explanation of policy outcomes can rarely neglect the roles played by groups.[59]

The opportunities for groups and coalitions to shape agendas, frame issues, and contribute to shifts in policy systems typically come about when policy windows are created by exogenous shocks or changes in public attention.[60] Actors search out solutions to a given policy problem and decide upon a course of action during these critical junctures. Policy change can be rapid, followed by longer periods of path dependence, relative stability, and incremental change.[61] As Margaret Levi notes regarding path-dependent processes, "Once a country or region has started down a track, the costs of reversal are very high. There will be other choice points, but the entrenchments of certain institutional arrangements obstruct an easy reversal of the initial choice."[62] Path dependence does not necessarily mean that a policy choice is locked to the point that further evolution is not possible – only that this evolution is constrained by past choices.[63] These past choices can create positive feedback effects, expressed through networks connecting organized groups and decision makers.

Later chapters of this book contrast the emergence of a stronger "policy community" in the United States with the development of a less cohesive and stable "issue network" in Canada. The distinction is made primarily for heuristic purposes to describe the structure and dynamics of network interactions between decision makers and religious and voluntary groups.[64] These dynamics support the reproduction of policy responses to refugees; in the United States, they strengthened feedback effects that generated path dependency, and weaker ties in Canada led to a more fitful developmental pathway.

In the United States, the structure of state cooperation with the country's major religious groups produced an institutional arrangement that resembles what Philippe Schmitter describes as corporatist: "a particular ... ideal-typical institutional arrangement for linking the associationally organized interests of civil society with the decisional structures of the state."[65] In this vein, I refer to a stable and relatively closed "policy community" that becomes more integrated with decision-making processes.[66] A key condition for the creation of a cohesive and stable community is a shared "policy image" (a set of beliefs and values concerning a particular policy) – a condition that was initially satisfied by a shared view of refugees as people fleeing from Communism.[67] In the United States, religious groups shared an anti-Communist position because of the association of Communism with atheism and religious persecution. The religious groups became "insiders" in relation to the evolving policy discourse around refugee resettlement, just as they became increasingly bound to the state in a transactional financial relationship.

Immigration policy was created by politics in Congress and the White House, and religious groups helped to overcome restrictionist barriers to early legislation. They did this by aligning themselves with anti-Communist themes, disabling antisemitic objections, and emphasizing the integration of potential immigrants in American religious life – in addition to their efforts to shift public opinion and mobilize grassroots constituents. The porousness of Congress to interest-group influence facilitated the entry of religious groups and their refugee coalitions into policy discourse. The result was the creation of a tight-knit policy community that included certain religious and voluntary groups and a corporatist partnership between the state and a segment of civil society. This partnership became embedded and routinized to the point where it was finally recognized in statute in 1980.

In Canada, on the other hand, religious groups were connected in a loose and informal "issue network" with each other and with immigration officials.[68] As Grant Jordan notes, an issue network is "the politics of the ad hoc and irregular" and the "loose-jointed play of influence."[69] It appears to consolidate during particular windows of opportunity but can scatter when the moment passes. These networks were less cohesive and stable than those in the United States, at least in part because they were not well institutionalized and did not share a common refugee policy framework with the bureaucracy. Religious groups viewed themselves as humanitarian actors in the refugee field, and they were critical of immigration officials' more instrumental view of refugees as mobile labour for the Canadian economy. Nevertheless, they had access to immigration officials and political leaders by virtue of their established role in refugee resettlement and used these spaces to advocate for policy changes.

Decision making was concentrated in the federal bureaucracy, where groups found it difficult to participate actively. The Westminster system of government in Canada creates a strong executive with little capacity by Parliament to check its policy initiatives.[70] Especially under majority government, the party in power is generally able to carry out a legislative agenda with few obstacles. In Canada's federated system, the provinces can contest national policy, even if they do not possess veto power. More to the point, relations with Quebec were often front of mind for prime ministers during much of the post-war period, and these concerns were doubly important in the volatile area of immigration policy.[71] Therefore, for much of this period, the executive was eager to avoid public debate over immigration, especially debate that would exacerbate political and popular tensions with Quebec. Immigration policy continued to be effectively delegated to the bureaucracy for the first several decades after the Second World War, as it had been before the war.

As other studies of bureaucratic politics have shown, the willingness of bureaucrats to "consult" with group leaders is not always accompanied by an eagerness to cooperate with their organizations.[72] At least until the 1970s, bureaucrats saw religious groups as naive, but occasionally useful, actors in their policy field. They sought to marginalize them from selection and resettlement in order to confine their role to "integration." Already under frequent pressure to accept more refugees by the Department of External Affairs – as part of the dynamic of inter-bureau politics[73] – immigration program managers saw their role as gatekeepers of the national interest, which meant admitting a fixed number of people of particular races and skills. This self-understanding hardened their unwillingness to accept an active role by religious groups in refugee policy. The path of private sponsorship was created essentially by accident and then further developed through iterative negotiations between bureaucrats and religious groups. Although kept at arm's length as outsiders, these religious groups managed to secure permission at the political level to carry out parallel private-sponsorship programs.

This book shows how similar kinds of groups, engaging states with comparable foreign-policy objectives, produced different modes of public-private cooperation in the field of refugee resettlement. Religious groups achieved an insider status within the refugee policy community in the United States because immigration decision making took place within Congress and the White House. These venues were more open to group pressure, and the principal actors viewed the role of groups in policy implementation to be aligned with state interests rather than in competition with them. Bureaucrats controlled immigration policymaking in Canada, and they sought to externalize religious groups from refugee resettlement because there was not a similar alignment in policy image.

The unexpected result of these domestic policy processes was the creation of a corporatist structure of private-public cooperation in the United States and a more pluralist, distributed one in Canada. In the United States, groups that engaged in the policy process immediately after the Second World War were able to consolidate their position, build organizational capacity, and create a significant barrier to entry by other groups[74] – exerting what Frank Baumgartner and Bryan Jones characterize as a status quo bias when groups engage with policy implementation.[75] While there is no evidence that these groups actively sought to exclude others from participation in refugee resettlement, membership in the policy community has remained relatively static, with movement only at the margins, since the 1940s.[76] In Canada, on the other hand, the system of private sponsorship has opened up the possibility for participation in refugee resettlement even to self-organized, informal groups of citizens, in addition to larger national groups.

RELIGIOUS GROUPS AND THE POLITICS OF REFUGEE POLICY

My argument has broader implications for our understanding of the forces driving the development of refugee policy. Religious and voluntary groups are commonly recognized to be important actors in the field of refugee aid,[77] and there is an emerging academic literature on the way in which secularism and religious thought have shaped a variety of responses to refugees.[78] A number of recent historical works on religious internationalism have shown how religious imperatives and U.S. foreign policy have often been intertwined.[79] However, the role of religious groups as protagonists in the refugee policy process has been either overlooked or minimized in most social scientific and policy studies.

In both the United States and Canada, strong foreign-policy rationales were, almost without exception, necessary but insufficient to shift and enact refugee policy. Accepting refugees is almost always good foreign policy: it increases international standing and fortifies international norms, in addition to condemning rivals (by highlighting their failures) or helping allies (through burden sharing).[80] The obstacles are principally domestic. Public opinion rarely favours increased immigration, let alone large refugee admissions. Racial, ethnic, or religious prejudices – whether expressed in official attitudes or in the fear of public backlash – have also been powerful impediments to the admission of refugees.[81] And, not least, refugees impose a net fiscal burden, certainly over the short term and often during the first generation.

These tensions play out within the state itself, with the foreign ministry urging the admission of refugees and immigration or justice departments resisting the approval of large programs; the former seeks to increase refugee admissions to boost international status, whereas the latter wants to regulate admissions in accordance with population goals.[82] In this context, the mobilization and engagement of pro-refugee groups – with numbers, influence, and organizational capacity far exceeding those of restrictionist groups – was essential to the transformation of refugee law and policy in Canada and the United States. Without their engagement, Canadian refugee policy would have been minimalist, focused essentially on meeting labour-market demand. American policy, on the other hand, initially sought to deter refugees and actively pursued resettlement in South America before initiating a partnership with religious and voluntary groups to bring displaced people to the United States.[83]

Major refugee programs have almost always followed upon some kind of international crisis or event that shifts public and political attention to the plight of refugees, galvanizing discourse and the search for solutions.[84] The first response of political leaders in this context is usually to shirk responsibility or to "internationalize" the program to the greatest degree possible – whether through regional solutions or other kinds of "burden sharing."[85] Where groups have mobilized to press for resettlement, they have presented a second option – that of privatization. Indeed, an internal U.S. government memo at the beginning of the Vietnamese refugee crisis crystallized these two principles for effecting resettlement: "1) Maximize internationalization of the problem; 2) Maximize dependence on international and domestic voluntary agencies and private resources."[86] In both the United States and Canada, the scale of refugee-resettlement programs – which, while modest in relation to the global problem, are significant among liberal democracies – has been achieved because of the development of cooperative partnerships with religious and voluntary groups.

The leadership of religious groups at the forefront of social mobilization for refugees also begs the question: Why religious groups? The simple answer is that they mobilized and engaged with the policy process before, during, and after the Second World War, and they remained embedded within evolving policy systems over subsequent decades. Other organizations, such as unions and international and national human rights groups, have not been the main protagonists of policy negotiation, despite what might be expected from bodies with transnational ties and a global outlook. Some have been occasional advocates for refugee resettlement and asylum seekers, but during the period under study they rarely led the way either in lobbying efforts or in the formation of coalitions and cooperative structures with the state.[87]

As the next chapter discusses, Jewish, Catholic, and Protestant groups were influenced by changes in religious thought and action that responded to perceived crises of modernity and secularism in the mid-twentieth century. Refugees were emblematic of the failures of the false gods of nationalism, Fascism, and Communism to attend to the basic requirements of the human person.[88] Church leaders interpreted this crisis as a moral and ethical challenge demanding a religious response; it was imagined that religion supplied a more universal ethos than could be expressed by the narrow interests of the state. Granted, this ethos was initially directed toward co-religionists, but it nevertheless challenged the more limited allegiances of national patriotism. The mobilization of religious groups was strengthened and directed by institutional hierarchies as political opportunity structures for effective action appeared.

Religious groups were unexpected protagonists of policy evolution during this particular time. José Casanova famously claimed that religion "went public" after the 1980s, following an extended period of "privatization" and retreat from the public sphere in the West.[89] Indeed, the 1960s were the heyday of secularization, according to its most noted theorist, Peter Berger.[90] T.S. Shah claims that secularization through "the subordination of religion to the power of the state" can be most clearly seen between 1917 and 1967.[91] The widespread consensus among social scientists that religion padded a hasty retreat from the public sphere during the mid-twentieth century makes it all the more notable that religious groups exerted an enduring influence on refugee policy during this period.

In addition to the fact of their public mobilization, religious groups also possessed characteristics that facilitated cooperation and partnership in resettlement programs. These included a shared culture, structures of hierarchical authority, and the presence of strong purposive incentives, which helped them to overcome collective-action problems when there was leadership from religious institutions.[92] By virtue of their extensive social and institutional networks – both transnationally and domestically – many had the capacity to identify, select, distribute, and settle refugees across the country. Policymakers who sought to avoid the concentration of refugees in particular locations – often to militate against popular backlash – viewed these networks and organizational structures of religious groups in a positive light. The membership bases of such groups were also an important segment of public opinion, which religious leadership sought to educate and at times mobilize. Furthermore, most of these groups had independent sources of funding and human resources – drawing both from among their own members – which presented the government with cost efficiencies it could not accomplish on its own.

Religion continues to be a variable of political importance, even in Western secularized democracies. Although the primary space available to religious groups in these countries is in the public sphere of civil society (now that preferential institutional access to the highest levels of political power is no longer commonplace), analytical leverage is lost when they are conflated with non-governmental organizations (NGOs), interest groups, or other social movements. The power of religious groups often resides in their own internal sets of ideas, practices, and social networks.[93] Religion has the capacity to tap into human motivation by appealing to non-material principles and purposes,[94] organizing individuals and resources through structured institutions, and connecting them with transnational social networks.[95]

As I argue in this book, the evolution of refugee policy in the United States and Canada was shaped by the political engagements of religious groups that mobilized in defence of moral and ethical ideals about international (and often non-sectarian) human solidarity. The institutional configurations that govern refugee policy in both countries would not be the same without the continued engagement of religious groups. Indeed, it is entirely likely that the scale of refugee admissions in both countries would be substantially diminished without them.

However, even when similar kinds of religious groups mobilize to advocate for a particular public policy, the outcomes of their efforts can be significantly different. Indeed, to take religion seriously as a political variable in comparative politics requires explaining how different outcomes can result from efforts by similar groups in separate political settings.[96] To argue for the political relevance of religion in Western countries cannot mean assigning it the status of a master variable that magically transforms policy areas that fall within its purview. As can been seen in relation to gay marriage and abortion, even when religious groups adopt a unified and well-resourced public position on a key policy question, they can fail dramatically in the context of hostile culture and political forces. Religious groups have shown that, even when they have significant public support for their policy positions and use tremendous resources to achieve their preferences, they frequently fall short.[97] The reasons for their relative success in the case of refugee policy include a number of contingent factors during the period after the Second World War, which created institutional arrangements that became path dependent.

Furthermore, religious groups themselves are not static entities or faithful emanations of an eternal theology. They are also shaped by their surrounding ideas, societies, and political contexts.[98] Although there are traditions of Christian and Jewish thought that call for love and solidarity with "the other," this altruistic ideal was not the only impetus for mobilization on behalf of refugees during and after the Second World War. It was more complicated than that. There were family ties, concern for co-religionists, an abstract struggle against godless Communism, internationalist idealism, interreligious competitiveness, and other motivations that all contributed to the early engagement of religious groups with refugee policy. The next chapter explores some of these reasons, situated within an evolving political context, to explain why religious groups initially mobilized politically to support refugee resettlement in the wake of the Second World War.

The book then proceeds in chapter 2 to analyze the shifting role of religious groups within the policy processes that led to the passage and implementation of landmark refugee law in the United States and Canada. This chapter begins with a close analysis of the post-war period, when religious groups became central actors in the implementation of resettlement policy targeting displaced people. The institutional configurations that developed through this time created different structures of cooperation. As chapter 3 shows, these structures became replicated through positive feedback effects as other Cold War refugee crises emerged. A policy community developed in the United States, connecting a small number of groups with key decision makers; whereas, in Canada, a relatively loose issue network tied religious groups to bureaucratic structures that were ambivalent about their involvement. Chapter 4 traces the consolidation of this policy community in the United States, alongside its attenuation in Canada throughout the 1960s and early 1970s. However, by the 1970s, as recounted in chapter 5, the Indochinese crisis created an influential context within which major immigration and refugee reforms were undertaken in both countries. The passage and implementation of significant legislation toward the end of this decade marked the crystallization of resettlement-policy models that had evolved since the Second World War.

I

A Moral Alternative to Power Politics

Why Religious Groups Mobilized for Refugee Resettlement

The prevalent attitude among North American Christians toward European refugees during and immediately after the Second World War has been described as "apathetic" and "indifferent."[1] Jews, for their part, supported refugee admissions "as quietly as possible."[2] Jewish advocacy was ineffective, Protestant and Catholic mobilization was virtually non-existent, and immigration in both countries was virtually frozen. Soon, however, Protestant, Catholic, and Jewish groups organized to become effective public advocates for refugee resettlement. This transformation was remarkably rapid. By 1948, it was possible for a prominent historian to call an American interfaith coalition for refugees "one of the largest and best-run lobbying groups in the nation."[3] Similarly, by 1947 in Canada, a newly formed Christian ecumenical refugee group was granted a say in the selection and resettlement of European refugees, alongside a Jewish counterpart.[4]

These groups brought a humanitarian discourse around refugees into the policy arena, a discourse that was at times in tension with the more strategic interests of decision makers. This was reflective of the broader rise of a discourse of personalism and "the crisis of man" among intellectuals in Europe and North America.[5] Mark Greif traces the ways in which these intellectual trends infused a whole generation of writers in the mid-twentieth century, with their mature expression in the thought of Hannah Arendt – a significant and enduring theorist of statelessness and the refugee condition.[6] Samuel Moyn describes the rhetoric of "the human person" – "a moral alternative to power politics, and likewise defined against the totalitarian spectre" – as a shared characteristic of ecumenical Protestant and Roman Catholic thinking in this time that would leave its mark on the genealogy of human rights.[7]

DIMENSIONS OF POLITICAL MOBILIZATION

The emergence and public mobilization of religious groups concerned with refugee resettlement cannot be explained as a matter of intellectual history alone. It invites an explanation that engages with the conceptual and analytical tools of social-movement theory to show how mobilization occurred so rapidly in the 1940s.[8] In this vein, I argue that political mobilization became sustained when it engaged three dimensions: religious and cultural motivation, resource mobilization, and political opportunity structures.[9] This process can be distinct from the mobilization of conventional (secular) interest groups, which typically focus on engaging individuals who share similar material interests or public concerns through the use of entrepreneurial tactics and selective incentives.[10] Religious groups have pre-made constituencies of members and congregations formed out of solidarity and purposive incentives, which are guided in most cases by hierarchical institutions and leadership.[11] However, religious leadership generally is concerned with the spiritual and social welfare of members, and political engagement is an exception rather than a rule. I outline below some of the salient features of their mobilization, which brought certain religious groups out of political obscurity and into the forefront of post-war refugee advocacy.

First, with regard to religious and cultural motivation, these groups did not form and engage with refugee issues as a simple result of spontaneous activism in response to Scriptural imperatives, as some lay histories claim.[12] For many of them, the initial motivation came from concern for the well-being of co-religionists and family members. Religious leadership with ties to international affiliates in Europe recognized the humanitarian crisis created by massive displacement during the Second World War and proceeded to initiate the creation of structures capable of lobbying on behalf of refugees and assisting with their resettlement. To connect these structures with existing national social networks, they invoked feelings of religious solidarity and moral and ethical commitments derived from religious ideas.[13] Some of these commitments related to humanist ideas of "personalism."[14] However, for Protestants, Catholics, and Jews alike, the strongest motivation arose from concern for the welfare of co-religionists and from an interest in buttressing the membership of their own religious communities.

Second, with regard to resource mobilization, religious communities often have access to a broad range of resources, including shared culture, religious leadership, material resources, community networks, and physical space.[15] The support of religious leadership is often crucial. Groups that are connected to the institutional structure of religious communities have the capacity to access networks of members and congregations that can distribute information, facilitate fundraising, and promote grassroots lobbying. The social capital of religious communities includes networks and institutions devoted to providing voluntary aid and social services. Mobilizing resources within religious groups, therefore, has involved not just fundraising but also the engagement of existing community institutions for the purpose of supporting refugee resettlement.

A third dimension of mobilization was the interaction of nascent groups with emerging political opportunity structures. In other words, there is a demand side to group mobilization.[16] As Beth Leech et al. explain, "we should expect mobilization to occur not when an opinion or need exists in the world, but when that opinion or need *and the possibility of government action* intersect."[17] Many religious groups initially focused on sending material relief to refugees in Europe, and their focus turned to resettlement as government action seemed more likely. Further, as they engaged with political opportunity structures, many groups also merged and consolidated their operations to achieve greater coherence and effectiveness in their work. Group mobilization and consolidation were accelerated by government attention to refugee issues, when initiatives of decision makers created policy windows for the participation of religious groups.[18]

When referring to "religious groups" in this chapter, I mean any organized group that is institutionally affiliated with a religious community. I consider Jewish, Lutheran, and Mennonite groups, which are sometimes referred to by scholars as "ethnic groups," as religious groups.[19] The term "religious group" encompasses a broader range of associations and public activity than might be captured by other terms, such as "interest group" or "pressure group." It is also preferable to the term "sectarian group," which suggests an exclusive concern with advancing the interests of a religious denomination. The descriptions above are not always inaccurate, but they obscure the theological and institutional sources of religious groups' responses to refugees, as well as their particular capacity for overcoming collective-action problems. The groups under study here include immigrant-aid societies, official representative bodies of religious communities, humanitarian-relief organizations, and coalitions of grassroots organizations that are connected with a religious denomination or ecumenical council. While some of them may also be fairly categorized as pressure groups and others can be called ethnic or sectarian groups, the term "religious group" most accurately describes the common thread that ties them together. Later in the book I also use the term "voluntary group" in a way that includes religious groups along with other membership-based associations, following the emergence of the concept in the U.S. refugee policy discourse.

This chapter considers each country in turn, identifying the primary groups in the refugee policy field and tracing the process by which they mobilized and emerged as political actors. Beginning with the United States, the chapter briefly introduces the context of refugee policy during the war before analyzing the mobilization of Protestant, Catholic, and Jewish groups across the three dimensions introduced above. The analysis of the Canadian case proceeds along similar lines.

UNITED STATES

Political Context: Refugee Policy during the War

The political environment in the United States during the Second World War was generally hostile to refugees. The small number of refugees admitted during this time reflects how impenetrable the United States was to refugees, even for those with compelling moral claims for asylum.[20] After several decades of essentially unchecked European immigration, population scares and racial theories propelled the imposition of national quotas on immigration in 1921. The United States, for the first time in its history, became a country of net emigration between 1933 and 1944.[21]

One of the primary sources of opposition to a resettlement program was Congress, where legislation had to be passed to admit any significant number of refugees. In part, restrictionist positions responded to overwhelmingly negative public opinion. A *Fortune* magazine survey in 1938 indicated that 86 per cent of Americans opposed increasing immigration quotas for German, Austrian, or other refugees.[22] Much of this was based on antisemitism.[23] Popular sentiment was reflected in government policy, as made clear by the failure of the 1938 Évian Conference to open pathways to emigration for Jews seeking to leave Germany and Australia. Congress generally aimed to limit the number of refugees admitted to the country while refusing to enact any quota or legislative commitment to refugees.[24] Initial plans by the Roosevelt administration to propose refugee-relief legislation during the war were quickly set aside after it concluded that the power of restrictionists in Congress would prove too strong to overcome.[25]

While President Franklin Roosevelt privately expressed sympathy toward refugees, he regarded the large-scale expansion of refugee admissions to be politically impractical. There were two constraints: Roosevelt needed Southern Democrats (who opposed refugee admissions) to support his New Deal, and public opinion was implacably opposed.[26] Roosevelt made some effort to overcome both, soliciting the participation of religious leaders in an effort to shift public attitudes. In October 1939 he outlined a plan to his secretary of state to promote engagement with the issue "on a broad religious basis, thereby making it possible to gain the kind of world-wide support that a mere Jewish set-up would not evoke."[27] During Christmas that year, he sent a telegram to the leaders of the Federal Council of Churches (FCC), the Jewish Joint Distribution Committee (JDC), and his Vatican envoy, "outlining what he hoped would be an attitude of cooperation between religious groups active overseas and the US government."[28] Roosevelt invited these leaders to meet with him in Washington to "discuss the problem which all of us have on our minds," which principally referred to refugee aid.[29] Yet, despite these overtures to religious groups, the president distanced himself from efforts to liberalize immigration policy in a way that would enable refugees to reach the United States.

The State Department also impeded the modest efforts made by the White House to try to open the door to refugees during the war. The State Department was allied with restrictionists,[30] and its officials were able "to close the doors at will" to Jews in Europe.[31] Before the war, the State Department claimed that admitting German Jewish refugees would damage relations with Germany, and consular personnel were obstructive when ordered by President Roosevelt "to interpret admissions guidelines liberally."[32] A 1944 report by the U.S. Treasury Department found the State Department to be guilty of "wilful attempts to prevent action from being taken to rescue Jews from Hitler."[33] Though not an impartial observer, Treasury Secretary Henry Morgenthau, Jr asserted in a briefing to Roosevelt that "plain Anti-Semitism" motivated the actions of State Department officials.[34] After the meeting, Roosevelt created the War Refugee Board to oversee refugee affairs outside of the State Department.[35] The board worked on a number of fronts to help rescue as many as 200,000 European Jews, often in collaboration with the JDC.[36] However, relatively few were permitted to enter the United States, and the board was disbanded in September 1945.

Despite the scarcity of political support for refugee resettlement during the war, religious groups began to mobilize in different configurations to promote refugee relief and assistance in Europe. According to Claudena Skran, "private voluntary groups" were responsible for facilitating the emigration and settlement of most refugees leading up to the war.[37] Most were primarily focused on assisting refugees "with whom they shared a common religion and culture."[38] During and after the war, many of these groups evolved into new agencies that worked in cooperation with each other to advocate a broader set of humanitarian policy goals – albeit still with a focus on helping their co-religionists in Europe. They came of age during this time, when their efforts became integrated into government policy.

The key window of opportunity for the mobilization of religious groups was President Harry Truman's 1945 Directive. In 1944 Congress was in a "decidedly anti-immigrant mood,"[39] and a coalition of religious and secular groups[40] was organized to focus attention on "close consultations with the Executive Branch" in order to open up refugee admissions by the United States. These efforts found a receptive audience among White House internationalists, who wanted to see the president push back against the isolationists and restrictionists in Congress. Introduced as an executive action intended to open up refugee admissions in a way that avoided seeking congressional approval, the Directive was limited in its immediate impact but tremendously important in its long-term effect. With this measure, President Truman allocated unused immigration quotas for European countries toward admitting displaced persons and refugees under the sponsorship of voluntary groups. The Directive did not change basic immigration law, but it created a path for the admission of refugees who possessed a "corporate affidavit" from "responsible welfare organizations" that assured that they would not become public charges.[41] Virtually all such organizations were religious groups that were engaged, in one way or another, with refugee relief in Europe. It created the opportunity for religious groups to designate, sponsor, and settle European displaced people. By specifying a particular role for voluntary groups to implement refugee resettlement on behalf of the state, this executive action set an important precedent for future refugee policy.

Table 1.1
Religious groups in the United States

Group	Affiliation	Dates Active
Hebrew Immigrant Aid Society (HIAS)	Jewish	1891–Present
American Jewish Committee (AJC)	Jewish	1906–Present
Federal Council of Churches (FCC)	Ecumenical Protestant	1908–50
Jewish Joint Distribution Committee (JDC)	Jewish	1914–Present
National Lutheran Council	Protestant	1918–66
National Catholic Welfare Conference (NCWC)	Roman Catholic	1919–66
American Christian Committee for Refugees (ACCR)	Ecumenical Protestant	1934–47
Catholic Committee for Refugees (CCR)	Roman Catholic	1936–47
World Council of Churches	Ecumenical Protestant	1939–Present
War Relief Services (WRS)	Roman Catholic	1943–55
American Council of Voluntary Agencies for Foreign Service (ACVA)	Interfaith Coalition	1943–84
United Service for New Americans (USNA)	Jewish	1945–54
Citizens Committee on Displaced People (CCDP)	Interfaith Coalition	1946–53
Church World Service (CWS)	Ecumenical Protestant	1946–Present
National Council of Churches (NCC)	Ecumenical Protestant	1950–Present
Catholic Relief Services (CRS)	Roman Catholic	1955–Present
United States Catholic Conference	Roman Catholic	1966–2001
United States Conference of Catholic Bishops	Roman Catholic	2001–Present

Having set out aspects of the political context surrounding refugee policy during and immediately after the war, the following sections trace the mobilization of Christian and Jewish groups within this environment.

Protestant Groups

During the 1930s, the emerging refugee crisis in Europe was met with indifferent silence by the rank and file of American Protestant churches.[42] Early efforts to inspire grassroots interest in helping Christian refugees were largely unsuccessful. As a few Protestant leaders and church organizations developed new structures to advocate for and raise money on behalf of refugees, they found themselves without any substantial support among local churches.[43] However, the support of Protestant groups would later become crucial to the passage of DP legislation. The transformation of Protestant groups was propelled by the influence of ideas and structures generated by the transatlantic ecumenical movement and the window of opportunity created by the Truman Directive of 1945.

In 1934 a number of Protestant church leaders and Christian humanitarians founded the American Christian Committee for German Refugees (ACCR), a branch of the International Christian Commission for Refugees.[44] Although it was an ecumenical Christian organization, the ACCR was financed by the American Jewish Joint Distribution Committee.[45] The driving force behind its creation appears to have been James G. McDonald, an American who served as the League of Nations high commissioner for refugees.[46] Upon his appointment, one of his first initiatives was to organize a committee that would serve as a liaison between his office and American religious groups.[47] The group described its purpose as follows: "To cooperate in the United States with James G. McDonald, High Commissioner for Refugees Coming from Germany, in an educational effort to evoke a sense of responsibility toward the needs of refugees from Germany ... and to enlist [the churches'] sympathetic participation in campaigns for funds as may later be projected."[48] It declared that it would work on behalf of "all refugees, without distinction of religious affiliation."[49]

The ACCR's initial efforts to raise funds to support the work of the high commissioner met with disappointment. Less than a year after the group's formation, its executive committee noted "the evident failure of Christians to rise to their opportunity and duty," and ACCR officers were "at a complete loss to understand why Christian leaders and Christian groups did not respond more generously."[50] Failing to provide much support to the League of Nations refugee program, the committee then proceeded to appeal to churches to support the refugee-fundraising efforts of the United Jewish Appeal. It succeeded only in revealing Christian indifference. The fundraising effort generated just $6,000 out of the $1.8 million raised by Jewish groups.[51] Despite eventually attracting some funds and sending aid to support a handful of refugees abroad, the ACCR fell far short of its ambitions. When a review of more than a decade of its work was conducted in 1946, it "revealed anew the prevailing apathy on the part of the American people regarding the non-Jewish German refugees."[52]

As the ACCR struggled, the gathering momentum of a transatlantic Protestant ecumenical movement created a new impetus for church responses to the refugee problem. This movement crystallized at a major conference in Oxford in 1937 that brought together prominent thinkers from the United States and Europe to deliberate on the future role of the church in society. It helped shape Protestant thinking about personalism, a discourse about the centrality of the human person for philosophical inquiry and political projects.[53] This intellectual movement help to lay the foundation for the World Council of Churches (WCC), which was formally established after the Second World War. One of the leaders of this movement, J.H. Oldham, wrote that Western civilization was on the threshold of a new historical epoch, entering "the end of the Christian era, or the end of the Protestant era."[54] He asserted that under the secularizing conditions of modern society, Christians must engage in "open conflict with the assumptions on which modern societies are organizing and directing their life."[55] They should work to build a "post-national world" where the dignity and freedom of the individual would be protected from the controlling influence of the state and the corrupting effects of capitalist markets.[56] The outlook Oldham describes became influential among certain Protestant leaders, although it took time for it to manifest in institutional structures and church culture.[57] Nevertheless, it was fertile ground for political mobilization in support of refugee resettlement.

The World Council of Churches was informally established in February 1939, and in April that year it set up an Ecumenical Secretariat for Refugees at Bloomsbury House, London. The tasks of this secretariat included coordinating Christian aid to refugees, helping Christian refugees emigrate, and "remind[ing] churches in the Ecumenical Movement of their responsibilities [to refugees]."[58] When the WCC was formally launched in 1948, this vision was expressed in part in resolutions to cooperate with states in the resettlement of European refugees.[59] It created a Department of Inter-Church Aid and Service to Refugees, which became a major agency in Europe for the assessment and relocation of refugees seeking resettlement.

Before its formal establishment, the World Council of Churches' influence on refugee issues was already beginning to be felt in the United States. In 1945 Samuel McCrea Cavert, the general secretary of the Federal Council of Churches, wrote to the Leland Rex Robinson, president of the struggling ACCR, to suggest that in the near future the World Council would assume greater responsibility for "representing the American churches in relation to the overseas aspect of the refugee problem."[60] "The main thing to bear in mind," he wrote, "is the growing strength of the World Council of Churches and the increasing recognition of the World Council as the center through which the churches of many different countries can be united in an international program of service."[61] He emphasized the need to coordinate refugee-relief and resettlement efforts with European churches. On 4 May 1946 the Federal Council of Churches, the Foreign Missions Conference, and the American Committee of the World Council of Churches jointly created Church World Service (CWS), with representatives of various Protestant denominations serving on its board.[62] It became the American affiliate of the WCC's refugee-relief and resettlement efforts in Europe. Today, Church World Service is the largest Protestant refugee organization in the world.

The relationship between the two ecumenical Protestant groups was initially strained, although the Federal Council of Churches effectively supervised them both. The council expressed its support for President Truman's December 1945 Directive to give preference for refugees within existing immigration quotas, provided they could secure an "assurance" from a voluntary agency.[63] In response to this support for the Directive, the ACCR and CWS each appointed seven members to work out a plan of service to displaced people who would be resettled in the United States through church sponsorships.[64] The ACCR took responsibility for operations in the United States, and CWS liaised with its World Council of Churches affiliates in Europe and oversaw transportation. This collaboration was unsuccessful, however, as ACCR funds continued to run low and CWS noted "slackening interest" from its member denominations.[65]

In 1947 Church World Service assumed full responsibility for refugee issues on behalf of the Federal Council of Churches (later the National Council of Churches [NCC]), and the ACCR and a handful of other small Protestant refugee-relief organizations were effectively dismantled. Church World Service formalized collaboration with the World Council of Churches and the Lutheran World Federation to advance a more ambitious program involving local churches in refugee-resettlement advocacy and cooperation. In addition to working with individual congregations, they engaged local and state ecumenical councils. Later that year, this transatlantic coalition announced a "greater unification of our services" to serve refugees in Europe and "to call upon Christian churches, organizations and individuals to recognize afresh what is happening and what needs to be done."[66] It urged local churches to pressure their governments "to open doors to immigration not to cheap labour but to human families."[67] The following year, CWS announced that it had enlisted the "active cooperation" of ecumenical councils of churches in 36 states and 633 cities across the United States to help with the resettlement of displaced people.[68] It promised action "on a much broader scale" should Congress approve larger admissions of DPs.[69]

The mobilization of Church World Service was closely connected to the development of transatlantic Protestant ecumenism. Early Protestant groups had only limited success at generating grassroots support for refugee relief and resettlement, and they were marginal to the immigration policy process in Washington. However, Church World Service emerged from an intellectual and organizational ferment within Protestant ecumenism that was characterized by humanist ideas, visions of social change, and the creation of transnational civil-society networks.[70] With support from Protestant, Orthodox, and Anglican churches within the Federal Council of Churches, CWS tapped into an ecumenical movement that extended to local and state inter-church councils. This became the foundation on which it built a major refugee-resettlement program that brought more than 50,000 DPs to the United States under the Displaced Persons Act between 1948 and 1952 – a significant accomplishment in light of the widespread apathy and indifference to refugees among mainline Protestants in the previous decade.[71]

Catholic Groups

Similar to their Protestant counterparts, Catholic groups initially gave an ambivalent response to the plight of refugees. During the war, the church hierarchy supported modest measures to assist certain Catholic refugees – many of whom were of Jewish ancestry – to settle in the United States. Establishment Catholic publications like *Commonweal*, *Catholic Worker*, and *Catholic Action* published positive stories about refugees, emphasizing the responsibility of American Catholics toward their European co-religionists.[72] On the other hand, however, "anti-Semitism was never far from the surface in the consciousness of American Catholics."[73] George Murray observes that, based on the general opinion of American Catholics at this time, "there can be no doubt that the Bishops faced an enormous challenge as they called for assistance in resettling refugee newcomers."[74] The scale of the challenge became evident as Catholic responses to the Truman Directive fell short. Anticipating further opportunities to sponsor refugees from Europe, the church hierarchy ignored anti-refugee sentiment at the grassroots and set up national structures that could manage refugee resettlement and shift opinions among lay Catholics.

Although Catholic humanitarianism stretches far back in time, a series of steps were taken by the Vatican in the early twentieth century to bolster Catholic humanitarian programs.[75] Gradually, these evolved to include an interest in resettlement. In 1939 Pope Pius XII established the Vatican Information Service, which operated under the auspices of the Holy See's Secretariat of State, with the purpose of gathering and responding to requests for assistance by Catholics affected by the war. In 1947 the Information Service was replaced by another office – the Pontifical Commission for Relief – which was charged with coordinating papal humanitarian services. This commission was joined by the creation of an Office of Migration that same year, intended to deal with both "voluntary migration" and displaced people. In 1948 Pius XII made one of his most significant and categorical statements on the subject of refugees: "You know indeed how preoccupied We have been and with what anxiety We have followed those who have been forced by revolutions in their own countries, or by unemployment and hunger to leave their homes and live in foreign lands ... The natural law itself, no less than devotion to humanity, urges that ways of migration be opened to these people. For the Creator of the universe made all good things primarily for the good of all."[76] A few years later, in July 1951, the pope established the International Catholic Migration Commission (ICMC), with the purpose of coordinating Catholic efforts on behalf of migrants around the world.[77]

The initial efforts of the American bishops to support the arrival of Catholic refugees from Europe built on past immigrant-aid initiatives.[78] The Catholic Committee for Refugees (CCR) was formed in 1936 under the auspices of the bishops' National Catholic Welfare Conference (NCWC). The CCR was headquartered in New York City, and it was set up "to aid, materially and spiritually, Catholic refugees coming to the United States who for racial, religious, or political reasons were victims of persecution and involuntary exile from their homeland."[79] The committee worked with German bishops to provide social services to the few hundred refugees who settled in New York City each year. These refugees arrived through special exemptions or normal immigration procedures.

In 1943 the stateside efforts of the CCR were complemented by a new U.S. Catholic agency, War Relief Services (WRS), which was also created by the bishops to operate under the NCWC as its overseas relief agency. It registered with the president's War Relief Control Board to participate in government-led efforts to help war-affected people. Registration with the board gave WRS access to funds generated by government-administered charity appeals. It expanded significantly with the support of these funds and assumed greater responsibility for Catholic aid and relief in Europe. This relief work included helping refugees who were cleared to enter the United States with the first stages of their resettlement process.

The signing of the Truman Directive was applauded by the Catholic bishops and proved to be a key moment for the consolidation of Catholic groups engaged with refugee issues. At the bishops' 1946 annual meeting, they passed a resolution that condemned the forcible repatriation of displaced persons, and they called for the entry of large numbers of refugees into the United States.[80] However, the response of Catholic refugee agencies to the Truman Directive was slow and ineffective. As Haim Genizi notes, before 1948 "the indifference towards refugees that characterized the prewar years prevailed not only among rank-and-file church members, but also among Catholic immigration organizations."[81] Out of 3,452 refugees who initially arrived under the Truman Directive, Catholic groups sponsored only 292.[82] Their lack of will or capacity to respond to a window of opportunity created by the White House prompted steps by the bishops to strengthen structures and coordination.

In 1947 WRS called for new coordination between the national, diocesan, and community levels, to be overseen by a proposed National Catholic Resettlement Council.[83] This council was established in November 1947, with representatives of the major national Catholic welfare organizations on its board. A 1947 WRS memo frames the organization's response to displaced people as follows: "The Holy Father has recognized the problem of Displaced Persons as one of the most serious facing Christian civilization. On several occasions he has made public pronouncements on this problem, calling upon all men of good will to take positive action. There has been established the Vatican Migration Bureau under the Vatican Secretary of State. The purpose of this Bureau is to encourage the development of favourable opportunities for Displaced Persons to migrate and re-establish themselves in new homelands."[84] The memo went on to underline the importance of Catholics in the United States assuming responsibility for responding to the refugee crisis in Europe: "If the United States is to play an active part in solving the problem of Displaced Persons it is quite clear that the Catholic Church will be required to establish a national plan for large-scale immigration ... It is a problem so wide in scope and importance as to require the assistance of all Catholic organizations – nationally, on a diocesan basis, and as well on a community level."[85] The National Catholic Resettlement Council became a key agency in the coordination of this effort, undertaken at the behest of the U.S. bishops and the Vatican. Despite widespread anti-refugee sentiment among the Roman Catholic laity, the religious hierarchy responded to Vatican directives to create structures for resettlement and educational programs intended to shift that sentiment.

Following the creation of the National Council, it and WRS assumed shared responsibility for the Catholic refugee-resettlement program.[86] WRS designed a plan to promote a significant increase in refugee resettlement by the church: "This plan had as its first objective the carrying out of an educational program which would more fully acquaint the laity with the real Christian issues involved in the Displaced Persons problem. This plan also called for the establishment of a coordinated program whereby all the various Catholic organizations, the nationality organizations and other interest groups would find an opportunity to participate."[87] WRS worked with the bishops and church hierarchy to establish a system of regional and diocesan resettlement directors whose offices would constitute a nationwide network of Catholic resettlement agencies. By 1948, 111 diocesan committees with resettlement directors were created, covering most Catholic communities across the United States.[88]

In summary, the mobilization of Catholic refugee groups was primarily stimulated and led by the church hierarchy, which had to overcome indifference and antisemitism among the laity. Statements by Pope Pius XII and U.S. bishops framed the refugee crisis with reference to fundamental beliefs and to the Holy Family, who were described as exiles and refugees.[89] They referenced "personalist" themes that became influential within the evolving Christian discourse on human rights.[90] They also focused exclusively on resettling fellow

Catholics.[91] Following the Truman Directive, the bishops consolidated and refocused the refugee work of the church through the establishment of the National Catholic Resettlement Council and the elevation of War Relief Services to the role of lead resettlement agency. The creation of diocesan resettlement directors and committees across the United States generated the institutional capacity to carry out large-scale resettlement.

Jewish Groups

A number of Jewish groups lobbied unsuccessfully for expanded refugee admissions before and during the Second World War; however, they became instrumental advocates for resettlement after the conflict ended. A key reason for this was a broad shift in strategy. The strategy of Jewish groups during the 1930s and early 1940s emphasized sectarian alliances and "quiet politics" that relied on interventions by Jewish members of Congress and cabinet officials.[92] The shift toward public, coalition-based advocacy followed the 1945 Truman Directive, which started to open up refugee admissions, and reports of deteriorating conditions in DP camps soon afterward. In 1946 Jewish groups developed closer coordination between operations focused on refugee admissions and resettlement and entered more openly and confidently into the arena of public political engagement. In the process, they spearheaded the formation of one of the most influential coalitions to shape changes to refugee law and policy after the Second World War.

The American Jewish Committee (AJC) led organized political advocacy on behalf of the Jewish community. The AJC had been established after the turn of the century in response to pogroms against Russian Jews, and it aimed to uphold the civil rights of Jews and to alleviate the consequences of their persecution.[93] It collaborated with other Jewish groups, such as the Hebrew Immigrant Aid Society (HIAS), which was created around the same time to facilitate emigration from Russia, and the Joint Distribution Committee, which was founded in 1914 and developed a network of some 2,000 local Jewish organizations across the United States to raise funds for Jewish humanitarian relief.[94] Together, these groups represented significant capacity and resources within the American Jewish community.

During the 1930s and early 1940s, the AJC and other Jewish organizations quietly advocated for changes to immigration laws.[95] A 1938 letter from the chairman of the JDC to the Canadian Jewish Congress

(CJC) reflects the prevailing sentiment of national Jewish groups at this time: "The Jews of America ... must necessarily take a leading part in the attempt to solve the refugee problem. While it is true that the problem is one which affects Christians as well as Jews and that it should not be regarded as specifically Jewish, we would be deluding ourselves if we did not realize that our co-religionists the world over, and particularly the United States, must be prepared – *as quietly as possible* – to take the initiative."[96] A favoured strategy included regular meetings with Jewish members of Congress (including Sol Bloom [D-NY] and Emanuel Celler [D-NY]) and occasional entreaties to the White House. However, this approach generated disappointing results. The 1945 Truman Directive was seen by the AJC to be a response to its private representations to the secretary of state, and yet it initially led to the admission of only 2,400 Jewish DPs (many more were later authorized under the Directive).[97] Around the same time, Truman appointed Earl Harrison to prepare a report on the DP camps in Europe. Harrison's 1945 report likened the treatment of Jewish DPs to the Nazi concentration camps: "We appear to be treating the Jews as the Nazis treated them except we do not exterminate them."[98]

The year 1946 was a turning point for Jewish political mobilization. Following Harrison's report, the AJC undertook its own tour of the DP camps in Europe. It warned of "catastrophic consequences" if the United States did not begin large-scale refugee resettlement.[99] Its findings coincided with a wave of antisemitic mob violence in Poland, during which dozens of repatriated Holocaust survivors attempting to re-establish themselves in their hometowns were slaughtered. It became apparent, as the historian of the AJC notes, that "the only way to get any large numbers of Jews into the [United States] would be for Congress to pass emergency legislation."[100] The growing sense of urgency generated by the deteriorating situation in Europe propelled the AJC, in collaboration with other Jewish organizations in the United States and Europe, to push for the admission and resettlement of refugees to the United States.[101]

On 2 October 1946 the AJC passed a formal resolution to "undertake to devote its utmost efforts to the promotion of a liberalized policy of immigration in this country."[102] In response to this resolution, fifteen Jewish organizations began to openly lobby Congress to admit 100,000 Jewish refugees to the United States.[103] This was an unprecedented show of unity and public political advocacy. Representative Celler, a vocal advocate for immigration reform and the ranking Democrat on the House Judiciary Committee, responded to a letter from AJC President Joseph Proskauer with his personal support for such legislation. He strongly recommended, however, that the Jewish coalition "be broadened to include representatives from Gentile groups such as the Federal Council of Churches."[104] Indeed, it was becoming clear to refugee-advocacy groups that, without the support of Christian groups, Congress would be reluctant to pass legislation admitting large numbers of displaced people.[105]

The AJC proceeded to refocus its campaign to downplay the demands of Jewish refugees and instead draw attention to the refugee population as a whole.[106] The group's Immigration Committee resolved "to work closely with non-Jewish organizations ... such as the Federal Council of Churches, the National Catholic Welfare Conference, etc.," in addition to other Jewish organizations.[107] On 25 October 1946 the committee decided to take steps to initiate an interreligious "citizen's committee" that would be a "political action and propaganda group which would swing public sentiment in favor of relaxing immigration laws in order to admit a fair share of displaced persons to this country."[108] They recruited Earl Harrison, the author of Truman's DP report, to head up a new Citizens Committee on Displaced Persons (CCDP). The AJC envisioned that the committee would have as its primary objective the passage of new immigration legislation to admit 400,000 DPs (of whom 100,000 would be Jews). The committee met for the first time on 20 December 1946. Four-fifths of its members were Christians, and it was outwardly non-sectarian – although, as Genizi notes, it was "initiated, organized, and directed by members of Jewish organizations."[109]

In summary, many of the Jewish groups engaged with refugee issues were established around the turn of the century, although most of their efforts were focused on immigrant aid and lobbying through quiet politics. They were headed by community leaders and prominent citizens, embedded in transatlantic networks, and connected with local community groups and social-welfare organizations. In the late 1940s, the futility of diplomacy finally led national Jewish groups to convene and finance an interfaith coalition to lobby Congress for the large-scale admission of displaced people. The CCDP became regarded as "one of the largest and best-run lobbying groups in the nation" in 1947 and 1948.[110] It succeeded in helping to break the immigration deadlock, eventually contributing to the passage of the Displaced Persons Act of 1948 – the first post-war refugee legislation, which authorized the admission of some 205,000 DPs over a period of two years. By 1950, about 40,000 of the refugees resettled under this act were Jewish.[111]

American Council of Voluntary Agencies for Foreign Service

The leading Protestant, Catholic, and Jewish groups informally cooperated with each other in ways that have been cursorily described above and that will be further elaborated in later chapters. In addition, however, their collaboration became formalized with the creation of the American Council of Voluntary Agencies for Foreign Service (ACVA) in 1943. The council was established with the aim of coordinating the planning of relief and rehabilitation abroad following the end of the Second World War. The major agencies identified above were early members, along with other organizations such as the International Rescue Committee (IRC), the YMCA, Save the Children, and a host of other religious and voluntary groups concerned with post-war relief.

The formation of the ACVA was led by Joseph P. Chamberlain, chairman of the board of the National Refugee Service (later to become the United Service for New Americans [USNA]). During the war, relief groups were required to register and report their overseas work with the government under the 1939 Neutrality Act. In January 1943 Chamberlain addressed a memo titled "Private International Service Organizations in Post-War Relief" to many of these groups, outlining a proposed role to be played by Protestant, Catholic, Jewish, and other relief agencies in the post-war setting.[112] It underscored the value of their relief work during the war and projected a continued relationship with foreign-aid issues, organized through a formal coalition. The council was formally established on later that year, on 7 October.[113]

Within the council, the three main religious groups (NCWC, CWS, and USNA) formed a specialized committee to focus on the particular problem of displaced people.[114] This Joint Council on Resettlement, chaired by Chamberlain, was a space in which information was shared between the Protestant, Catholic, and Jewish groups about their advocacy efforts. It also became a point of increasing interaction with government agencies, Congress, and the leading resettlement organizations. Internal memos indicate agreement that "there is a need to have a body that gives a unified view from the three faiths."[115] The three religious groups viewed their role as "a spearhead to carry out the burden of the [resettlement] work in the US."[116] They saw themselves as the agencies responsible for carrying out the future operations of the DP program waiting to be approved by Congress.

Therefore, in addition to becoming the major coordinating agency of American non-profit relief organizations after the Second World War, the ACVA found itself at the centre of an emerging policy community connecting the major religious groups engaged with refugee-resettlement advocacy and implementation. In addition to facilitating information sharing and joint statements, the ACVA Joint Council on Resettlement also became a resource for government agencies looking to engage the voluntary sector on refugee issues. The Displaced Persons Commission (DPC), created by Congress to oversee the implementation of the Displaced Persons Act of 1948, sought out members of the ACVA Joint Council to serve on its advisory committee to aid in the coordination between private and public agencies.[117] In subsequent decades, it would serve as the primary voice of the religious refugee groups in testimony before Congress.

CANADA

Political Context: Refugee Policy during the War

In Canada, as in the United States, immigration ground to a virtual halt leading up to and during the Second World War. Restrictive policy extended back to the 1906 Immigration Act, which imposed additional racial and ethnic criteria for admission to Canada – a process that had been advancing since the 1885 Chinese Immigration Act and the 1885 Electoral Franchise Act, which were geared toward limiting Asian immigration. The 1910 Immigration Act prohibited immigrants "belonging to any race deemed unsuitable to the climate and requirements of Canada."[118] It invested cabinet with the authority to discriminate on the basis of race and ethnicity and to block the admission of refugees. Immigrants sponsored by welfare organizations were disallowed. The 1919 Immigration Act Amendment continued the expansion of the cabinet's authority in matters of immigration by allowing it to prohibit immigrants of any background owing to their "peculiar customs, habits, modes of life and methods of holding property."[119] Other measures targeted Chinese and black American immigration. Cabinet finally closed Canadian immigration almost completely in 1931 with Order-in-Council PC 695. It barred entrance to anyone non-American or non-British, without agricultural experience, or without a husband or father as a Canadian resident.[120] PC 695 was used in 1939 to justify Canada's infamous refusal to allow entry to passengers of the *St Louis*, a ship bearing Jewish refugees, which was forced to return its passengers to Europe, where many perished in the Holocaust.

In general, the public supported the restrictive stance taken by the government, with only "religious leaders and some newspaper editorials" voicing opposition.[121] As Kelley and Trebilcock note in their history of Canadian immigration policy: "The mechanisms for setting policy, primarily through executive orders and Immigration Branch directives, enabled the Prime Minister, Cabinet, and bureaucrats within the Immigration Branch to shape immigration policy quickly and relatively easily in response to public and personal biases, in the absence of parliamentary scrutiny."[122] Gerald Dirks adds that Parliament has rarely been an important actor in defining refugee policy, as decision-making processes are driven by "the stature and effectiveness of the responsible Cabinet ministers."[123]

William Lyon Mackenzie King, prime minister from 1935 to 1948, resisted admitting refugees because of apparent personal prejudices and worry about political backlash.[124] Privately, he recorded his concern that resettling refugees meant admitting Jews, and "we must ... seek to keep this part of the Continent free from ... too great an intermixture of foreign strains of blood."[125] Jewish leaders repeatedly lobbied him in private meetings during the 1930s and 1940s to admit refugees. In response to one such meeting, where the Canadian Jewish Congress provided assurances of sponsorships for refugees, he recorded his reply as follows: "I pointed out the sympathy we felt with the Jews and their plight ... but we had to consider the constituencies and the view of those who are supporting the government."[126] A key consistency that impeded the admission of refugees were voters in Quebec, where King was loathe to strengthen the position of Maurice Duplessis and his nationalist party.[127] However, opposition to refugees and the admission of Jews was not restricted to Quebec. While Canadian public opinion grew to be more sympathetic toward refugees, a majority – 61 per cent – remained opposed to admitting them to Canada. The meagre 21 per cent in favour of admitting refugees after the war expressed a preference for Scandinavian, Dutch, and French refugees.[128]

Following the war, one of the primary tensions in cabinet over refugees was between the Department of External Affairs and the

Department of Mines and Resources, within which the Immigration Branch was located. Whereas the foreign ministry became increasingly engaged with refugee issues and wished to see Canada make some contribution to European resettlement as a sign of post-war international leadership, the Immigration Branch resisted it.[129] Frederick Blair, director of immigration from 1936 to 1943, notoriously restricted the admission of Jews, making Canada "arguably the worst of all possible refugee receiving states" in this respect.[130] As one diplomat commented, "External Affairs battered vigorously against what they regarded as the defensive mentality entrenched in the Immigration Branch, sought to warn the cabinet of the desperate realities they saw in Europe, and to encourage an imaginative approach to population policy for Canada."[131] The keys to unlock immigration were held by the gatekeepers, and the gatekeepers were Immigration Branch bureaucrats.

Bureaucrats exerted a disproportionate amount of control over immigration policy, compared with other government departments.[132] There was little appetite among political leaders to make immigration a subject of public discussion, so an unusual amount of policy authority was delegated to public servants. The concentration of authority over refugee policy within the Immigration Branch of the Department of Mines and Resources made this venue a focus of advocacy efforts to reform refugee-resettlement policy.

In Canada, religious groups mobilized more slowly than in the United States in part because the political opportunity structures did not materialize as quickly. Whereas the 1945 Truman Directive gave an impetus for religious groups to consolidate and organize their resettlement schemes in response to an opening for cooperative sponsorship with the government, Canada offered no such opportunity. Furthermore, lobbying legislators was of no use. Authority over immigration and refugee policy was concentrated in the hands of bureaucrats animated by the conviction that "people should be kept out of Canada instead of being let in."[133]

When displaced people began to be admitted in larger numbers in the late 1940s, they were primarily selected and resettled through a government-run "bulk-labour" scheme tied to specific labour-market needs. Religious groups subsequently lobbied bureaucrats to create a complementary scheme of refugee resettlement focused on humanitarian admissions and family migration. As Tanya Basok and Alan Simmons observe, the idea of admitting refugees as a special class

Table 1.2
Religious groups in Canada

Group	Denomination	Dates Active
Canadian Jewish Congress (CJC)	Jewish	1919–2011
Jewish Immigrant Aid Services (JIAS)	Jewish	1922–Present
Canadian Mennonite Board of Colonization*	Mennonite	1923–59
German Baptist Immigration and Colonization Society*	Baptist	1929–54
Catholic Immigrant Aid Society*	Roman Catholic	1928–57
Canadian National Committee on Refugees (CNCR)	Interfaith Coalition	1938–48
United Jewish Relief Agencies (UJRA)	Jewish	1938–74
Canadian Council of Churches	Ecumenical Protestant	1944–Present
Canadian Lutheran World Relief (CLWR)*	Lutheran	1946–Present
Rural Settlement Society	Roman Catholic	1946–57
Canadian Christian Council for the Resettlement of Refugees (CCCRR)	Ecumenical Coalition	1947–57
Catholic Immigration Service	Roman Catholic	1957–1980s

*Members of the CCCRR.

– outside of "population policy" – was advanced primarily by religious groups: "The explicit recognition by the Federal government of humanitarian considerations was promoted by church groups and their allies within Canada, and at the same time tended to legitimize and empower those same groups to act as spokespersons for refugee interests."[134] Even though they shared similar motivations and resources as their American counterparts, the difference in political opportunity structures encountered by religious groups marked an early divergence between the two cases that will be introduced below and further examined in the next chapter.

Having set out aspects of the context surrounding Canadian refugee policy, the following sections trace the mobilization of Christian and Jewish groups within this environment.

Christian Groups

As in the United States, the majority of Christians in Canada responded to the refugee crisis in Europe with indifference.[135] The mobilization of Christian groups and their engagement with refugee policy were advanced by two key developments. The first was the entrepreneurial initiative of leaders of religious communities with close ties to Germany – particularly Lutheran, Mennonite, Baptist, and Catholic groups. The second was the partnership between a number of these domestic groups and international affiliates with strong European connections, such as the World Council of Churches, the Vatican, Lutheran World Relief, and the Mennonite Central Committee.

Canadian Protestant churches were slow to rally to the cause of refugee relief and resettlement during the Second World War. A few clergymen became active in the establishment and advocacy of the Canadian National Committee on Refugees (CNCR), which will be discussed further below. However, in general, early public advocacy in favour of admitting refugees came primarily from a few outspoken clergymen and not from broad-based community support or strong institutional engagement by Christian groups.[136] A handful of senior clergymen from the Anglican Church and the United Church spoke up on behalf of refugees and sought to mobilize their reluctant denominations.[137] The Reverend Claris Silcox's outspoken advocacy led the United Church – the largest Protestant denomination in Canada – to submit a rather ambivalent statement to the director of immigration appealing to the government to "do its utmost for refugees" and informing him that the United Church "would favour a slightly more 'open door' policy in the matter of immigration."[138] This feeble advocacy for refugee admissions speaks volumes about the lack of enthusiasm for the idea among mainline Protestant church leaders.

The transatlantic ecumenical movement helped stimulate the Canadian Protestant churches to advocate for and participate in refugee resettlement, just as it did in the United States. A 1942 World Council of Churches report that recognized the initiation of a Canadian committee of the WCC – later, the Canadian Council of Churches (CCC) – also noted the priority it ought to give to refugee relief: "It is not by accident that one of the first new tasks which the Provisional Committee of the World Council took on after its formation was assistance to refugees. For it is our duty and privilege to show the Christian refugee who has lost his fatherland that wherever he goes he remains a member of the world-wide Christian community. Thus our ministry to the refugees is not merely a matter of philanthropy; it is a witness to the reality of the Church in which men of all nations and races are bound together by a deep solidarity."[139] This vision of solidarity was not immediately interpreted as applying to refugee admissions; rather, an initial focus was on fundraising to support relief efforts in Europe. However, over time, the Canadian Council of Churches became more closely associated with the international refugee-resettlement initiatives of the World Council of Churches.

The process of forming the Canadian Council of Churches began in 1942 at a meeting hosted by the Reverend W.J. Gallagher of the United Church. Its intention was to amalgamate and assume the responsibilities of the Christian Social Council of Canada and the Joint Committee for Evangelization of Canadian Life within the ecumenical framework developed by the World Council of Churches.[140] The CCC was formally established in September 1944 and held its first annual meeting at Yorkminster Baptist Church in Toronto. The new body "accepted the responsibility of serving as the agency of the ecumenical movement in Canada, and of pursuing the purposes and caring for the interests of the WCC" in Canada.[141] Its purpose was understood by its members to be primarily evangelical, with a global social mission. As Andrew Thompson notes of that first meeting, "all in attendance shared the belief that the elusive answer to war could be found in the gospel. Indeed, the initial function of the organization was to condition 'the mind of the world for peace' through Christ."[142]

The Canadian Council of Churches gradually embraced the idea of advocating for refugee resettlement as a result of policy direction given by the World Council of Churches. Initially, the CCC focused its refugee efforts on raising funds from its thousands of member churches to support the WCC refugee division.[143] There appeared to be no prospect in the early 1940s of Canada accepting significant numbers of refugees, and these funds were directed toward European aid and relief administered by the WCC. However, there is some evidence of early interest in advocacy for immigration reform. The CCC was a member of the Committee for the Repeal of the Chinese Immigration Act, whose aims were successfully achieved in 1947.[144] Initial lobbying on refugees was more measured in its advocacy. An undated memo (presumably between 1947 and 1948) presented to Prime Minister King stated:

> The Canadian Council of Churches has viewed with satisfaction the increasing movement of immigrants to Canada from Great Britain and from among the refugees and displaced persons of Europe. It welcomes the more generous policy which is now being developed for the entry of immigrants of the latter

classification. The Council believes that Canada should assume her full share of responsibility for the reception and settlement of refugees and displaced persons, not only to meet the economic and industrial needs of Canada, but on humanitarian grounds and as a matter of moral obligation as well.[145]

This position of the CCC and its member churches – that Canada should accept refugees on the basis of human need rather than economic utility – was repeated in communications with the government throughout the late 1940s and 1950s, as the policy discourse tended toward admitting refugees to meet specific occupational demands of a growing economy. The CCC became a "linchpin" of Canada's DP program, connecting refugees nominated by the WCC in Europe and boasting a network of denominational newsletters and some 6,000 member churches across the country.[146]

Similar to their Protestant counterparts, Catholic groups were not publicly active in efforts to advocate for the admission of refugees during the Second World War. In fact, the region of the country where the Roman Catholic Church exerted the strongest cultural and policy influence – Quebec – was also one of the primary barriers to the admission of Jewish refugees.[147] Neither the bishops nor lay Catholics mobilized publicly to advocate greater refugee admissions in the run-up to or during the Second World War. Had they done so, it would have been through quiet back channels of what Patrick Lacroix calls "elite conciliation" and "subdued visibility."[148] Until 1943, when the Canadian Catholic Conference[149] was formed, the church did not have a permanent episcopal body to coordinate approaches to national issues.[150] The Catholic Church in Canada was also in the midst of a shift from what Robert Choquette has said was a church "fragmented into a series of ethno-cultural and linguistic lobbies"[151] into one that "embraced a humanistic conception of society largely based on universal values and tolerance."[152]

The primary impetus for Catholic mobilization on immigration and refugee policy came from the Vatican. Lacroix notes the important role of "papal exhortation, shortly after the Second World War," in stimulating the Canadian Catholic Conference to organize its members into a committee for immigration.[153] Although Catholic refugee resettlement work would later be consolidated into a single Catholic Immigration Service (1957) to better facilitate collaboration with the Catholic Immigration Commission established by the Holy See in

Geneva, it began with two separate national entities. The first was the Rural Settlement Society (est. 1946), based in Montreal, and the second was the Catholic Immigrant Aid Society (est. 1922), based in Winnipeg.[154] The Rural Settlement Society focused on both the recruitment of famers and family reunification –especially facilitating the immigration of German and Italian women and children who had remained in Europe when their husbands and fathers had immigrated.[155] Its work grew to have a national scope. The Catholic Immigrant Aid Society tended to focus on specific regions and ethnic groups and was later subsumed under the Rural Settlement Society in 1951 as part of an effort to "provide a broader base to Catholic migration work."[156]

A number of denominational Protestant groups with strong ties to Germany were initiated or reformed in the late 1940s with the aim of supporting refugee relief in Europe. These included the Canadian Mennonite Board of Colonization, Canadian Lutheran World Relief (CWLR), and the German Baptist Immigration and Colonization Society.[157] Of the three groups, CWLR was "the most active, best funded, and well connected."[158] These groups had strong institutional networks in both Europe and Canada, and their motivations for mobilizing evolved over time. At first, they formed simply to raise funds to supply material relief to refugees in the occupied zones of Germany.

Cabinet's 1946 Order-in-Council PC 2071 authorized the resettlement of refugees who had close relatives in Canada. The Close Relatives Program was likely a reaction to a set of very critical Senate hearings on immigration policy during 1946, which found that "Canada, as a humane and Christian nation, should do her share toward the relief of refugees and displaced peoples."[159] Although the Canadian public still opposed accepting refugees from Europe, the Senate committee recommended that Canada resettle displaced people "to hold [its] place abroad and maintain and improve [its] standard of living at home."[160] According to one scholar, the report "marked a watershed" in Canadian immigration policy by calling for the resettlement of refugees.[161] PC 2071 gave permission for certain categories of relatives of residents of Canada to immigrate as displaced persons; however, as J.M. Bumsted notes, "it was not intended to represent the opening of any floodgates."[162] The definition of a first-degree relative eligible for sponsorship was made narrow. And, as Parliament was told, "the amending of the regulations does not mean immediate action will be taken to admit immigrants from overseas."[163]

In fact, acting upon PC 2071 was more difficult than expected. The Canadian government relied on the International Refugee Organization (IRO) to facilitate arrangements in Europe for the resettlement of refugees and displaced persons. However, the IRO's definition of displaced people excluded ethnic Germans who were not German citizens, which left many close relatives of Canadians unassisted by the IRO. A third of the approved family-reunification cases submitted by Canada were rejected for resettlement on these grounds.[164] The policy failure of PC 2071 unexpectedly created a crucial window of opportunity for religious groups advocating for increased resettlement.

In response to problems with the government's program to admit family members of Canadians, Christian groups began to lobby immigration officials to allow them to work with their international affiliates in Europe to facilitate cases of family reunification "as a matter of Christianity and humanity."[165] The Lutheran, Mennonite, and Baptist groups joined with the Catholic Immigrant Aid Society to form the Canadian Christian Council for the Resettlement of Refugees (CCCRR) in 1947. Their involvement in family reunification through the CCCRR gave them a foothold to increase their resettlement activity, with the aim of augmenting the membership of their churches.[166]

The CCCRR was formed to "overcome this deficiency and create an agency which could process the refugees who do not come under the Mandate of IRO."[167] One historian of Canadian refugee policy has called the creation of the CCCRR, in cooperation with immigration officials, a "marriage of convenience."[168] Canadian immigration officials did not have a strong field presence in Europe, and the partnership between religious groups and their international affiliates enabled them to overcome the IRO problem. Another historian called the partnership "extraordinary in the context of Canadian immigration history,"[169] which up to that point had been relatively insulated from interest-group lobbying.[170]

The purpose of the CCCRR was "to organize the assembly abroad, selection, presentation to Canadian immigration offices, and onward movement to Canada of refugees and displaced persons."[171] Through the European networks of its members, and with the cooperation of the Canadian authorities, it set up a processing camp in Hanover to facilitate the immigration of refugees who had close relatives in Canada. The leading member of the CCCRR (in terms of annual refugee sponsorships) was Canadian Lutheran World Relief, which received financial and administrative support from its international affiliate, Lutheran World Relief.[172] The Baptist group partnered with the Baptist World Alliance and later with the World Council of Churches.[173] The Mennonite group cooperated with the Mennonite Central Committee, the international relief agency of the Mennonites.[174] These international partnerships shaped the field presence, the policy direction, and in some cases the financial stability of the Christian groups in Canada.

Although the initial focus of the CCCRR was on helping close relatives, it generated a novel form of cooperation with the government on refugee resettlement. As Angelika Sauer notes, the success of the CCCRR was in part due to its willingness to work within existing political realities instead of pressing for parliamentary opposition or voicing criticism through the press.[175] It contributed to the creation of a policy field in which religious groups received authority to preselect refugees for resettlement in Canada and use private funds to support their relocation to targeted communities. The Immigration Branch would repeatedly try to repeal the privileges granted to the CCCRR, the Canadian Council of Churches, and Jewish groups.[176] But, as the following chapter elaborates in more detail, the CCCRR, the Rural Settlement Society, the Canadian Council of Churches, and Jewish Immigrant Aid Services (JIAS) later entered into a more formal partnership with the Immigration Branch that extended and formalized such cooperative arrangements through an Approved Church Program. Despite great reluctance by bureaucrats in the Immigration Branch to support these kinds of arrangements, they would slowly grow and consolidate in response to future refugee crises.

Jewish Groups

Efforts to create a national Jewish organization began in 1919, when the Canadian Jewish Congress was formally established. Soon after its formation, Jewish Immigrant Aid Services was created as a "voluntary pioneering organization, founded in response to a definite need to help Jewish immigrants obtain entry to Canada and assist them in their adjustment to their new surroundings in this country."[177] However, as Irving Abella and Harold Troper note, these organizations "foundered on the rocks of internal disharmony" and were essentially "moribund" until the rise of Hitler in Germany. Even after the CJC was resuscitated in 1934, it remained fractured between its three regions of Winnipeg, Toronto, and Montreal, and it was unable to bridge a divide between leftist factions and local Jewish elites.[178] And, despite the attempts to unify immigration aid efforts under the authority of JIAS, the private initiatives of "migration entrepreneurs" and consultants were perceived to undermine its efforts to pressure the government to accept more refugees.[179] In the 1930s, therefore, efforts to organize Jewish political advocacy and refugee assistance suffered from disunity and weak national organization.[180]

In the years leading up to the Second World War, Jewish advocacy for the expansion of refugee admissions was initially advanced through the informal efforts of a handful of influential Jewish citizens. Most prominent among them was a group of three Jewish members of Parliament, Liberals who had been elected in 1935.[181] The Jewish community in Canada, like that in the United States, was reluctant to press its case openly and publicly for fear of activating widespread antisemitism; instead, it sought the intervention of these men to try to moderate the government's restrictive immigration policy. Little of real consequence was achieved through this approach, aside from a few preferential admissions for prominent families. Furthermore, it reinforced the impression of government leaders that the brewing refugee problem in Europe was primarily a Jewish issue – and therefore one that political leaders saw as a threat to national cohesion.

The political engagement of the Canadian Jewish Congress appeared to reach a turning point on the eve of the outbreak of war with Germany in response to the *Kristallnacht*. In November 1938 it changed tactics from quiet diplomacy focused on the particular demands of Jews to embracing a public campaign that put non-Jews into more prominent positions of advocacy. The CJC "instructed its local organizations to insure that [public] meetings be non-sectarian, that non-Jewish community leaders play a prominent role and that most of the speakers be Gentile."[182] Successful demonstrations brought out national journalists, trade unionists, and church leaders to call on Canada to "provide havens of refuge for the victims of Nazi brutality."[183] Heartened by the show of public support, CJC representatives joined the Jewish MPs and JIAS in a meeting with Mackenzie King to ask him to admit 10,000 Jewish refugees – offering to guarantee them employment and assure the government that they would not become public charges. King denied their request, citing concern over the "forces of separatism" emanating from Quebec.

Before the meeting with King, the CJC had resolved to create a non-sectarian body that could "approach the Government and appeal to them directly for favourable consideration on a purely humanitarian basis."[184] Such a group was, in fact, formed independent of its own efforts and led by a number of the prominent non-Jewish citizens who had spoken at its public meetings. The Canadian League of Nations Society sponsored a national refugee conference in December 1938 under the leadership of Senator Cairine Wilson and with the support of the Canadian Jewish Congress. The formation of the Canadian National Committee on Refugees soon followed, with Senator Wilson as its chairperson. While Jewish involvement in the CNCR was intentionally kept in the background, the Congress played an integral role in expanding its membership, financing its operations, and even in providing printing and mailing services to facilitate its efforts. The CNCR became the most outspoken refugee-advocacy group during the war, exerting pressure on the government to adopt a humanitarian refugee policy that would include Jews. It pledged, in association with the CJC's United Jewish Relief Agencies (UJRA), to guarantee sponsorship of refugees that would be admitted.[185] The CJC also coordinated its advocacy with the CNCR, which could be counted on to make arguments for liberalizing immigration policy in line with Canada's national interest.

On the surface, the CNCR resembled the Citizens Committee on Displaced People. Both were interfaith coalitions that included secular groups and movements and were supported heavily by national Jewish groups determined to advocate publicly for refugee resettlement. However, the Canadian CNCR, unlike the American CCDP, was relatively ineffective at achieving its aims. Because decision making about immigration policy was concentrated within cabinet and the immigration bureaucracy, advocacy focused on parliamentarians and public opinion achieved relatively little. This will be discussed further in the next chapter.

The advocacy of Jewish groups produced little practical effect for refugee admissions and for European Jews. Between 1937 and 1945, less than 6 per cent of all immigrants and refugees admitted to Canada were Jews.[186] Many of these refugees were German and Austrian nationals (primarily students and rabbis) who had been living in the United Kingdom when the war erupted. They were transferred to Canada by Britain as "potentially dangerous enemy aliens" and were finally released and settled after the war when sponsors (typically JIAS) could guarantee their maintenance.[187] When Canada did begin admitting larger numbers of refugees in 1948, Jews constituted a fraction of those accepted by Canada; most were relatives, orphans, or workers in trades in demand. Even after the government started to accept displaced people, Ottawa instructed their "mobile immigration teams" responsible for selection in Europe to reject Jewish applicants.[188]

Jewish immigration to Canada only really accelerated after the creation of the State of Israel, once the Jewish emergency in Europe had diminished in urgency. As Jewish immigration rose, the JIAS continued to expand its operations to resettle refugees from Europe. The expansion of JIAS's operations was facilitated by collaboration between the CJC and the European headquarters of the Joint Distribution Committee, which helped identify refugees for resettlement in Canada under the sponsorship and assistance of the JIAS and the CJC.[189] This often meant following labour-market selection criteria set by immigration officials. The JIAS's work grew to such an extent that Hawkins deemed it "one of the best performers among the agencies which help immigrants," owing to its strong international network, integrated community ties, and well-funded professional staff.[190] After DPs began to arrive, the director of JIAS compiled a brief report on the range of its activities with the purpose of sharing its experience with other groups that were new to the field of refugee settlement in Canada. Its work included the following: helping refugees obtain a permit of entry to Canada; receiving them upon their arrival to Canada and escorting them to their destination; securing employment; providing needy refugees with shelter, food, medical care, and other necessities; and conducting night courses for language instruction and "the basic rudiments of citizenship."[191]

During the period after the Second World War, Jewish groups underwent a process of consolidation in relation to refugee assistance. A number of immigrant aid groups had been active in the early twentieth century, many of them with transatlantic ties and constituencies within pockets of the Jewish community in Canada. These groups included the Federation of Polish Jews, the Jewish Peoples' Relief Committee, the Joint Distribution Committee, the Jewish Immigrant Aid Society, and the United Jewish Relief Agencies.[192] Over time, the Canadian Jewish Congress emerged as the principal advocacy group, with the JIAS eventually assuming a growing responsibility for overseeing and coordinating refugee settlement in Canada.

To recapitulate, although a number of national Jewish groups existed prior to the Second World War and advocated for the resettlement of Jewish refugees, they were generally unsuccessful in achieving their goals. The primary reason was widespread antisemitism that either affected decision makers directly or shaped how they anticipated their actions would be received by the public. As in the United States, Jewish groups were led by prominent citizens, became embedded in transatlantic partnerships, and increasingly connected with local community groups that were part of the JIAS network. Although the advocacy efforts of the CJC led to dozens of meetings with the prime minister, testimony before parliamentary hearings, and expressions of sympathy by national civil-society leaders, they hardly moved the needle on refugee admissions. Even after Canada began to open its doors to DPs, only three of the first 2,900 refugees to arrive were Jews.[193] Nevertheless, by the end of the 1940s, the Jewish community was led by a well-organized and publicly engaged CJC and supported by a competent and professional JIAS. Both would play key roles alongside Christian groups in the refugee policy process, following the cooperative approach pioneered by the Canadian Christian Council for the Resettlement of Refugees – a nascent form of private sponsorship.

CONCLUSION

The religious groups described above were the primary groups to mobilize and publicly advocate for the resettlement of refugees in the United States and Canada during after the Second World War. However, religion did not automatically generate political action. Political mobilization followed when at least three dimensions were engaged: religious and cultural motivation, marshalling of resources and social capital, and response to political opportunity structures.[194] This chapter has discussed how religious groups formed, mobilized, and consolidated with reference to these three dimensions. In the next chapter, I compare in more detail the policy processes in the United States and Canada during the period from 1945 to 1955, when both countries formulated their responses to the refugee crisis following the Second World War.

2

Overcoming Restriction

Religious Groups and the Post-War Refugee Policy Process

The problem of European displaced people was one of the leading international issues of the post-war period as the Allied powers struggled to resolve a growing humanitarian crisis.[1] The decisions by the United States and Canada to resettle around half of the displaced people in Europe reversed decades of restrictive policy. Although foreign policy played a key role in both countries' decisions to admit refugees, other domestic factors shaped the precise nature of the policy response and the structures designed for implementation. This chapter traces the evolution of the policy cycle leading to the post-war resettlement programs in both countries. Programs that were intended to be temporary became more permanent as they started a pathway of institutional and policy development that continues to define refugee policy today.

The chapter tracks the advocacy of religious groups in the context of four major phases of the policy cycle. While these phases are discussed sequentially, this is primarily for heuristic purposes in order to highlight different features of the policy process.[2] The first relates to the efforts of groups and political actors to contribute to agenda setting by presenting policy problems and attempting to frame them in particular ways.[3] The second phase is policy formulation: a smaller set of actors – typically limited to experts, insider groups, and government decision makers – refines options to resolve a given policy problem. A third phase of decision making primarily takes place within what John Kingdon calls the "political stream" of the policy process.[4] This process of decision making, as a number of early theorists pointed out, is not strictly rational in the sense of choosing the most efficient means to achieve policy goals.[5] It is contingent and embedded in political and cognitive processes that limit the range of options that are considered to be feasible means by which to address a policy problem.[6] Finally, a fourth phase of the policy process relates to implementation and administration.

With regard to this fourth phase, most studies of policy implementation focus either on top-down, command-and-control management by policymakers or on the creative initiatives undertaken by "street-level" bureaucrats.[7] Where groups are included it is usually in relation to monitoring implementation and exerting pressure on the government to carry out (or to reverse) policy decisions.[8] This theory of implementation is incomplete, however. Groups can also influence policy implementation by aiding, and even expanding, the scope of authorized policies by executing them on behalf of governments. Refugee resettlement, as it came to be conceived in both the United States and Canada, demanded the delivery of an array of social services to ensure the identification, transportation, settlement, and integration of refugees. Religious groups assumed significant responsibilities at multiple stages in the resettlement process in both countries, becoming crucial actors in the implementation of policy decisions to accept refugees outside of normal immigration regulations. In the process, they created structures and processes that produced positive feedback effects leading to the replication of past programs.

UNITED STATES

Agenda Setting and Issue Framing

According to the standard history of U.S. refugee policy, lobbying by the Jewish community was a major influence on the decision to admit large numbers of DPs after the war. Gil Loescher and John Scanlan argue that refugees in European camps could have been there for decades with no permanent home were it not for "substantial segments of the American Jewish community ... [who had] become alarmed at the condition of Jewish survivors in DP camps and ... [began] lobbying for a new program of admission to the US."[9] They assert that the efforts of Jewish groups "were decisive in creating a new American attitude toward refugees, and a new legislative modality which would permit the entry of many as special immigrants."[10] Gibney repeats this claim, stating that "lobbying by domestic Jewish organizations ... led to the formulation of a position by the US Executive favourable to the resettlement of displaced persons."[11] He continues: "While a number of factors combined to make the admittance of the displaced persons an important issue for the US government in the mid 1940s, chief amongst them was lobbying by Jewish pressure groups."[12]

This conclusion needs to be qualified. Although Jewish groups played an early and leading role in putting the issue of refugees on the government agenda, their capacity to achieve legislative goals depended on expanding the issue frame of European refugees so as to encompass Christians. It also required reframing DPs as refugees from Communism rather than as victims of vanquished Nazism. To do this, they worked with Protestant and Catholic groups, which were in fact the crucial actors in the coalition advocating for refugee resettlement. Prejudice toward Jews was simply too widespread and too powerful for Jewish groups to succeed on their own.

As discussed in the previous chapter, the mobilization of Protestant and Catholic groups during the mid-1940s, accompanied by the formation of the American Council of Voluntary Agencies and the Citizens Committee on Displaced People, brought new and influential actors into the refugee policy process. Ultimately, the effort to frame the refugee crisis in Europe as a problem of Jewish Holocaust survivors was insufficient to secure major legislation. Widespread antisemitism was a clear impediment to achieving meaningful action. In 1944 the temporary admission of less than a thousand Jewish refugees from Eastern Europe generated a significant backlash from Congress and the conservative press. New and different approaches would be needed to secure the legislation required to admit large numbers of refugees.

After the termination of hostilities, the American Jewish Committee and other Jewish groups made statements emphasizing the specific injustice suffered by Jews at the hands of the Nazis: "This is not a question of charity," one statement read. "As long as the Jewish victims of fascism are denied justice, democracy and freedom generally are in danger."[13] Initially, the AJC focused on advocating the appointment of special liaisons within the U.S. Army to give particular attention to the needs of stateless Jews in the Allied zone. After several months of lobbying by the AJC and a coalition of Jewish congressmen, they received a reply from the War Department that allowed them to appoint, at their own expense, "a limited number of representatives who are satisfactory to the United States ... to assist with problems of Jewish stateless and nonrepatriable persons in the US zone in Germany."[14] The appointment of these liaisons, while of seemingly minor significance, was a step toward the development of an infrastructure to resettle Jewish refugees. It initiated a degree of formal cooperation between Jewish groups and government agencies responsible for refugees.

The AJC also pushed for the admission of refugees from Europe within the framework of existing immigration law. The 1945 Truman Directive directed consulates in Europe to give preferential access to visas for displaced people. While it authorized the admission of 40,000 people, only about half that number arrived in the United States – some two-thirds of whom were Jewish.[15] The AJC urged the secretary of state to open consulates in areas where DPs were concentrated in order to fill unmet country quotas that were specified in the Quota Law of 1924.[16] In December, Edwin Rosenberg, the director of the National Refugee Service – one of the leading Jewish organizations at the time – was called to the White House to discuss the measures President Truman intended to take. In a letter to his counterpart at the National Catholic Welfare Conference, Rosenberg explained: "We were told that the Government would count heavily on us in adjustment of the thousands of prospective new immigrants, and in preventing them from becoming public charges."[17] Although the Truman Directive targeted DPs, it admitted them under existing immigration law. Despite the relatively small number admitted under the Directive, it provided a framework for voluntary groups to nominate refugees for resettlement by issuing a "corporate affidavit," a guarantee that refugees would become self-supporting. This measure further stimulated the mobilization and consolidation of Catholic and Protestant refugee groups – opening the door for them to sponsor family members and co-religionists they wished to rescue from DP camps – and set an important precedent for future refugee legislation.

A year after the Truman Directive, the number of refugees admitted to the United States was still unsatisfactorily low. The AJC noted that only 2,400 Jewish refugees had been admitted by October 1946.[18] Furthermore, reports of atrocities committed against Jews who attempted to repatriate after the war were increasing the alarm over continued barriers to resettlement.[19] On 7 October 1946 the AJC resolved "to devote its utmost efforts to the promotion of a liberalized policy of immigration to this country."[20] This included a push to bring 100,000 Jewish refugees to the United States.[21]

Christian groups became more effectively organized during this time and also began to advocate more publicly and forcefully for the admission of refugees. The president of the Federal Council of Churches wrote to President Truman affirming support for his 1945 Directive,[22] and in September 1946 a resolution was passed urging the FCC to "give earnest attention to the proposals that are being made to obtain Congressional legislation that will at least temporarily increase the immigration quotas so that a larger number of Displaced Persons in Europe may be permitted to find a permanent home in America."[23] The National Catholic Welfare Conference likewise reported that it would publicly advocate for raising the immigration quotas in the United States to admit 100,000 DPs.[24]

As Christian groups mobilized in support of refugee resettlement, the AJC also resolved to advocate more publicly and to build interfaith coalitions with these groups.[25] In October 1946 the AJC Immigration Committee deliberated at length on the creation of a Citizens Committee on Displaced People, which would facilitate its collaboration with "non-Jewish organizations who have indicated support of this program, such as the Federal Council of Churches, the National Catholic Welfare Conference, etc."[26] It envisioned a "political action and propaganda group which would serve to swing public sentiment in favor of relaxing immigration laws in order to admit a fair share of displaced people to this country."[27] It recognized that the "most urgent" matter in forming the committee was obtaining "the support of Protestant and Catholic church leaders."[28] The committee decided to bring the proposal of the Citizens Committee to the following meeting of the American Council of Voluntary Agencies "to push the Citizens Committee idea and see whether it can be set up without further delay under the immediate auspices of that group."[29] The Citizens Committee on Displaced Persons was launched in December 1946 under the titular leadership of Earl Harrison, with thirty-two leading Protestants and Catholics on its board of directors.

A key strategic decision made by the CCDP was to reframe the refugee issue. Its advocacy marked a clear departure from the approaches of Christian groups, which emphasized charity and humanitarian action for needy refugees, and Jewish groups, which called for justice for their co-religionists. Instead, "its propaganda consistently identified the displaced persons in intentionally general language which downplayed Jewish and Eastern European origins and emphasized Christian and anti-communist characteristics."[30] Genizi notes that the shift in framing was partly designed to mobilize churchgoers, who viewed Communism with special hostility as an atheistic doctrine – "Christianity's archenemy."[31]

The CCDP assumed a leading role in mobilizing the public support of labour, veteran, religious, women's, and social-welfare groups for the cause of admitting DPs. Interest groups that had opposed the admission of DPs, like the American Legion and the American Federation of Labor (AFL), joined its call for "non-sectarian," "emergency," and "temporary" legislation to solve the displaced-persons problem.[32] It distributed fact sheets and editorials to try to influence thousands of decision makers. It attracted a handful of prominent patrons at the national level – such as Eleanor Roosevelt and Fiorello LaGuardia – and mobilized more than 150 local committees to foster more favourable public opinion.[33]

The creation of the CCDP was accompanied by a shift in issue framing of European refugees, away from survivors of the Jewish Holocaust to a larger group of Christians and Jews displaced by the circumstances of the Second World War. This shift proved to be significant for the creation of a political coalition needed to pass refugee legislation in Congress.

Policy Formulation

The three-year process leading to the passage of legislation in 1948 and 1950 to admit refugees from Europe was spearheaded by the CCDP and the religious groups in its coalition. In April 1947 the CCDP wrote a DP bill that was presented to Congress by Representative William Stratton (R-IL), reflecting the issue frame it had developed around the refugee crisis in Europe.[34] Stratton described the DP population as composed "primarily of Christians" who were "unsettled and homeless people who dare not return to their former homes where they would meet persecution, abuse, and even death at the hands of Communist-dominated governments."[35] The initiation of the bill marked the first serious attempt to bring legislation forward that reflected a phase of policy formulation in response to the DP crisis. It proposed a resettlement program that would admit 100,000 refugees a year, for four years, as non-quota immigrants. The bill's definition of a displaced person was strikingly similar to the definition of a refugee that would later be formalized in the 1951 Geneva Convention.[36] By the summer of 1947, the bill counted among its proponents some 120 national interest groups, the *Washington Post*, *Life Magazine*, the *New York Times*, Secretary of State George Marshall, and Secretary of War Robert Patterson.[37] Nevertheless, it foundered on the shoals of overwhelming restrictionism within a Republican-controlled House and Senate that President Truman was unable or unwilling to influence. Despite efforts to reframe the refugee population in Europe as predominantly Christian, internal reports indicate that a major obstacle to the bill among congressmen was the belief that "it will admit too many Jews."[38]

In the meantime, the situation of displaced people in Europe continued to deteriorate, and pressure increased on the U.S. government to launch a resettlement initiative. After the failure of the Stratton Bill, the *Washington Post* worried that the unwillingness of lawmakers to act on the problem of displaced people "will subject the United States to the charge that our professions of democracy and humanitarianism are [a] mockery."[39] In addition to the existing domestic pressure, the opening salvos of the Cold War also centred on refugees. The Soviet Union demanded repatriation of their prisoners of war, which the United States refused owing to reports of persecution that these POWs faced upon their return. The United States therefore led the way in the creation of the International Refugee Organization, which formally came into existence in 1948 (against Soviet protestations). The primary purpose of the IRO was to facilitate the international resettlement of refugees from Europe. "By taking these steps," note Loescher and Scanlan, "the Truman administration converted the refugee issue into an aspect of the emerging cold war, and thus provided a new basis for conservative support."[40] Nevertheless, Congress insisted that U.S. membership in the IRO be made conditional upon a guarantee that domestic immigration law would not be changed without further legislation. This was as much a defensive measure against the executive assuming congressional powers as it was a reassertion of restrictionism.

The leading role assumed by the United States in creating and financing the IRO, and its signalling of a new era of anti-Communist foreign policy, generated another set of arguments for resettling refugees. Secretary of State George Marshall declared that the refugees were an important weapon in the Cold War and that their resettlement would also hasten post-war economic recovery in Europe, thereby releasing the United States from continuing financial burdens.[41] The focus of the IRO on restricting forced repatriation and promoting third-country resettlement represented a moral victory of sorts for the religious groups, which had lobbied to establish these features as foundations of an international approach to refugee problems.[42] Congressional approval for participating in the IRO made it increasingly likely that the United States would have to accept a portion of the remaining displaced people in Europe. However, there were still a number of competing proposals to modify the provisions of the original Stratton Bill to make it more palatable to the restrictionists, whose votes were needed to pass the legislation.

Another displaced-persons bill, which retained many the features of the original bill while also adding a number of restrictive provisions, was tabled in April 1948 by Representative Frank Fellows (R-ME). The Fellows bill cut the number of admissions in half (from 400,000 to 202,000); linked eligibility for admission to entry into the Allied zone of Austria or Germany before 21 April 1947; and required that all admissions be "borrowed" against future national-origins quotas. In other words, it left the national immigration quotas and exclusions legislated by the Immigration Act of 1924 intact so that the admission of refugees in the short term would diminish future arrivals from their countries of origin in the future. Finally, the bill specified that every family admitted under the law required an "assurance" of a job and housing in the United States, effectively replicating the policy innovation introduced under the Truman Directive and mandating a role for the religious groups and voluntary agencies in implementing the intended legislation. The Fellows bill passed the House, but it needed to be reconciled with what would come out of the traditionally more restrictive Senate.

Decision Making

The process of passing workable and effective legislation would ultimately depend upon assurances and guarantees offered by Christian groups to wary legislators. Protestant groups banded together to try to mobilize their members to support refugee legislation, with the knowledge that this was a key constituency for passing a workable law. A widely published ecumenical statement commented on the scale and severity of the problem, emphasized the networks and resources of Protestant churches, and presented refugees in the language of personalism:

> Our first-hand knowledge of the situation in Europe and our personal contact with refugees themselves fills us with concern which no administrative reorganization can relieve, and we are impelled to call upon Christian churches, organizations and individuals to recognize afresh what is happening and needs to be

done ... The failure to solve the refugee problem is resulting in a widespread assault upon the value and dignity of the individual human personality. Economically biased policies of resettlement are shattering what is left of the integrity of family life ... We call upon [the churches] to urge unceasingly their governments to open doors to immigration, not to cheap labour but to human families. We call upon them to prepare themselves and their churches to receive with love and care those who may come to their lands.[43]

One of the political obstacles faced by proposed legislation was related to the question of how the admission and resettlement of refugees would be managed. Indeed, the capacity of Christian groups to help administer a large refugee program gradually became the key consideration for ambivalent members of Congress. The head of Catholic War Relief Services, Edward Swanstrom, reported in November 1947 that "there was a general feeling in Congress that the Christian bodies in the United States would have to demonstrate their ability to assist in the reception and resettlement of Displaced Persons before emergency legislation could be passed."[44] This sentiment was repeated in more direct terms related to underlying antisemitism in a newsletter to Catholic diocesan resettlement directors:

The biggest obstacle in Congress appears to be a feeling that if any legislation is passed the Christian groups of the United States are not prepared to take their full share of the people admitted under the bill. The line of reasoning that follows is that since only the Jewish group is adequately prepared to handle this problem, the vast majority of the people entering into the United States will be of the Jewish Faith. This opposition is not out in the open, and is subterfuged [sic] by using opposition on other points. We are convinced, however, that this single factor looms large in the minds of a great number of the members of Congress.[45]

Questions and statements made in congressional committees indicated that some legislators were unsure whether Christian groups had the infrastructure to handle resettlement. They wanted to "find out just how far the Christian organizations are prepared to go, and how capable they will be in meeting the actual job of resettlement."[46]

Catholic diocesan directors were therefore encouraged to contact their members of Congress to reassure them of their ability to "handle this problem" and to show that there was broad-based cooperation among Christian organizations to prepare for the resettlement of displaced persons.

As lawmakers debated legislation to govern the admission of refugees, therefore, religious groups prepared to assume responsibility for the resettlement process.[47] Christian groups in particular sought to publicize their readiness to manage large-scale resettlement. In December 1947 the CCDP wrote to its members that the religious groups were mobilizing to play their role in any forthcoming resettlement program: "Even now representatives of the three major faiths, Catholic, Protestant and Jewish, are meeting together to draw up a joint plan for the effective resettlement and distribution of displaced people throughout the country. It is understood that the plan will be completed soon and presented to the appropriate Congressional leaders and committees for its consideration in January."[48]

The Catholic Church had, by this point, created its National Catholic Resettlement Council to coordinate public advocacy and program implementation across every diocese and local community. Its intention was to "marshal the full resources of the Catholic Church in the United States for resettlement in this country of a substantial number of Displaced Persons."[49] Similarly, the Protestant ecumenical Church World Service reported in a press release that "the active cooperation of interdenominational Councils of Churches in 36 states and 633 cities and towns has been enlisted to help in the resettlement of DPs and assist them to become self-supporting."[50] It continued: "When Congress acts, Church World Service ... will be ready to carry through on a much larger scale than it has already demonstrated it is able to do under severe handicaps and restrictions. It now waits for Congressional action."[51]

The struggle to achieve a workable piece of legislation, however, strained the CCDP coalition. While the CCDP insisted on standing firm on the terms of the original Stratton bill, the Catholic NCWC was more willing to compromise.[52] It supported the less ambitious measures advanced by Fellows in the House of Representatives and then by senators Pat McCarran (D-NV) and Chapman Revercomb (R-VA), who served on the Senate Judiciary Committee. The Senate bill, sponsored by Alexander Wiley (R-WI), accepted the reduction in the numbers of DPs in the Fellows bill and added further restrictive provisions that were aimed at reducing the number of Jewish admissions. A displaced person would be recognized under the bill only if he or she had arrived in the Allied zone on or before 22 December 1945. Many Jews arrived after this date, following persecution upon attempting to return home to the Soviet Union, Poland, and other Eastern European countries. The bill also required that 30 per cent of DP visas be allocated to persons who worked in agriculture, a profession in which Jews were not well represented.

The DP Act of 1948 was finally passed on the last day of the session of the 80th Congress, and it included the restrictive provisions added by Wiley. President Truman reluctantly signed it on 25 June 1948, and his ambivalence was on full display in his public remarks:

> If Congress were still in session, I would return this bill without my approval and urge that a fairer, more humane bill be passed. In its present form this bill is flagrantly discriminatory ... The bill discriminates in callous fashion against displaced persons of the Jewish faith ... The bill reflects a singular lack of confidence by the Congress in the capacity and willingness of the people of the United States to extend a welcoming hand to the prospective immigrants. It contains many restrictive requirements, such as prior assurances of suitable employment ... [and] unnecessarily complicated investigation of each applicant.[53]

The CCDP joined the president in denouncing the bill's restrictive definition of an eligible displaced person, calling it "simply a transparent shield for racial and religious bigotry ... a betrayal of American principles."[54] The decision-making process that produced the DP Act of 1948, therefore, was ultimately the product of restrictionist forces in Congress modifying the policy formulation presented by religious and voluntary groups, within the context of an increasingly favourable foreign policy.

Despite the shortcomings of the act, the three main religious groups (HIAS, NCWC, and CWS) quickly gathered to plan their role in its implementation. Meeting under the auspices of the American Council of Voluntary Agencies, leaders of these groups proposed that their organizations "would serve as the spearhead to carry the burden of the work in the US."[55] In accepting this responsibility, they were reminded "that all through the legislation [debate] was based on the fact that voluntary agencies would take care of the situation in America

... We had gone to legislators and told them we would guarantee interest and enthusiasm" once they passed an adequate law.[56]

Although the act lowered the number of admissions and created a more restrictive definition of an eligible displaced person than was initially proposed in the Stratton bill, other primary features of the original bill remained intact in the DP Act. The act set up a Displaced Persons Commission to oversee the resettlement process, which involved receiving assurances from registered voluntary groups and recommending the issuance of visas to U.S. consuls in Europe.[57] It also – in contrast to the 1945 Truman Directive – specified that the government would pay for the costs of travel from Europe to the United States port of entry. This was the first in a series of government concessions to pay an increasing amount of the costs of resettlement undertaken by religious groups.

The active participation of Christian groups in the legislative process was necessary to secure the passage of the DP Act. Although they worked in concert with Jewish groups, the coalition required to pass the bill needed to see certain assurances from the Protestant and Catholic groups. In early 1948 Church World Service, the NCWC, and the Jewish United Service for New Americans formed the Joint Council on Resettlement as a subgroup of the American Council of Voluntary Agencies.[58] This council served as a "united front" in making representations to Congress. Indeed, during the six months leading up to the passage of the act, members of the council participated in regular meetings with the leaders of the Senate and House to establish "certain basic principles ... to assure the passage of the legislation."[59] The first of these principles was that "the Christian churches would establish organizations which would be national in character, [because] the Jewish groups were recognized as well organized for this type of work, whereas the Christian churches were not."[60] An underlying concern was that Christian groups would need to help select and resettle refugees in order to ensure that the majority of arrivals were non-Jews. Other principles emphasized the responsibility of voluntary agencies to aid in finding housing and employment for refugees, to assist with the process of "Americanization," and to help select refugees in the European camps.[61]

After the passage of the DP Act of 1948, the members of the Joint Council on Resettlement worked to administer the new refugee program. As CWS was quick to recognize, the law governing admissions of DPs now "placed upon the three major religious groups in this nation large responsibilities for the effectiveness of this legislation."[62] By September 1949, most of the resettlement work had been done by the Catholic and Jewish groups, despite concerns about the discriminatory provisions of the DP Act. Just a year into the program, CWS, NCWC, USNA, and HIAS had provided assurances for about 56,000 DPs.[63]

At the same time, the three groups consolidated their primary criticisms of the DP Act and worked with the CCDP to lobby for the expansion of its provisions. First, they sought government financial support to cover the transportation costs of moving refugees toward their sponsoring groups and congregations.[64] Second, they asked for an increase in the number of DPs to 400,000 over four years – the same number specified in the original Stratton bill. Third, they sought the elimination of quota mortgaging, whereby the admission of DPs would enable the restriction of future immigration from their countries of origin. Fourth, they aimed to remove references in the act to the exclusion of "persons of German ethnic origin" who were non-German citizens.[65]

Together, many of these provisions were taken up as the Ferguson-Graham-Kilgore DP amendments, which were intended to make the DP Act a "workable, just and humane displaced persons law."[66] Although the quota mortgaging was not ultimately removed, the new amendments pushed back the date of eligibility in the legislation to 1 January 1949. This was the provision initially criticized as anti-Jewish; however, it also prevented refugees fleeing Communism from accessing the DP program, and linking refugee policy with growing anti-Communism sentiments helped facilitate the passage of the change.[67] In April 1950 the amendments were passed by both Houses and signed into law by President Truman. The CCDP was able to write to its members: "At long last, the three-year effort to obtain just and workable DP legislation has triumphed."[68] Whereas the 1948 DP Act reflected a partial victory for the coalition of refugee advocates, the CCDP had accomplished virtually all of its legislative goals by 1950. The protracted negotiation yielded this successful result primarily because of the participation of Christian groups and the evolving politics of the Cold War, which together helped secure the support of crucial conservative and restrictionist votes in Congress.

Policy Implementation

With the passage of the DP Act of 1948 and its 1950 amendments, the fourth phase of the policy cycle moved ahead: implementation and administration. On the government side, this responsibility fell to the Displaced Persons Commission, which was established by Congress under the original legislation to operate from August 1948 to August 1952. The DPC was mandated to provide general oversight of the program, which involved accrediting voluntary agencies to provide assurances for eligible DPs. Its role was that of "an international and domestic coordinator," as one member of the commission put it.[69] It ensured coordination between the various government agencies responsible for issuing visas and conducting security and health reviews and the registered voluntary agencies that were providing sponsorships.[70]

The DPC was established outside of the regular bureaucracy, with a small staff of less than two dozen people. Three commissioners headed it: Edward M. O'Connor, Harry N. Rosenfield, and Ugo Carusi (replaced by John W. Gibson when he voluntarily stepped down). The three were selected pragmatically by the White House according to their religion – O'Connor was Catholic, Rosenfield was Jewish, and Carusi and Gibson were Protestants – because of "the need of assistance from the religious groups in providing sponsorship."[71] Carusi and Gibson, the two Protestants, held the chairmanship. This reflected the emphasis that was placed on "maintaining some degree of religious proportionality among refugees arriving" and the importance to the program of retaining the active support of Protestant churches.[72] In addition to the three commissioners, the DPC also appointed an advisory committee comprised of members of the AVCA's Joint Council on Resettlement, with the aim of facilitating close coordination between government agencies and the voluntary groups.[73] As the DPC noted in its final report, the role of federal government in the resettlement program was remarkably limited, compared to the "indispensable" non-governmental agencies that assumed the primary burdens.[74]

The DPC was responsible for accrediting voluntary agencies to sponsor refugees. In October 1948 it accredited nine agencies to the commission, including HIAS, USNA, CWS, and NCWC.[75] These nine agencies submitted about 90 per cent of the assurances needed to facilitate the resettlement of DPs under the two pieces of legislation.[76] The four religious groups above, along with the National Lutheran Council, generated the lion's share of the assurances. Toward the conclusion of the program, they had carried out the resettlement of the following numbers of DPs: CWS (50,784); NCWC (135,350); National Lutheran Council (32,000); USNA (38,327); HIAS (20,788). The DPC called the involvement of these groups in the resettlement program "a continuous chain of efforts."[77] Without their participation, it said, "there never would have been a displaced persons program to begin with. Without their continuous and active participation, the program would never have been able to succeed."[78]

CANADA

Agenda Setting

In Canada, refugee advocates found it challenging to penetrate the decision-making structures around immigration policy. Their advocacy, such that it was, focused on the press, Parliament, and the odd meeting with the prime minister. However, the real gatekeepers were in the bureaucracy, where policy development was sequestered among guardians of the Canadian population and workforce. There is little to suggest, therefore, that religious groups exerted a significant influence on policy development throughout the early phases of the policy cycle; however, they began to play a more central role in the later implementation process, once Canada began to admit refugees from Europe.

In the months and years after the end of the war, business, media, and religious leaders called on Canada to seize the opportunity to show international leadership on the DP crisis in Europe and attract much-needed labour to fuel a growing economy. However, the Immigration Branch at first resisted accepting large numbers of refugees from Europe. The discretionary powers of the branch to restrict and select immigrants were entrenched in law as well as custom. Furthermore, the culture within the department produced a widely held view, as the director claimed in 1946, that immigration was as a "problem" to be managed.[79] To resist domestic pressure to open up immigration to displaced people, the department claimed (disingenuously) that all available shipping was occupied with repatriating Canadian soldiers and their families from Europe.[80]

The earliest and most persistent pressure to resettle refugees from Europe came from religious and internationalist groups, which had been campaigning for refugee admissions since the mid-1930s. As discussed in the previous chapter, these lobbying efforts were led primarily by the Canadian Jewish Congress and the Canadian National Committee on Refugees, the latter of which included a number of Protestant clergy among its leadership. Together, they played a role in agenda setting and problem formation by presenting to the government and the Canadian public the humanitarian problem of refugees in Europe and framing Canada's moral responsibility to respond with resettlement. Before the conclusion of the war, a primary focus of the advocacy of both groups had been the admission of Jews from Europe. The CJC primarily pursued quiet diplomacy through discrete interventions by Jewish members of Parliament, until the scale of the emergency in Europe became clear and public advocacy was more widely embraced. The formation of the CNCR in 1938, through cooperation between the League of Nations Society and the CJC, created new public voices that took a position described by one Jewish group as follows: "It would be a just and wise policy for this country to open its doors more widely for the admission of men, women and children who in their search for freedom and human dignity would join us to build our country and our people."[81] By 1943, the government had recognized that, apart from Jewish appeals, there was evidence of "an uneasy public conscience over the Canadian record with respect to refugees."[82] Nevertheless, pressure by Jewish groups and the perception of an uneasy conscience were insufficient to cause any real shift in immigration policy.

The humanitarian appeals by these groups were complemented after the war by an influential argument within the government that admitting DPs from Europe would allow Canada to assert an international role for itself as a country newly in control of its foreign policy.[83] As early as January 1946, the Department of External Affairs wrote to the Immigration Branch of the Department of Mines and Resources, advocating the admission of refugees from Europe.[84] The timing suggests that External Affairs was influenced by the Truman Directive, which was issued in late December 1945: "Something has to be done for the refugees of Western Europe," one such memo read. "Provision might be made to permit the entry of some and to open processing and medical operations again in Europe, as the United States is doing."[85] The Immigration Branch resisted these entreaties, responding that "the [refugee] problem just bristles with difficulties."[86] The CNCR noted these emerging foreign-policy themes and began to incorporate them into its own arguments. In her January 1946 letter to the minister of mines and resources, the chairman of the CNCR, Senator Cairine Wilson, wrote: "Surely in this problem, Canada will also want a position of equal leadership among her partners who have already taken positive action in these enterprises, motivated by the selfless desire to alleviate the hardships of those who are suffering so grievously."[87]

Following these interventions, Labour, Health, and External Affairs officials, along with the Immigration Branch, convened a small interdepartmental committee in March 1946 to begin generating recommendations to cabinet.

The humanitarian and foreign-policy arguments for admitting refugees were further buttressed – and perhaps overtaken – by the increasingly prevalent view of interest groups representing business leaders and railroad companies that Canada needed to expand its economy by attracting workers to build its population. The refugees in Europe were identified as primary targets for meeting this goal. In 1946 the government began to open up immigration through a few special programs to bring in several thousand Dutch farmers and a similar number of Polish ex-servicemen living in Britain.[88] While these were not refugee programs, they indicated a new willingness to accept European immigrants to address labour shortages in the Canadian economy. At this time, Alan Green notes, "Canada still saw immigration as a means of satisfying excess demands for labour in the basic industries, especially on farms."[89] When C.D. Howe – an energetic and powerful member of King's cabinet – assumed responsibility for the Department of Reconstruction and Supply, he acquired temporary jurisdiction over the Immigration Branch and proceeded to push the idea that the government could admit refugees from DP camps to meet needs for unskilled labour on Canadian farms and other industries experiencing worker shortages. In the words of Abella and Troper, Howe viewed DPs as "the simplest, cheapest and quickest way to find labour."[90] The shift in issue framing – from the humanitarian case for "moral responsibility" to resettle refugees, advanced by the CNCR, toward Howe's description of DPs as mobile labour – would prove to be critical to changing government policy.

Policy Formulation

By 1946, pressure from foreign and domestic sources was pushing the government toward opening up its borders to displaced people from Europe. The interdepartmental committee convened by the Immigration Branch reviewed submissions from "pro-refugee" pressure groups, such as the CNCR and religious entities, and considered the growing international concern shared by External Affairs.[91] However, it still saw the primary goal as "devis[ing] a high-profile, low-commitment program" to deter international pressure and pacify domestic groups, without actually admitting refugees.[92] Prime Minister King assured the CNCR that "the problem of refugees is one which is continually before the Canadian Government, which shares the concerns of many citizens of Canada over the fate of thousands of people now homeless in Western Europe."[93] He added that "the Canadian Government will be prepared to bear its proper share of the responsibility for solving the refugee problem," although he claimed that United Nations negotiations needed to advance further before Canada would act.[94] Expectations ran high within the CNCR that Canada was preparing to launch its own refugee program, despite the fact only 21 per cent of Canadians favoured the immigration of large numbers of refugees from Europe.[95] When cabinet finally approved a resettlement program, however, it did not reflect the aspirations expressed in Senator Wilson's letter to the minister of mines and resources, which called on him to resettle DPs out of "a selfless desire to alleviate the hardships of those who are suffering."[96]

During this period of policy formulation, the concept of "absorptive capacity" became more prevalent within policy discourse.[97] The term reflected the idea that refugees resettled from Europe should be accepted in proportion to the capacity of the economy to ensure their employment. It affirmed Howe's framing of refugees as a source of labour, not simply as a population demanding humanitarian assistance. As the idea of European refugees as a solution to the growing labour demand in Canada took hold, a variety of other interest groups began to push for a resettlement program. Railway and banking executives joined the CNCR in lobbying, although they advanced a contrasting view of the refugee as a worker.[98]

King finally made a major immigration policy statement to the House of Commons on 1 May 1947. In his remarks, he asserted that Canada was under no legal or other obligation to accept European refugees as a result of membership in the United Nations or the International Refugee Organization. He emphasized that it was Canada's right to select its future citizens and that it was not "a 'fundamental human right' of any alien to enter Canada."[99] King continued: "The policy of the government is to foster the growth of the population of Canada by the encouragement of immigration. The government will seek by legislation, regulation and vigorous administration, to ensure the careful selection and permanent settlement of such numbers of immigrants as can advantageously be absorbed in our national economy."[100] King's declaration about an immigration policy oriented toward population growth resurrected an old policy of settler immigration that had been inactive in recent decades. In addition to directing future immigration policy under King's Liberal government, the most immediate application of this directive was to frame the rationale and criteria for the resettlement of displaced people. A leading consideration was the assurance that refugees admitted to Canada would not become a public liability and would work in sectors where there were identified labour shortages.

Decision Making

Cabinet approved two refugee-resettlement initiatives – a Bulk Labour Program and a Close Relatives Program. Both originated in the bureaucracy, not from parliamentary debate or public deliberation. The former program required the repeal of an order-in-council that disallowed contract labour from outside the country, so that Canadian industries might select workers from the refugee camps in Europe and bind them to work agreements for their first year of residency in Canada. Starting in June 1947, cabinet approved a series of orders-in-council that authorized a steadily expanding stream of refugee labourers in cooperation with the IRO. This program was designed to meet particular labour demands of the Canadian economy while also demonstrating Canada's commitment to the international effort to clear the refugee camps in Europe. H.L. Keenleyside, deputy minister of mines and resources, explained the rationale for the program as follows: "The reasons for the Canadian action were both humanitarian and pragmatic. The Government desired to make a contribution to the solution of a sad human problem both directly and by setting an example for others. It also wished to add a new and valuable element to the Canadian economy."[101] The first order-in-council, PC 2180, signed on 6 June 1947, authorized the admission of 5,000 refugees from refugee camps in Europe. Within this movement there were to be 2,720 woodworkers, 2,000 garment workers, 100 textile workers, and 400 laundry workers.[102] As the program expanded, it targeted a range of other professions: miners, railway workers, steel workers, foundry workers, fur workers, and aluminum workers, among others.[103]

An Immigration-Labour Committee was convened by the Department of Mines and Resources to approve the admission of specific numbers of refugees in light of existing labour conditions. Canada sent mobile immigration teams to Europe to identify suitable refugees from the camps. Representatives of industries also joined the teams to "trade test" refugees whom they agreed to support with work contracts. Refugees resettled through this scheme had their transportation paid for by their prospective Canadian employers, for whom they were bound to work at prevailing wages for one year, after which they could seek other employment.[104] Labour groups and the IRO, which did not favour resettlement countries selecting only the most economically desirable refugees, criticized the program. Nevertheless, between 1947 and 1948, 40,000 displaced persons were authorized to come to Canada under the Bulk Labour Program. By the time it ended in October 1951, some 100,000 refugees had arrived in Canada under its general provisions of industry sponsorship.[105]

Under the Bulk Labour Program, Canada refused to take any refugees with intellectual or professional occupations, causing the head of the IRO to remark sardonically that Canada had an "embargo on brains."[106] This was not hyperbole. David Wyman describes the process of selecting refugees for resettlement as follows: "Several DPs told of being forced to show Canadian authorities the callouses on their hands; a Ukrainian noted that Canadian railroad representatives examined his father's arms and shoulders to see if he was fit for railway labour. The aim was to recruit workers, not to prove their humanitarianism."[107] Those with higher education who remained in the camps sought training in skills needed to do physical labour, and young women disguised their education to seek positions as domestic help. The latter problem became so widespread that the Canadian Labour Department sent a memo to missions in the field that they ought to reject any young woman applying for employment as a domestic who might be suspected of having higher education.[108] A particular irony was that the "mobile immigration teams" sent to Germany and Austria to identify refugees for resettlement also screened for ethnicity. Canadian officials on these teams routinely rejected Jewish applicants (while accepting non-Jewish Germans) based on instructions from Ottawa.[109]

The close-relatives scheme was the second resettlement program, developed in parallel with the bulk-labour one. It began as a general immigration program, much to the disappointment of refugee-advocacy groups. Order-in-Council PC 2071 was announced on 28 May 1946, and it granted permission to Canadian citizens to sponsor first-degree relatives from Europe. There was no mention of refugees. A first-degree relative was defined narrowly to be a parent, unmarried child under eighteen, an unmarried sibling, or an orphan

Table 2.1
Canada: bulk-labour movement (1947–48)[1]

Date	Order	Authorized number
6 June 1947	Order-in-Council PC 2180 – Admission of people from the DP camps	5,000
1947	Order-in-Council PC 2856 – Admission of additional people from DP camps	5,000
1 October 1947	Order-in-Council PC 3926 – Admission of additional people from DP camps	10,000
22 August 1948	Order-in-Council PC 1628 – Admission of additional people from DP camps	10,000
5 October 1948	Order-in-Council PC 3721 – Admission of additional people not from DP camps	10,000

1 Annual Reports of the Department of Mines and Resources, 1947–49.

niece or nephew under sixteen. The program appeared to be intended to keep the movement of family refugees as small as possible. The sponsoring relative had to pay all costs of transportation and care and had to guarantee that the immigrant would not become a public charge. Furthermore, the processing of applications was sure to be slow because of the understaffing of Canadian immigration posts in Europe; it was estimated that the first relatives would not arrive before the spring of 1947.[110] Subsequent hearings before the Senate Committee on Immigration and Labour provided an occasion for refugee groups to express their continued displeasure with the restrictive policy.[111]

Policy Implementation

In November 1946 the government announced that it would accept applications from close relatives of refugees as well as other immigrants from Europe. Tens of thousands of applications poured in from relatives and from religious groups in the months following the announcement.[112] However, many of them found that their relatives were ineligible for sponsorship because ethnic Germans who were not German citizens were considered to be enemy aliens under Canadian regulations. They also were outside the mandate of the International Refugee Organization. The policy looked like a failure.

In response, an entrepreneurial Lutheran layman, T.O.F. Herzer, brought together a coalition of church groups to meet with immigration officials to determine how to overcome these obstacles. In June 1947 the Canadian Mennonite Board of Colonization, Canadian Lutheran World Relief, the German Baptist Union, and the Catholic Immigrant Aid Society met with the government and transportation agencies to determine how to facilitate the movement of refugees who qualified under the Close Relatives Program. This meeting led to the creation of the Canadian Christian Council for the Resettlement of Refugees.[113]

The CCCRR quickly found itself playing a key role in the close-relatives scheme. The agreement reached with immigration officials was for the international affiliates of CCCRR members to find refugees who fell outside the mandate of the IRO and who had Canadian relatives and assemble them for screening by Canadian authorities. However, they faced practical obstacles to efficient movement to Canada, and the CCCRR complained to government authorities about the cost of their work and the logistical challenges involved.[114] Cabinet then approved a grant of $10,000 a month to support the CCCRR and made available a ship (the *Beaverbrae*) to facilitate transportation to Canada. The government attempted to claim that it was not subsidizing a church-sponsorship program but simply "accept[ing] the assistance of voluntary organization in searching out people to come to Canada."[115]

As the number of relatives brought to Canada by the CCCRR gradually diminished, the organization asked the Immigration Branch for an expanded role in the resettlement effort to sponsor refugees without Canadian family members. Already, the Canadian Jewish Congress had lobbied for and been permitted to resettle 1,000 orphan children, and the Catholic Immigrant Aid Society had likewise been permitted to sponsor 1,000 refugees.[116] In January 1949 the CCCRR was authorized to assume responsibility for resettling 500 farm- and woodworkers as a trial program. The success of this initiative opened the door to the CCCRR receiving permission to bring to Canada refugees who were co-religionists of its member churches and who met certain occupation criteria.

The CCCRR, which was created to cooperate with the government's close-relatives scheme, parlayed this relationship into a church-sponsorship program. It recognized the change in its role from a voluntary agency assisting government programs for family sponsorship to one that had a broader mandate to help resettle refugees from Europe: "At the last meeting, official recognition was given to the change and status of the CCCRR ... It has now become the official agency for groups interested in relief and immigration, appointed and recognized in the participating church bodies ... The CCCRR [is] ... pledged to process all refugee immigrants eligible for admission to Canada, regardless of creed and race."[117] The approval given to the CCCRR to expand the category of people who were eligible for its sponsorship would later be extended to other approved religious groups. This marked the first appearance after the war of an ongoing government-approved program of private sponsorship of refugees nominated for resettlement in Canada. About 60,000 of the 163,984 displaced people who resettled in Canada between April 1947 and March 1952 arrived through the evolving sponsorship program.[118]

In 1949 the Canadian Council of Churches took steps to initiate its own refugee-sponsorship program. Until this time, the Canadian Council of Churches had campaigned for refugee admissions but had not yet entered into the field of resettlement alongside the denominational groups of the CCCRR. Most members of the council were also part of the CCCRR.[119] However, in response to the urging of the World Council of Churches, which recognized new openings for resettlement in Canada through the sponsorship of religious groups, the CCC started its own project of refugee assistance. In September 1949 the Reverend Canon Judd wrote on behalf of the CCC to the deputy minister responsible for immigration, H.L. Keenleyside, to request authorization to "take advantage of arrangements now allowed by the Canadian government" for church congregations to sponsor displaced people.[120] In January 1951 the Immigration Branch decided to encourage the WCC and CCC to sponsor refugees in Germany and Austria in order to try to assist with the resolution of the refugee problem in Europe. The director of immigration informed field officers that "where the application is made under the sponsorship of the World Council of Churches or the Canadian Council of Churches, as long as employment is guaranteed for one year and settlement arrangements are in order for that period, such applications should be approved."[121] This marked the beginning of a key element of Canada's private refugee-sponsorship program – that sponsors assume responsibility for the care of refugees in their first year of arrival.

The Canadian Jewish Congress also launched a similar program in collaboration with its European counterparts affiliated with the Joint Distribution Committee. Despite support for their applications provided by the Canadian Jewish Congress, Jewish refugees continued to face obstacles with obtaining visas. The JDC wrote to Saul Hayes, head of the CJC, asking that someone from the Congress come to Austria to help Jewish refugees pass their selection interviews. They would often be told by immigration officers that Canadian employers "don't want this type of person."[122] The Canadian Jewish Congress was urged to assume greater responsibility for sponsoring refugees so that they did not have to pass through the more selective Bulk Labour Program. However, there was some confusion within the Congress about what it meant to sponsor a refugee and whether this also meant paying for all future health-care costs, old-age pensions, and other social services provided to citizens. Nevertheless, the CJC helped to accompany and resettle thousands of Jewish refugees from Europe through both the bulk-labour and sponsorship schemes.

When the IRO mandate ended in December 1951, Canada's refugee program for displaced people also concluded, along with the immigration regulations that distinguished between immigrants and refugees. However, there remained a "hard core" of refugees in Europe who were difficult to resettle, whether because of old age or illness. The Canadian Council of Churches urged the government to continue the arrangement it had developed in the latter years of its refugee program through cooperation with religious groups: "We feel deeply that there should be a place in Canada for a Christian enterprise like ours. May we not hope that in your general immigration scheme, this Church Sponsorship Plan of the Canadian Council of Churches may continue to find a place? We think this attitude could be accompanied by a return to the cooperative attitude which prevailed prior to the demise of the IRO."[123] Just two months after receiving this letter, the Immigration Branch rescinded its cancellation of the church-sponsorship program. The CCC agreed to guarantee employment for one year and to ensure other settlement requirements for sponsored refugees. They were relieved of the ambiguous requirement to guarantee that sponsored refugees would not become public charges. A directive to field officers from the immigration director noted that sponsorship would be given for refugees, and not standard immigrants, and that their files should "be given first degree of priority in examination."[124] Initially, the Canadian Council of Churches was restricted to sponsoring forty cases a month, but this limitation was later lifted provided that employment and housing were guaranteed.[125]

In 1953 the Department of Citizenship and Immigration sought to rationalize a number of practices that had developed through its continuing sponsorship programs with different religious groups. A memo was sent to four religious groups informing them that they would henceforth be considered members of a new Approved Church Program. These groups were the Canadian Jewish Congress (with the Jewish Immigrant Aid Service), the Canadian Council of Churches, the CCCRR, and the Rural Settlement Society (the Catholic group based in Montreal). The memo explained: "To ensure closer coordination between the activities of recognized agencies of the Protestant, Catholic and Jewish faiths and this Department with respect to immigration, it is desirable that such activities be governed by uniform procedures."[126] The groups were given authority to sponsor refugees for admission to Canada without having to demonstrate any definite employment or accommodation being prearranged.

Although the Approved Church Program developed relatively quickly in response to demands from these voluntary groups, the immigration bureaucrats were uneasy about the program because of the authority it gave the groups over the selection of immigrants to Canada.[127] The crux of the tension between the religious groups and the immigration officials was the criteria used to select refugees. The government remained focused on selecting immigrants who met labour demand in specific sectors of the Canadian economy, whereas the religious groups wanted to select refugees based on humanitarian need. Furthermore, the religious groups thought that their selection process allowed them to discern the "moral and religious aspect" of desirable refugees, which the government might overlook.[128] Immigration field officers complained about the requirement to grant visas to refugees under the sponsorship of members of the Approved Church Program, which often targeted the "hard core." One such complaint read as follows: "[They] appeared almost to specialize in undesirable immigrants of this kind ... 'Hard core' means just that; the final, ultimate dregs, the scrapings of the very bottom of the barrel. I do not wish to be and am not inhumane, but have never regarded our work in any other light than that the interests of our country must be paramount; which means that every immigrant should possess some desirable qualification, at the very least."[129] In response to such complaints, the Immigration Branch sought to limit the authority of religious groups to select refugees by imposing an Occupational Selection List of desired professions.[130] In a 1954 meeting with the deputy minister, Laval Fortier, the four approved voluntary groups vented their displeasure, noting their opposing views of refugee resettlement: "The Government selected these people for their occupation – skilled labour. That differs entirely from the Voluntary Agencies who have a different view – that of a charitable nature."[131]

By late 1954, the Department of Citizenship and Immigration was looking to reassert complete control over the selection and placement of refugees without sacrificing the valuable role played by religious groups in the settlement and integration process. Senior civil servants feared that the continued involvement of the four approved religious groups in the selection process would give the department no basis on which to resist pressure by ethnic groups that sought to carry out similar programs.[132] This slippery slope, it was feared, would leave the department powerless over the selection of new Canadians.

In October 1954 the four groups participating in the Approved Church Program were invited to meet with the minister of citizenship and immigration, J.W. Pickersgill, and his deputy minister. The minister outlined his plans to abandon the involvement of the groups in overseas selection, "stating that in the interest of administrative ease and efficiency, the agencies should abandon this function and restrict themselves to the integration process of people of their confessional group on arrival and during the period of adjustment."[133] The joint response of the four groups was to protest vociferously: "This humanitarian and welfare aspect of refugee and migrant services overseas cannot be continued if present procedures are radically changed as proposed in the discussions with the Deputy Minister and his officers."[134] The government once again backed down, delaying a final decision on the matter and instructing field officers to grant visas to immigrants sponsored by the four groups "if they are qualified in an approved occupation list ... and meet the usual requirements."[135]

Despite the instrumental role played by religious groups in Canada's response to Europe's displaced people, the government was not eager to applaud their humanitarian work publicly. Their very inclusion in Canadian efforts to identify, transport, and settle refugees was a reluctant concession of the government – one that it was compelled to defend repeatedly and protect from bureaucratic jealousy. The two parties forged a cooperative relationship that was guided by government policy directives, but there ultimately existed an unresolved tension over the scope of authority and freedom given to the religious agencies to play their part in Canada's response to Europe's refugee crisis. By 1955, this struggle had reached a stalemate of sorts as the displaced-people problem was winding down – just in time for the next major refugee crisis to hit when millions of Hungarians fled to Austria in response to a Soviet crackdown.

CONCLUSION

During the post-war period, refugee policy emerged in the United States and Canada as a distinct policy field – and refugee policy meant refugee resettlement. The generation of this new policy field made the response to displaced people a critical juncture – a "crucial founding [moment] of institutional formation that [sends] countries on different developmental paths."[136] During such periods of policy innovation, the foundations for institutions are laid through historically contingent processes. Actors engage in structured negotiation that is shaped by timing, events, and a particular constellation of factors. Policy choices become the first step along a pathway that continues to be shaped by politics but that is constrained by past choices.[137] Political actors adapt to the logic of the new system. In the case of refugee policy, the post-war response to displaced people was crucial because it initiated separate developmental pathways for the United States and Canada. The framework of refugee resettlement today is an institutional legacy of these political struggles.

In the United States, decision making with regard to refugee resettlement was primarily reserved to Congress, which had to pass legislation to admit significant numbers of displaced people. Lobbying members of Congress, therefore, became a key aspect of the advocacy efforts of religious groups. The foreign-policy reasons to resettle displaced people were not sufficiently convincing to carry a majority in both Houses of Congress. Both political parties had members who held restrictive views of immigration and were reluctant to open the border to destitute refugees. A good number were also influenced by anti-semitism. The participation of Christian groups in the policy process – and the guarantees of sponsorship they provided – became essential to gathering enough votes to pass the 1948 Displaced Persons Act. The act itself intentionally narrowed the definition of a refugee in order to exclude as many Jews as possible. However, the positions of some of these conservative members of Congress shifted in response to the changing dynamics of the Cold War, which created a policy window for the religious groups' advocacy coalition to advance its full policy agenda of expanding the number and eligibility of refugees to resettle from Europe.[138]

Although the Canadian decision-making process was more insulated from group pressure than that of the United States, it was not entirely closed off to advocacy. Business interest groups exerted a great deal of influence over the policy discourse leading to the Bulk Labour Program. Furthermore, the policy failure of the Close Relatives Program opened the door for religious groups to present themselves as government partners in successfully implementing the scheme. By insinuating themselves into the process of implementation, these groups succeeded at generating "policy conversion" – a mode of institutional change that tends to occur when the "status quo bias" of the political environment is high (as it was in the Immigration Branch in the 1950s).[139] As Jacob Hacker, Paul Pierson, and Kathleen Thelen note, conversion happens when "political actors are able to redirect institutions or policies toward purposes beyond their original intent."[140] In this case, the relevant political actors were not bureaucrats or politicians but policy entrepreneurs representing Protestant, Catholic, and Jewish groups. They successfully redirected a family-sponsorship scheme into a religious-sponsorship scheme, without altering the basic rules of the original order-in-council.

In both cases, the response to the DP crisis in Europe after the war was intended to be a temporary refugee program. After the expiration of the mandate of the IRO in 1951, it was thought that most of the resettlement needs would be met and the exceptional measures taken to admit refugees could be wound down. However, the refugee crisis in Europe took longer to resolve than initially expected, in part because of a new wave of refugees fleeing Soviet oppression in Eastern Europe. Then, in 1956, a sudden influx of refugees into Austria from Hungary, following brutal Soviet repression of an uprising in that country, triggered an urgent policy debate in both the United States and Canada. At the forefront of these debates were the same religious groups. However, by this time, they had established relationships with decision makers and a structure of cooperation with the state. They adapted their advocacy to recommend the preservation of existing patterns of cooperation, generating strong feedback effects that initiated a process of institutional-path dependency.

3

A Continuous Chain of Efforts

Issue Networks and Policy Communities

On 4 November 1956 the Soviet army entered Hungary, provoking a new European refugee crisis right on the heels of the displaced people of the Second World War. A popular uprising against Soviet-imposed policies led to the formation of a new government led by Imre Nagy. That government fell on 10 November. About 180,000 Hungarians fled across the Austrian border, and some 20,000 escaped into Yugoslavia, until both borders were closed in early 1957. With the support of the Intergovernmental Committee for European Migration (ICEM) and the United Nations High Commissioner for Refugees, many of these Hungarian refugees were resettled in Western countries.[1] The United States and Canada took the largest numbers of any country – about 38,121 and 37,565, respectively.[2] Their responses to the Hungarian crisis were shaped by the policy logic and frameworks developed in the context of the post-war European refugees.

The Hungarian uprising, Soviet crackdown, and subsequent refugee crisis attracted broad public and political attention in both Canada and the United States. Scenes of the popular uprising were broadcast on television, exposing Western audiences to current events through a new, powerful medium and generating widespread public sympathy for Hungarians. Western governments also were looking to seize opportunities for symbolic victories over the Soviet Union, and accepting refugees who fled Soviet violence was quickly understood as one such way to signal political and cultural superiority.[3] Anti-Communism played an important role in strengthening grassroots support for religious groups working in resettlement. The resettlement of Hungarian refugees in both the United States and Canada proceeded rapidly in late 1956 and early 1957. The United States further embedded these groups as leading implementers of government programs, and Canada continued to elaborate features of private sponsorship.

Both Canada and the United States present classic features of path dependency, although the effects were stronger in the United States owing to that country's more cohesive policy community. The success of the DP programs generated positive feedback for the initiation of a Hungarian program. The ad hoc institutional arrangements created to facilitate refugee resettlement after the Second World War did not completely disappear after the major displaced-persons movements had finished. The policy innovations developed in the late 1940s were moral, conceptual, and administrative blueprints that became the templates upon which resettlement was designed in the second half of the 1950s. In other words, they generated increasing returns to the reproduction of institutional arrangements.[4] Indeed, the success of the DP programs altered the sense of what was possible in the arena of refugee policy. The religious groups yielded a kind of power in these settings by exploiting their administrative know-how, vast social networks, and interfaith coalitions to present possibilities for policy action that, several decades before, were off the table for decision makers.[5] The Hungarian movement revived the policy responses to displaced people, consolidated the related institutional arrangements, and reiterated the exceptional admission of refugees outside of still-restrictive immigration laws.

A close examination of the policy process leading to the admission of Hungarian refugees and the implementation of the resettlement program reveals strong learning and coordination effects based on the DP programs developed in both countries. While shorter in duration and smaller in magnitude, the Hungarian resettlement program consolidated key features of the resettlement systems in both countries. In the United States, it introduced, for the first time, government subsidies for accredited voluntary agencies to resettle refugees, further entrenching them in a system of government cooperation with religious groups. The emergency program required efficient replication of past practices. Catholic, Protestant, and Jewish agencies resettled 96 per cent of Hungarians accepted into the United States.[6] In Canada, the participating groups in the Approved Church Program leveraged their consultative relationship with the government to push for the admission of Hungarian refugees outside of normal immigration channels. When the government initiated its resettlement program, it consolidated their role as private sponsors of refugees. Catholic groups, JIAS, and the Canadian Council of Churches sponsored about 90 per cent of Hungarian refugees resettled in Canada.[7]

Following closely on the heels of the Hungarian refugee crisis was the transnational movement associated with World Refugee Year (WRY), the global "campaign to save the world's refugees."[8] The idea for WRY originated with the head of the U.S. Catholic Relief Services (CRS, successor of War Relief Services), Edward Swanstrom, at the 1957 International Catholic Migration Congress and was carried forward most notably by the Catholic Church and the World Council of Churches through their transnational religious networks.[9] Although the purpose of WRY ostensibly was to raise private funds for refugees – thereby attracting the support of governments, which recognized that it could save them "a great deal of money"[10] – it also came to focus on securing resettlement for the remaining "hard core" of displaced persons in Europe. It generated another opening for policy discourse about the protection of refugees, an issue that was increasingly recognized as a permanent feature of the post-war world.

By the time World Refugee Year concluded in 1960, the United States and Canada had emerged as major countries of refugee resettlement, without initiating major immigration reform to alter racial, ethnic, or national restrictions.[11] Refugee admissions, in this way, were the leading edge of the process of liberalizing immigration law in practice if not legislatively. Of course, this claim has to be qualified by the acknowledgment that refugee programs were also shaped by racial thinking that continued to restrict admissions for Chinese refugees and migrants seeking resettlement.[12] Refugee resettlement was accomplished by layering one set of institutions on top of another: a more liberal program for the admission of refugees was created on top of a more restrictive one for immigrants.[13] This layering process created a tension that contributed to the process of immigration policy reform during the subsequent decade. However, it also entrenched the concept and category of the refugee as an exceptional kind of immigrant whose admission is decided according to different criteria and who requires extra support in the process of settlement.

UNITED STATES

Following the conclusion of the DP program in the United States at the end of 1952, a number of policy developments generated an important context for the response to the Hungarian refugee crisis.

The first was the passage of the Refugee Relief Act (RRA) of 1953, which was referred to colloquially as the "church bill" owing to the support it received from religious groups.[14] The bill extended many of the programs of the DP Act and complemented the 1952 United States Escapee Program (USEP), which created refugee reception camps near Eastern European borders to host escapees from Communist countries. Under USEP contracts, the religious refugee groups provided reception and care for refugees fleeing across the border. Church World Service, Catholic Relief Services, and the Joint Distribution Service were the first three organizations to receive government contracts. The Refugee Relief Act authorized the issuance of 214,000 visas outside of the national-origins quota system to permit the resettlement of escapees hosted in these camps.

With the passage of the Refugee Relief Act, refugees could apply for special immigration visas to come to the United States. They had to present an "assurance" of suitable employment and proof that they would not displace an American from a job, measures similar to those first introduced under the 1945 Truman Directive. Assurances, however, had to be provided by individual citizens, and arrivals were extraordinarily slow. In an era of McCarthyism, the head of the selection process was an ideological anti-Communist who imposed a restrictive set of additional requirements, including "political cleanliness." These criteria added major challenges to securing sponsorship.[15] When a new administrator was finally added to the program, he immediately altered the selection process by allowing the religious refugee groups to endorse sponsorships, reviving a key aspect of the DP program.[16] Ideological issues became less important in the selection of refugees. This instantly accelerated the process and, in the final year and a half of the program, most of the authorized visas issued were the result of the involvement of the religious groups in program administration and implementation.[17] As the program approached its conclusion toward the end of 1956, only a few thousand of the 214,000 authorized visas were left unused. These would be employed to resettle Hungarians fleeing the Soviet invasion.

Within a month of the overthrow of the Nagy government in November 1956, President Dwight Eisenhower appointed Tracy S. Voorhees to be his personal representative and coordinator for Hungarian refugee and relief work. On the day of his official appointment, Voorhees was briefed by the State Department that the key to the efficient aid of Hungarian refugees in the United States would be the unity and engagement of the religious groups. "There will be problems," one official commented, "if the voluntary agencies who represent the different religious groups do not get together from the start in handling the aid program for the refugees."[18] Others noted that the United States would prefer to see more refugees settled in other countries, whereas the religious groups want to help with resettlement of refugees in the United States. Voorhees commented that his next meeting would be with those agencies and that he would help them become involved "perhaps largely in fundraising" for relief in Europe.[19] He would quickly learn that this was not their primary area of interest.

Eisenhower initially announced the resettlement of just 5,000 Hungarian refugees in the United States, using most of the remaining visas authorized under the RRA. However, he faced growing public demands, especially from the religious groups (as State Department officials had anticipated), to expand admissions to the United States instead of promoting resettlement elsewhere.[20] On 1 December 1956 Eisenhower announced that the United States would accept 21,500 refugees from Hungary. The additional refugees would be admitted under the parole authority of his attorney general. This was an unprecedented use of executive power in immigration, which attempted to wrest control of refugee policy away from Congress. The Immigration and Nationality Act of 1952 (INA) included a little-noticed and never-before-used statute (section 212[d][5]) that permitted the attorney general to authorize the admission of refugees: "In his discretion [the attorney general may] parole into the United States temporarily under such conditions as he may prescribe for emergent reasons or for reasons deemed strictly in the public interest any alien applying for admission to the United States."[21] According to this statute, parolees were to be returned to their home country after a temporary period of residence in the United States. The legislation included a provision for exceptional cases in which an individual needed to be admitted on an emergency basis and where securing congressional approval was impractical.[22] In other words, Eisenhower's use of parole authority to admit tens of thousands of refugees clearly went against the intentions of the original legislation. While parolees were to be admitted temporarily, it was understood that the president would later seek from Congress the necessary legislation to grant them permanent residence in the United States.

The significance of Eisenhower's decision to use the parole authority created by the INA to admit Hungarian refugees is hard to overstate. It shifted primary authority over refugee admissions from Congress to the executive, giving a freer hand to the White House to authorize the admission of refugees outside of normal immigration channels and national-origins restrictions. This move increased the salience of foreign-policy considerations in refugee policy because the countervailing power of domestic restrictionists in Congress was effectively sidelined. It also reinforced the conceptual and political (if not yet legal) distinction between an immigrant and a refugee, each subject to different statutes and regulations for their admission to the United States. The use of executive parole authority henceforth became the primary way in which refugees would be admitted to the United States until the passage of the 1980 Refugee Act.[23]

Following Eisenhower's announcement of large-scale Hungarian refugee admissions, Voorhees received a letter from his close confidant, former president Herbert Hoover. Hoover urged Voorhees to work closely with the religious voluntary agencies in his refugee work: "The voluntary agencies have a vital spiritual part and an important administrative function in the solution of the whole of this problem. The heads of the useful voluntary agencies should be appointed by the President into a Refugees Relief Council, which will cooperate with [the administration] in securing coordination of all activities … The major burden of resettlement of the refugees in the United States should be undertaken by the voluntary agencies and the coordination of this task should be directed by the Refugees Relief Council."[24] From December 1956 to March 1957, Hoover continued to meet with Voorhees and corresponded with both him and President Eisenhower, offering advice on refugee issues.

Apparently influenced by Hoover's advice,[25] the president announced on 12 December 1956 that he was appointing a President's Committee for Hungarian Refugee Relief (PCHRR) with the responsibility of working with Voorhees to coordinate the national resettlement effort of the voluntary agencies.[26] The committee was comprised of a small group of people, including "representatives of the principal religious faiths currently concerned with this problem," and was given the mandate to coordinate and "support in every way possible the various religious and other voluntary groups" engaged in refugee resettlement.[27]

Almost immediately, the religious groups identified an area where they required government support – subsidies to support the resettlement of refugees. The PCHRR advanced the request, and Voorhees put his weight behind the proposal of an expanded budget to support the work of the voluntary agencies. The initial allocation he requested from the State Department was for $1.5 million to pay $40 per resettled refugee. Voorhees noted that this was an exceptional arrangement made under the conditions of an emergency program undertaken in the national interest: "They [the subsidies] do not in any way constitute a precedent for Government payment of similar costs for other refugee movements."[28] In fact, they set a precedent for government subsidies to voluntary groups on a per-refugee basis that continue to this day.

The operation to resettle Hungarian refugees was rapid and efficient, in large part because it replicated the program of cooperation between government and religious groups developed in response to the DP crisis. The program of resettlement began in mid-November, with chartered planes flying Hungarian refugees from Austria to a reception area set up at Camp Kilmer, a U.S. Army camp in New Brunswick, New Jersey. The first plane arrived on 21 November 1956, by which time the National Catholic Welfare Conference had already set up its operations to facilitate resettlement. By mid-January, over 22,000 Hungarian refugees had been received in the United States, and 20,000 of them had left Camp Kilmer under the sponsorship of religious and other voluntary agencies. The religious agencies and members of the American Council of Voluntary Agencies for Foreign Service played the "principal role," according to Voorhees, in the resettlement program: "Following government examination and registration at the Reception Center, the refugee goes to his voluntary sponsoring agency. The agencies include the major religious denominations. Others are non-sectarian ... the large church agencies resettle refugees through both clergy and lay workers in local communities in the United States. Generally, it is the responsibility of these local representatives to find housing and jobs for the refugees, and to integrate them into American communities."[29] By the first week of February 1957, the total number of refugees resettled by voluntary agencies were as follows: NCWC (14,321), CSW (4,469), HIAS (2,633), International Rescue Committee (1,189), and Lutheran World Federation (1,182).[30] The program of resettlement eventually expanded to over 38,000 refugees, and most of the arrivals took place within the first ninety days.[31]

The religious groups were not just engaged with resettlement from Camp Kilmer; they also helped in the selection of the refugees who applied to leave Austria for the United States. Initially, representatives of the groups were assigned to U.S. consulates, where they selected and sponsored applicants as they arrived. In an effort to create a plan, the U.S. consul asked the groups to agree to a quota between them as a working expedient. Naturally, the quota broke down along religious lines: 62 per cent Catholic, 25 per cent Protestant, 9 per cent Jewish, and 4 per cent other (i.e., non-sectarian).[32] Refugees began to submit questionnaires that identified their religion. The groups' representatives sought out co-religionists to sponsor and send to local congregations in the United States.

The press criticized this religion-based selection process as potentially favouring churchgoing people.[33] The novelist James Michener, who was covering the flight of Hungarians to Austria, publicly accused the religious refugee groups of imposing religious tests to select devout immigrants. His accusations were so widely publicized that the Immigration and Naturalization Service was compelled to release a statement affirming that religious groups were essential to the success of the Hungarian program but that they "operated under standards and criteria set by the Service."[34] Indeed, the public criticism led to the progressive removal of sponsoring agencies from the selection process.[35] Toward the conclusion of the program, refugees began to be resettled by congregations with which they did not necessarily share a religious identity. This was a significant evolution from the displaced-persons program, which was explicitly designed to manage the religious composition of the refugee population.

Voorhees resigned from his position as coordinator of the Hungarian program on 28 February 1957, by which time almost 30,000 refugees had arrived at Camp Kilmer. To mark the end of his tenure, an editorial titled "The 90-Day Wonder" appeared in the *Washington Post*: "American immigration laws were ill-suited to the unexpected need, but they have been made to serve. The two dozen or more religious and other private agencies which have found homes and the jobs and guided the refugees to them were not equipped for so gargantuan an effort, but they have brought it off in a heartening display of cooperative, voluntary endeavours."[36] The PCHRR issued its own final report on 14 May 1957, when its members met with the president and leading members of Congress to brief them on the results of the program.

Notwithstanding the continuity between the resettlement of displaced people and the Hungarian program, refugee policymaking continued to evolve in a number of ways. First, the locus of decision making over refugee admissions shifted from Congress to the executive branch through the novel use of the parole admissions under the 1952 Immigration Act. This in turn enhanced the salience of foreign policy in refugee resettlement and helped reinforce the connection between refugees as escapees from Communism. Anti-Communist sentiment was not only a context for executive action on refugee resettlement; it also helped strengthen the mobilization of religious groups that were increasingly tied to refugee programs. These groups had first emerged to help displaced co-religionists in post-war Europe and were now directed to aid refugees, regardless of religion. Their growing organizational capacity had given them a powerful position in relation to an expanding and contested field of immigration and refugee policy. The Hungarian program consolidated their pre-eminent role in implementing and administering refugee resettlement (with increasing government financial support) and further situated them as leading experts on immigration and refugee policy. In the coming decade, immigration reform would be a major area of policy debate – one to which religious groups, by virtue of their political contacts, organizational size, and experience, were well placed to contribute as members of an emerging policy community.

In the wake of the Hungarian program, the leading religious refugee groups turned their focus to advancing legislative reform. Congressional action was required to bring about any ongoing legislative commitment to refugee resettlement. When delivering the final report of the PCHRR, its members (representatives of the voluntary agencies) used the opportunity to "push ahead for basic immigration changes" that would address the particular needs of refugees and do away with national-origins quotas in the basic immigration law.[37] While they left these initial meetings feeling discouraged about the immediate prospects for legislative reform, they were assured by leading members of Congress (like Pat McCarran [D-NV]) that the refugees admitted under executive parole authority would be made permanent by an act of Congress.[38] Over the subsequent months, papers circulated among the main religious refugee groups progressively articulated a general consensus on a legislative agenda for future immigration and refugee reform.

One such paper was a policy note prepared under the auspices of the National Council of Churches titled "Improve Our Immigration

Law: A Job for the Churches." Drafts were widely circulated and commented upon throughout 1958 before a final version was signed by the leaders of the major Protestant denominations in the United States and appraised positively by Catholic leaders. The note was a response to a December 1957 NCC General Assembly Action, which called for the focused attention of churches "to support Congressional action to improve our Immigration Law" so that it would "be more in accord with principles which we as Christians can fully support and its procedures may testify more favourably to our nation's character and its sense of world responsibility."[39] Therefore, the note presented a policy agenda to promote an end to racial, national, or religious discrimination in immigration policy; a path to citizenship for immigrants to the United States; and cooperation to provide "a fair share of resettlement opportunities in the USA."[40] It observed that the refugees admitted to the United States since the Second World War would never have been allowed entry under the restrictive provisions of the basic immigration law. The experience of the churches with resettlement fortified their belief that they have "a special responsibility for making their position in immigration clearer."[41] The churches, the note concluded, "have a right to expect that Congress will strengthen the leadership of the United States toward more adequate opportunities for all in the Free World and will continue the tradition of our country to show compassion for the oppressed."[42]

The decision of religious groups to lobby for reform to the basic immigration law occurred within the context of a broader realignment in immigration politics. The 1955 merger of the American Federation of Labor and the Committee of Industrial Organizations (CIO) brought about a significant change in the role of unions in relation to immigration. The AFL had been one of the more powerful groups advocating the erection and preservation of the national-origins system, whereas the CIO was a long-time supporter of refugee resettlement and the end of national-origins quotas.[43] The changes in leadership and ideas brought about by the merger of the two groups led to the adoption of immigration reform as a top priority – namely, the "abolishment of the national origins quota system entirely."[44] The Democratic Party also began to examine immigration reform as a policy plank in the mid-1950s – which it later adopted officially in 1960. Despite the achievement of a Democratic majority in the House in 1958, however, according to Emmanuel Celler (D-NY), immigration reform remained obstructed by "a coalition of Southern

Democrats and Midwest Republicans whose opposition is strong and precludes action."[45]

Lacking a clear policy window to generate political movement on immigration reform in Congress, the voluntary groups turned the transnational campaign to mark 1959 as World Refugee Year into a point of focus for their refugee-related lobbying efforts.[46] Initiated and primarily advanced by religious groups, WRY was endorsed by the United Nations as an opportunity to "clear the camps" of the estimated 110,000 displaced people remaining in Europe. Most were sick (often tubercular) or elderly. The idea gained the support of Western governments, which believed that it would foster an "international division of labour" by generating private funds from religious charities to facilitate the resettlement of "hard core" refugees in South America or Australia.[47] Catholics and Protestants, in particular, mobilized global constituencies in support of World Refugee Year. Pope John XXIII called on governments to "open their frontiers" and "to speedily bring about the human and social resettlement" of refugees.[48] Leading figures of the World Council of Churches rearticulated their vision of a "post-national" global order, calling on the ecumenical movement to see migrants as "orphans" to whom they had particular duties as Christians.[49]

A general theme of WRY was the instrumental role of voluntary action within the global-refugee regime. Hugh Samson, a leader of the WRY movement, remarked that mobilization around the year would "impress upon the public that the few existing 'official' organizations (such as UNHCR ...) are virtually non-operational and depend upon the voluntary organizations for the actual machinery of relief, integration and resettlement."[50] In the United States, religious groups framed voluntary action within an anti-Communist discourse. As one statement indicated: "if the US could offer anything that the Russians couldn't, it was the concept of voluntarism carried on by agencies which are religiously oriented."[51] They saw the new use of executive parole as simply an expedient measure to admit refugees, which also failed to adequately recognize the role of private, voluntary action in enabling its effectiveness.[52] The religious agencies, therefore, identified WRY as a window of opportunity to promote a more permanent process for resettling refugees in the United States in which they would be embedded.

The voluntary groups urged Congress to pass immigration legislation that would demonstrate international leadership during a symbolic period of time.[53] The American Jewish Committee's statement on WRY outlined its vision for liberalizing immigration, "based on the recognition that our present immigration laws reflect an attitude of distrust toward aliens, discriminate unjustly on grounds of the racial and national origins of aliens, and impose a self-defeating rigidity on efforts to promote our foreign policy."[54] Roland Elliott, head of Church World Service, in testifying before the Senate Subcommittee on Immigration, noted that "the refugee problem is dynamic and recurrent; it is not static and temporary." He argued, "Refugee immigration should be recognized as a valid part of our permanent Immigration Legislation as a normal means of serving our own national interest and expressing our leadership for world order and stability."[55] Other coordinated actions were taken under the auspices of the American Council of Voluntary Agencies, which urged legislators to pass immigration reform before the end of World Refugee Year in 1960.[56]

Mobilization around World Refugee Year generated some political focus on refugee resettlement. President Eisenhower issued a proclamation in May 1959 in support of WRY and convened a meeting at the White House to call for renewed efforts by governmental and voluntary groups to care for refugees. Representatives of CWS, Lutheran World Service, IRC, HIAS, and Catholic Relief Services also testified before the House Subcommittee on Immigration, presenting four legislative actions to undertake during World Refugee Year: creating a pathway to admit refugees as permanent residents, not temporary parolees; extending the recognition of refugees beyond those falling under the mandate of the UNHCR; removing the dateline of eligibility set under the DP Act; and providing for the admission of those "difficult" to resettle, such as those with tuberculosis.[57]

Ultimately, the pressure exerted on Congress did help generate one piece of legislation, although it fell far short of the ambitious goals set out in the wake of the Hungarian program. Congressman Francis Walter (D-PA), one of the authors of the restrictive 1952 Immigration and Nationality Act and a staunch anti-Communist, led the passage of the 1960 Fair Share Act (Public Law 86–648). The act did not incorporate any of the legislative changes set out by the religious groups. It simply gave the State Department additional power to negotiate with other governments to induce them to admit more refugees by strategically increasing admissions to the United States under temporary parole authority. This applied only to European refugees who fell under the mandate of the UNHCR, and by 1961 it had led to the admission of fewer than 2,000 refugees.[58] It passed into law, uncelebrated by refugee groups.

Throughout the late 1950s, the advocacy of religious groups became oriented toward replicating and extending the patterns of refugee resettlement that had been established in the displaced-persons program. The 1948 DP Act and its amendments were intended to be temporary measures, carried out in cooperation with a handful of registered religious groups. However, the Soviet invasion of Hungary and the flight of refugees to Austria created another opportunity to deliberate over refugee resettlement. With leadership from the White House this time, a refugee-resettlement program rapidly evolved in close collaboration with the same groups – mirroring the main features of the DP program. The program also evolved in a number of other important ways: government subsidies per refugee were introduced, and the religious-sponsorship scheme was set aside to require all agencies to resettle refugees of any faith. As the religious and voluntary agencies became more firmly embedded alongside government decision makers in a policy community, their focus turned toward advocating a more liberal immigration law and a more universal and permanent refugee program.

CANADA

During the 1950s, the resettlement of European refugees in Canada continued to follow two parallel tracks – an Approved Church Program, sponsored by religious groups, and a government-run program that was designed meet labour-market needs. Religious groups and immigration officials were connected in a loose issue network, which meant that they met regularly to discuss refugee and immigration policy. However, these meetings were often uneasy, owing to contrasting views of how refugees should be identified, selected, and resettled in Canada. This tension came into focus in the context of the Hungarian refugee crisis. Initially, the Canadian government resisted launching a resettlement program; however, external pressure finally led it to open a path to resettlement that relied heavily on selection and sponsorship by religious groups. Even though these groups faced repeated efforts by immigration officials to exclude them from government programs, the Hungarian crisis helped them to retain their role in implementing privately sponsored refugee resettlement.

The Canadian response to the Hungarian refugee crisis has been wrongly described by a number of scholars as the product of decisive action by Jack Pickersgill, the minister of citizenship and immigration. Hawkins says that the crisis "awoke the nobler instincts of the Liberal government."[59] She continues: "It was a perfect liberal cause and they responded swiftly to it. The issue of Hungarian freedom seems to have been particularly appealing to Mr. Pickersgill."[60] This narrative of government leadership has been reiterated in another recent historical analysis of the development of Canadian refugee policy.[61] Valerie Knowles, while acknowledging the role of public pressure, also presents the Department of Citizenship and Immigration as the leading agent in the policy process – trying one thing after another before the minister stepped forward as the "commandant" of the operation to come.[62] In fact, the primary impulse for policy change came from outside of government.[63]

When the Hungarian refugee crisis started, the Canadian government was slow to react. The foreign minister, Lester Pearson – who was, at the time, deeply involved with the Suez crisis – issued a message "to show that the Government was deeply sympathetic to the cause of the Hungarian people."[64] However, the initial policy of the government did not extend far beyond the expression of sympathy. The UNHCR appealed to the Canadian government to go beyond financial assistance to the Hungarian refugees in Austria and to grant temporary asylum "to the greatest possible number of political refugees from Hungary."[65] But, initially, resettlement was not in the cards. Instead, the government helped to convene a meeting of the Hungarian Federation, Catholic and Protestant groups, and the Red Cross to coordinate a national Hungarian relief organization.[66]

As media coverage of the events in Hungary saturated the public sphere, the government adopted a policy of giving priority to immigration applications from that country. This was explicitly not a policy of refugee resettlement. At first, Pickersgill dismissed public criticism from religious groups and the Hungarian Federation, both of which observed that the government's response fell far short of responding to the demand for asylum coming from Austria. He noted to cabinet that "there had been very few [immigration] cases coming forward" to the Immigration Department, suggesting that the demand for resettlement was not there.[67] In all likelihood, however, the limited number of immigration applications was due to Canada's unwillingness to relax its normal immigration procedures, which emphasized employability.

In the years before the Hungarian crisis, Canada was focused on reorienting its immigration program toward the general objective of finding "people with skills and abilities which are scarce in Canada."[68] The economic recovery in Europe had made it more difficult to attract immigrants defined by the government as "desirable," as fewer Europeans sought out emigration opportunities. Religious groups continued to sponsor refugees from Europe under the Approved Church Program, but that program remained a point of some contention with bureaucrats who were reluctant to open the doors too widely to refugees who appeared, on the surface, to offer little to the Canadian economy. This point of tension surfaced repeatedly, including in dialogues with the immigration minister. During one such meeting in 1956 – which became heated at certain moments – Saul Hayes (Canadian Jewish Congress) asserted: "Immigrants should be regarded from the humanitarian as well as the economic point of view ... Canada has obligations in the post-war world ... and we shouldn't look at immigration solely from the point of taking the very best people out of Europe."[69] The crisis in Hungary brought this disagreement over the purpose of refuge policy to the fore.

The religious groups led a public outcry (through media commentary and telegram campaigns) against the government response to the flight of refugees from Hungary.[70] Jewish Immigrant Aid Services, the Catholic Immigrant Aid Society, and the Canadian Council of Churches urged the government to replicate its response to the displaced people by initiating "a sizeable emergency scheme to bring refugees from the reception centres of Austria."[71] They noted, in a meeting with bureaucrats at Citizenship and Immigration, that the policy response of the Canadian government to the plight of the Hungarians was vague, and that some "definite plans" were needed to coordinate private and government action in the field of resettlement.[72] Across the country, clergy delivered sermons calling on the government to bring "anti-communist freedom fighters" to Canada.[73]

Ottawa initially resisted the pressure from the UNHCR, religious groups, and the opposition parties in Parliament. Pickersgill declared at a meeting with various groups in Toronto that "I do not think it would be of advantage to the Hungarian refugees to bring them all the way across the Atlantic only to set them up in special camps here."[74] He claimed that the national interests of Austria, which was hosting most of the Hungarians, should be considered alongside those of Canada, which should be wary of admitting large numbers of refugees with unknown health problems, employment prospects, or accommodation needs. Other reasons surfaced later. Security advisers were concerned about Soviet infiltrators, and immigration advisers worried about the adaptability of Hungarians to Canadian life.[75] The director of immigration suggested that there would be no way to prevent the arrival of "non *bona fide* refugees," whom he described as "members of the Hebrew race."[76]

In the meantime, the department was receiving a "flood" of offers of assistance to Hungarian refugees from across the country. These offers came from organized groups, as well as from citizens who were sending "chain telegrams" to the government.[77] Faced with organized pressure to resettle Hungarian refugees, immigration officials recommended expanding Canada's existing program of cooperation with religious groups. An internal memo from the director of immigration proposed the following: "I suggest to communicate with those national voluntary agencies with which we have dealt for some time and which have offered to help in this instance, namely: RSS, CJC/JIAS, CCCRR, CCC ... and ask them to coordinate all offers to assist or sponsor unnamed Hungarian refugees and indicate to us what specific commitments they can make."[78]

The memo also recommended not working directly with the Hungarian Relief Fund, which the government had helped establish under the Red Cross. It suggested instead that religious groups and their affiliates in Europe could "present to us refugees who would be sponsored by the Canadian voluntary agencies."[79]

On 27 November, almost a month after the beginning of the Hungarian refugee crisis, the Department of Citizenship and Immigration called a meeting with the leading religious and voluntary groups to consult about refugee relief and resettlement.[80] The director of immigration outlined the government's intention to bring together refugees in Austrian hostels, from which it hoped that voluntary organizations would "let the branch know immediately what assistance they can give in taking these people out of the hostels and putting them in homes at the very earliest possible moment."[81] The expression of support from the four religious groups allowed Minister Pickersgill to announce a change in policy in Parliament. Under the 1952 Immigration Act, the minister of citizenship and immigration was granted broad discretion to waive regulations for a specific group or class of immigrants if it was viewed to be in the national interest.[82] Accordingly, Pickersgill announced that Canada would take all

Hungarian refugees who elected to apply for Canadian immigration, transport them at government expense, and waive most of the formalities overseas.[83]

The government decision was reached only after "significant pressure from within and beyond Parliament" had been applied to Pickersgill and his colleagues.[84] An upcoming election in mid-1957 made the Liberal government more sensitive to public criticism, as the main opposition parties increasingly advocated a more open door to refugees from Hungary.[85] The religious groups – which had the capacity to administer a resettlement program and grassroots networks that could tap into and further mobilize public opinion – were another source of this pressure, as well as the means for alleviating it through a sponsorship program.

By early December 1956, the government estimated that more than 30,000 refugees could arrive in Canada within the space of four or five months under the new program.[86] The Department of Citizenship and Immigration instructed its district offices to identify the local affiliates of the agencies "regularly associated with immigrant movements: RSS, CJC, CCC, CCCRR" to coordinate settlement in Canada. As the minister commented, he viewed the role of the department as simply to "recruit immigrants" and not to "handle social problems," a responsibility that would fall to "social agencies and organizations."[87] By 25 January 1957, Pickersgill was able to report to the House of Commons the progress made by the government in collaboration with these groups: "I should like to say a word or two about something that is really a good deal more relevant to the estimate here, and that is the problem of settlement. We have had the most magnificent cooperation from voluntary organizations all over this country and I cannot speak too highly of them."[88] Pickersgill later noted the significance of the leading role of religious groups in the process of resettlement in the context of restrictions in Hungary on the operation of churches. "There is no other organization," he observed, "which can do as much as the churches to assist in the social integration of these refugees."[89]

By April 1957, Canada had begun to slow its admission of Hungarian refugees, and by June it counted the arrival of 31,269 Hungarians in Canada under the program.[90] The program was, on the whole, successful. Within a year of arrival, an insignificant percentage of Hungarians were receiving welfare payments.[91] And, despite some initial criticism from the United Steel Workers in the early days of the program, by the time of its conclusion both major parties and a broad base of public opinion supported it.[92] At the conclusion of the program, 37,565 Hungarian refugees had arrived in Canada at a cost to the federal government of more than $14.4 million.[93] Virtually all of the refugees arrived under the sponsorship of one of the four religious groups, part of a resettlement scheme that Dirks describes as "a useful precedent for those who pressed the government in later years for equally generous programs and policies."[94] Troper adds that it was "a watershed event" and "a model for a series of Canadian refugee initiatives during the next twenty years."[95]

The conclusion of the Hungarian program coincided with a June 1957 general election that saw the Liberal government of Louis St Laurent defeated by the Progressive Conservatives under John Diefenbaker. The new acting minister of immigration, E.D. Fulton, was advised by the director of immigration within a week of the government's taking office to adopt more restrictive measures with respect to the Hungarian refugees.[96] Two weeks later, a memo to cabinet noted that the Hungarian program, if "unchecked," would "result in serious problems" and would "prejudice future prospects for successful programs."[97] Such claims were premature and speculative, reflecting a tenacious restrictionist impulse within the department.[98] Nevertheless, they received a hearing from the new and inexperienced acting minister, who recommended to cabinet that "the granting of visas to those who are sponsored by friends, voluntary agencies or church groups, be discontinued."[99]

Successful lobbying by the religious groups had long preserved their role in refugee resettlement, a position they appeared to consolidate through the Hungarian program. Nevertheless, in mid-1957, the director of immigration expressed a desire to end the Approved Church Program, an objective that the department had pursued repeatedly since 1954. He was advised by the deputy minister, however, to hold off "pending review of Immigration policies and procedures."[100] Indeed, Acting Minister Fulton sought the input of the approved religious groups in his review of immigration policy, continuing the "consultative and cooperative" relationship that evolved during the Hungarian program.[101] During this meeting, the groups were advised of an upcoming slow-down in immigration during the winter months. Interpreting this as yet another move to close down the sponsorship stream, the groups stressed to the acting minister the continuing value of the Approved Church Program.[102]

In May 1958 the deputy minister finally acceded to the requests of the director of immigration to recommend the end of the Approved Church Program. In his memo to the acting minister, he traced the origins of the program to the cabinet's recognition of the CCCRR and other voluntary agencies in June 1947. He noted that a multiplicity of schemes subsequently developed in relation to a handful of religious groups, which were rationalized and coordinated under the Approved Church Program in June 1953. This program, the memo observed, was "initiated with a view to achieving closer coordination between the activities of the various agencies of the Protestant, Catholic and Jewish faiths and the Department, and to ensure that their activities were governed by uniform procedures."[103] These approved groups could sponsor immigrants (almost always refugees) through a process of pre-selection. The deputy minister proposed new procedures that would eliminate the "administratively cumbersome" arrangements with the religious groups in favour of treating them the same as a family sponsor "in the ordinary case of immigrant sponsorship."[104] The goal would be to have "no special and separate procedures for church cases and perhaps the involvement of the voluntary agencies in recruitment, movement, etc. of immigrants would be confined to advising or assisting the immigrants themselves."[105] The government sought to maintain the "moral assistance" of the groups in settlement while securing greater control over the process of selection and admissions.[106] The acting minister was more easily persuaded by his officials than were previous ministers, and the department quietly ended the Approved Church Program in May 1958.

Soon after the Approved Church Program was discontinued, Minister Ellen Fairclough replaced Acting Minister E.D. Fulton. She assumed office as efforts to stimulate Canada's involvement in World Refugee Year were beginning to crystallize in a civil-society coalition and more active government engagement. A Canadian Committee for World Refugee Year (CCWRY) formed in February 1959, and it included the main religious groups, the Red Cross, the Canadian Labour Congress, the National Council of Women, the YMCA, and the United Nations Association of Canada among its forty-four members. Its initial goal was to raise funds for the UNHCR, as there were differing views on the committee as to whether to press for refugee admissions to Canada.[107] The government of Canada, however, was reluctant to offer early support to the initiative, declining to co-sponsor the UN resolution on World Refugee Year (although Canada did vote in favour of it). Diplomats noted that the Department of Citizenship and Immigration did not favour relaxing immigration regulations or making special arrangements for refugees in European camps, and so they were loathe to offer public support for World Refugee Year.[108]

Following the formation of the CCWRY, the External Affairs Department approached the Department of Citizenship and Immigration to explore possible government action during World Refugee Year. The under-secretary of state noted that the positive response from the Canadian public and some allies suggested that "significant pressure may develop both domestically and in the field of our international relations" to do something for World Refugee Year.[109] In a subsequent interdepartmental meeting, External Affairs officials noted that WRY could become "a public relations problem which might have important political overtones."[110] Despite some urging on their part for Canada to encourage the committee of voluntary groups to sponsor refugees from Europe, immigration officials replied that the "Minister was not in favour of Canada accepting any large number of refugees this year."[111] The meeting ended without any decision on Canadian action for World Refugee Year. Indeed, nothing would be done for several months to come.

The four religious groups seized the opportunity of World Refugee Year to push for the reinstatement of the Approved Church Program. They collectively wrote to Minister Fairclough, advocating the creation of a sponsorship program that would allow them to select refugees from abroad without consideration for employment prospects.[112] The groups were invited to meet with Fairclough and other senior immigration officials. At this meeting, the deputy minister attempted to rebuff any proposal to recreate the Approved Church Program. However, "the Minister interjected at this point, stating that it might be a good idea to call semi-annual meetings with these particular groups in order to have a general discussion on immigration matters, especially pertaining to refugees."[113] The groups also appeared to stimulate a change of perspective at the Department of Citizenship and Immigration regarding its commitment to World Refugee Year. Immediately after the meeting, the director of immigration observed that "unless the Federal Government takes some initiative in the WRY, public interest and enthusiasm will become a wave of criticism and the Government might eventually be forced into some action for which it will be impossible to gain any credit."[114]

Following the meeting with the minister, all four groups submitted proposals to resurrect the Approved Church Program sponsorship scheme. The proposals reserved a role for the agencies in selecting refugees to resettle and committed them to assuming responsibility for accommodation, travel, reception, and employment on arrival. The director of immigration continued to resist these proposals, noting that "it will mean that immigrants [i.e., refugees] who would not otherwise be approved will be able to come to Canada" and expressing concern that if they fell out of employment they would become a public liability.[115] The deputy minister proceeded to recommend to the minister that the department relax its occupation and age restrictions when one of the recognized agencies agrees to "complete and continuing responsibility after arrival in Canada."[116] The term of "responsibility" was a major sticking point for the agencies, which were concerned about taking on an indefinite liability for the refugees they sponsored. Such a commitment could become an unreasonable drain on their future resources. They pushed back on this point and finally received a proposal from the department to reinstate a sponsorship program that would be conditioned on sponsors agreeing to a one-year term of support for refugees before they would become eligible for public assistance.[117]

The terms of this scheme were subject to several further exchanges and meetings with the four religious groups, although the main features can be traced back to the Approved Church Program. Internal memos from within the Department of Citizenship and Immigration reveal a great deal of frustration with the groups, which were publicly criticizing government policy while also resisting the sponsorship terms they were offered. The Canadian Council of Churches, in particular, voiced its displeasure that the government would not allow refugees to access welfare services for their first year, calling it "an amazing suggestion and one which we cannot accept."[118] This did not stop the minister from publicizing the new private-sponsorship program. In one public address, she identified the recognized voluntary agencies,[119] noting that the government would accept as part of its WRY commitment any number of privately sponsored sick or handicapped refugees. "It would be difficult to find a more rewarding project for a church group or private agency than the sponsorship of a refugee during Refugee Year," she added. "Action by government agencies alone will not solve our refugee problem – there must be in addition a multitude of individual efforts which spring from the deep roots of our religious and democratic faith."[120]

Initially, in fact, supporting private sponsorship appeared to be all the government would do for World Refugee Year. The foreign minister pushed for some kind of government commitment to a special resettlement program, but Fairclough (acting on the advice of her department) was firm: "I have considered this matter very carefully indeed, and it is a most difficult problem. As a matter of fact, I feel Canada has done her share in accepting some 38,000 Hungarian refugees."[121] As World Refugee Year began,[122] Canada's commitment was limited to government plaudits for a civil-society WRY committee and a relaunched private-sponsorship program. Editorials began to appear in the daily newspapers criticizing the government for its inaction. One proposal became the focus of some advocacy – that Canada should admit refugees diagnosed with tuberculosis and commit to their treatment and rehabilitation. Finally, at the meeting of the UN General Assembly in late 1959, the Canadian government announced that it would resettle one hundred refugees with tuberculosis along with their families.

By the conclusion of World Refugee Year, some 3,000 refugees had been resettled from the remaining camps in Europe. About half of these were refugees with tuberculosis and their families, a number that was increased twice after it became apparent that their treatment and the burden on public funds was far less than initially estimated. The other half were privately sponsored by the recognized voluntary groups – mostly sick or disabled refugees who were otherwise ineligible for immigration to Canada.[123] Finally, the Canadian Committee for World Refugee Year raised $1.8 million for the UNHCR, which contributed to the resettlement of more than 1,200 displaced people in Western Europe.[124] This all occurred within the context of shrinking immigration to Canada, owing to an economic downturn and pressure from unions to decrease admissions.[125]

Between 1956 and 1960, the relationship between the handful of religious groups concerned with refugee policy and the Department of Citizenship and Immigration became more routinized yet also increasingly adversarial. It became routinized in the sense that regular meetings and exchanges between the leaders of the CCC, CCCRR, CJC-JIAS, and the Catholic groups, on one side, and senior officials in the department, on the other, became a part of the normal policy discourse. Together, they retained a loose network around refugee issues. However, these relationships also became more contested over time. Although the department had broken out of its highly restrictive policy stance of the interwar period, it remained reluctant to cede control over admissions of refugees who did not present tangible benefits to the Canadian economy. The cooperative arrangements with religious groups led to the admission of a greater number of "humanitarian" cases. Religious groups also exerted pressure (often unsuccessfully) on the government to accept refugees from non-European countries such as China – something that, although no longer blocked by law, was still viewed as undesirable by bureaucrats steeped in early-twentieth-century race thinking.[126]

As the terms of the Approved Church Program were repeatedly renegotiated, frustration mounted on both sides. The religious groups – especially the Canadian Council of Churches – wanted a liberal refugee policy that would enable them to select and resettle refugees with access to welfare support from the government. However, the Department of Citizenship and Immigration saw things differently. It valued the role of religious groups in "reception and integration" but sought to exclude them from "selection and movement processes."[127] If groups were to have a role in selection, the department thought they should provide guarantees that the refugees they were bringing into the country would not become an immediate burden on public finances. By July 1959, the department had formally replaced the Approved Church Program with a private-sponsorship scheme. Under private sponsorship, one of the major religious agencies could sponsor refugees who would not ordinarily be approved for immigration to Canada, provided the costs of their first year of accommodation and maintenance were paid.[128] The groups protested the new terms, claiming they unduly shifted the "full burden of risks" onto the churches.[129] Nevertheless, they participated in the resettlement program approved during World Refugee Year, sponsoring some 1,500 sick and disabled refugees who were remaining in Europe's displaced-persons camps.

By 1960, the relationship between the religious groups and the Department of Citizenship and Immigration was evolving from its early mode of close cooperation. The church groups in particular saw themselves as custodians of a set of universal values and as advocates for upholding these values within refugee policy. The government, in their view, was simply pursuing its own interests within the framework of a flawed international order, and it had to be asked to subordinate these interests to a higher truth.[130] At first, the religious groups thought they could satisfy their humanitarian impulses by helping resettle refugees admitted by the government, but over time they became frustrated with what they thought was an abdication of government responsibility to pay the full cost of refugee resettlement. These frustrations increasingly led to a more critical stance toward the government, which fractured the issue network that developed during the 1940s and 1950s. Although private sponsorship flourished during the 1950s, many of these groups would distance themselves from government in the decade to come.

POLICY NETWORKS AND FEEDBACK EFFECTS

During the 1950s, the development of refugee policy in the United States and Canada continued along separate pathways. The temporary responses to displaced people were made continuous by structured interactions between the state and religious and voluntary groups, within the context of the Hungarian refugee crisis. The United States government renewed its relationship with the same religious and voluntary agencies that, with its cooperation and support, had resettled displaced people after the war. Canada, on the other hand, retained two programs – one managed by immigration bureaucrats and another implemented by religious groups at their own expense.

The continuity of these programs was reinforced by the advocacy of religious groups, which focused on retaining and reproducing systems of post-war resettlement. As Jürgen Beyer notes with regard to path-dependent processes, "a chosen 'path' is stabilised by the fact that actors keep referring to it in their actions" and "a cumulation of mutual commitments results."[131] Religious groups and government officials had produced relatively stable and structured relationships in order to implement post-war resettlement programs, and these became the foundations on which future programs were designed. In both countries, refugee programs continued to evolve, but they did so along the paths already charted during the post-war period. Feedback effects arising from structured interactions with implementing groups were one of the significant mechanisms generating path dependency in both countries, and these effects were stronger in the United States because of its more cohesive policy network.

In the United States, religious groups achieved insider status with decision makers in Congress and the White House as members of a policy community that coalesced around shared beliefs and a single agenda.[132] According to Martin Smith, policy communities are highly coordinated, and they are "more likely to develop where the state is dependent on groups for implementation."[133] Leaders of these groups were invited into advisory positions of government refugee programs, were routinely asked to testify before congressional hearings as expert witnesses, and operationally and financially worked hand-in-glove with executive agencies with responsibilities for refugees. They shared a common set of ideas related to a fight against Communism, albeit for different reasons: religious groups were focused on the struggle against the forces of atheism and secularism, while government officials had more political motives.

Membership in the policy community was primarily mediated through the American Council for Voluntary Agencies and its various committees, which concentrated expertise and shared interests among its members. The role of religious and voluntary groups as partners in the implementation of refugee resettlement became essential to sustaining the continuity of government programs. By 1963, more than 50 per cent of the $41-million budget of Church World Service came from government sources. Similar ratios pertained in the other major religious groups. This marked a significant change from the early 1950s, when most contributions were from internal sources.[134] It reflected the dependence of the government on the implementation capacity of the religious and voluntary groups to carry out resettlement programs. It also indicates the growth and potential influence of these groups within the field of refugee policy.

What developed in Canada over the course of the 1950s resembled the characteristics of an issue network far more than a policy community. An issue network, Martin Smith notes, tend to develop in areas "of lesser importance to government, or high political controversy, or in new areas where interests may not have had the time to establish institutionalized relationships."[135] They can be characterized by high participation but lack a great amount of interdependence among members. Members also lack a common set of beliefs, each participating in the issue network for different reasons. Canada did not have a formal coalition between religious groups, which interacted with immigration program managers who were reluctant to embrace formal partnerships.

Religious groups in Canada gradually became outsiders within the refugee policy process, despite being in regular dialogue with decision makers. Although there were a small number of groups who played a recognized, authorized role in refugee resettlement, they were not connected with each other through a formal coalition entity. They retained the position of external advocates, seeking to pressure the government to liberalize its immigration and refugee policies whenever the moment seemed ripe for a policy intervention. As administrators and implementers of resettlement programs, they were reluctantly granted authority to select and resettle displaced persons by the Department of Citizenship and Immigration, which also tried to limit their role as much as possible. In other words, they forged an issue network that connected the group members to each other but that lacked any strong coordination, resource exchanges, or shared beliefs and ideas with officials in government.

In Canada, private sponsorship evolved in the context of a continuing tension between religious groups and immigration officials over the policy image – the core beliefs and values concerning refugee policy – and how to select refugees for resettlement. As a result, these groups did not receive any government funding and were required to self-finance their resettlement work. The extent of this financial burden became a source of significant frustration and debate in the late 1950s. The groups wanted to select and resettle refugees from Europe with access to government welfare services, but they were refused – at least for the first year of residency. Immigration officials repeatedly tried to prevent them from taking an active role in the selection and transportation of refugees, but they faced difficulty securing political support. The Approved Church Program finally was ended in favour of a private-sponsorship arrangement that required registered voluntary groups to maintain sponsored refugees for the first year of their residency. However, the adversarial process leading to this decision alienated the leading groups from participating heavily in private sponsorship in much of the subsequent decade.

Over the 1960s, relationships in both countries between religious and voluntary groups and government officials would be reconfigured and fragmented. In the United States, religious groups joined new political coalitions that mobilized around an emerging human rights discourse and pushed for immigration and refugee policy reform. Despite the liberalization of immigration law during this time, the main elements of the refugee-resettlement policy framework were retained and became further entrenched. In Canada, most Christian groups retreated from cooperation with private sponsorship and began to embrace the outsider tactics of public criticism of the government's refugee policy.

4

Shifting Alliances

Refugees, Human Rights, and Policy Reform

World Refugee Year was an inflection point marking the end of the post-war European refugee crisis and the emergence of a more global perspective on refugees and their demands for protection and resettlement. It also coincided with the beginning of the end of racial restrictions on immigration in the United States and Canada. Immigration reform became a major legislative issue in both countries during the 1960s, as changes in domestic coalitions and international normative contexts empowered decision makers to promote liberalization.[1] Explicit racial and national barriers to immigration were removed. And, within this context, refugee policy was debated as a permanent aspect of immigration policy rather than as a temporary emergency response to a crisis.

During this period, relationships between the state and religious and voluntary groups were reconfigured. In the United States, religious groups continued to embed themselves in the refugee-resettlement system through the operation of a stable policy community, while at the same time joining new political coalitions to advocate immigration reform. The post-war framework of cooperation on refugee resettlement remained stable because of shared beliefs about anti-Communism and the role of religious groups in resettlement. In Canada, on the other hand, the issue network sustaining dialogue and cooperation on resettlement virtually disintegrated because of diverging views about the purpose of refugee policy and the criteria used to select refugees for resettlement. Religious groups moved away from refugee resettlement during much of the decade; as a result, labour-market criteria came to the fore in Canadian government-run refugee programs. The parallel system of private sponsorship was intact, but little used, alongside the deteriorated issue network.

In the United States, the mass arrival of Cuban refugees beginning in 1960 initiated another major resettlement program in which religious groups took the lead for relocating and settling refugees across the country, with the support of an expanding government subsidy. These same groups also partnered with leading unions, civil-liberties associations, and ethnic and nationality groups to campaign for immigration-law reform, which eventually achieved the elimination of national-origins quotas under the 1965 Hart-Celler Act.[2] The act also established, for the first time, an annual quota for refugee admissions.

In Canada, on the other hand, religious groups in the 1960s largely abandoned refugee resettlement and retreated into an outsider position of advocacy against government policy. The loose issue network that had formed around post-war refugee resettlement and the Approved Church Program effectively broke down soon after the program was terminated in 1959. Although religious groups remained engaged with certain refugee issues (Jewish groups with Soviet Jews, and Christian groups with Chinese refugees in Hong Kong, among others)[3] during this time, they dramatically reduced refugee sponsorship.[4] They were virtually absent from the policy discourse around the Czechoslovakian refugee program in 1968 and the Ugandan program in 1972, both of which were government-led initiatives that were (at least initially) undertaken principally for utilitarian reasons of selecting talent and skilled labour, in the context of Cold War politics.[5] The Christian groups re-engaged more strongly with public-refugee advocacy in 1973, however, following the coup in Chile that year.[6] Their adversarial, "outsider" advocacy tactics generated sufficient pressure to provoke a policy change, leading to the resettlement of thousands of Chilean refugees, many of them with church sponsorship.[7]

In this chapter, I explain why, during the 1960s, cooperation between the state and religious and voluntary groups strengthened in the United States but radically diminished in Canada. A cohesive policy community in the United States, held together by shared beliefs and clear roles set out for the actors involved, served to reproduce institutional responses to refugee resettlement – even in the context of a volatile national policy debate over immigration. In Canada, the weak issue network binding together religious groups and the immigration bureaucracy finally broke down over disagreement about the purpose of refugee policy and the division of responsibilities, costs, and authorities between actors. As a consequence, many of these groups retreated to the public sphere, where they became more openly critical of government policy. Private sponsorship was retained as a regulatory policy, but it was virtually unused during this time.

UNITED STATES

Cuban Refugees

In early 1959 the United States became a country of first asylum. Soon after Fidel Castro assumed power in February 1959, Cubans began to arrive in Dade County, Florida. They were admitted under the president's parole authority. The government observed a "passive policy" in response to these early arrivals, waiving the need for any sponsorship or guaranteed employment: the Coast Guard did not intercept ships, commercial flights were permitted to land, and the Immigration and Naturalization Service did not initiate deportation hearings.[8] The asylum seekers were initially aided by Catholic charities based in Miami, but the number of arrivals soon outpaced their capacity for voluntary service. Some 500–2,000 arrived per week.[9] About 125,000 Cubans arrived between January 1959 and April 1961.[10] One hundred and fifty thousand came between 1961 and 1962.[11]

By 1960, the Cuban refugees were beginning to overwhelm local schools and religious charities in Miami. A group of civic and religious leaders, including Bishop Coleman Carroll of the Roman Catholic Diocese of Miami, organized the Cuban Refugee Committee and wrote to President Eisenhower to request federal funds to support aid and resettlement.[12] In November 1960 Tracy Voorhees, who had been President Eisenhower's representative to coordinate the Hungarian resettlement program, was once again pressed into service as Eisenhower's personal representative for Cuban refugees. Voorhees reported to the president that the continued arrival of Cubans required a more coordinated response, with federal support. His report and recommendations shaped the initiation of the Cuban Refugee Program in 1961 and the passage of the 1962 Migration and Refugee Assistance Act, which authorized appropriations for the program.

The development of the Cuban Refugee Program was shaped by the refugee-policy community, which shared a common view of the refugee as someone fleeing Communist rule.[13] This was the general view held by the U.S. government, as expressed in the 1957 Refugee-Escapee Act, which defined a refugee to one who "has fled or shall flee ... Communist-dominated, or Communist-occupied" areas. It was also embraced (mostly without criticism) by the religious and voluntary groups that were part of a cohesive group operating under the American Council of Voluntary Agencies.

When Voorhees met with the ACVA's Migration and Refugee Affairs Committee, he underscored that the lessons learned during the Hungarian program "have been helpful to us now."[14] He drew comparisons between the two refugee movements as rapid arrivals to the United States that required close cooperation between government agencies and voluntary groups. Voorhees stressed the importance of the Catholic Church in responding the Cuban movement, in view of the number of Catholic arrivals and the church's organizational capacity. In response to his request for the assistance of resettlement agencies "to contribute their experience and skills," four leading agencies signed on to implement the program: Church World Service, Catholic Relief Services, HIAS, and the International Rescue Committee.[15] Voorhees assured them that they would be reimbursed for expenses incurred during the transportation of Cubans and that they would receive an additional amount of $60 per refugee to cover administrative costs. They were required to agree that they would facilitate the participation of refugees in the religious communities of their choice.[16]

Soon after Voorhees's meeting with the voluntary agencies, Eisenhower launched the Cuban Refugee Emergency Center on 7 December 1960. The design of the program was left to Voorhees, who in turn consulted closely with Catholic, Jewish, Protestant, and other implementing partners. Initially, however, many Cubans expected their sojourn in Miami to be temporary, and few accepted resettlement. Nevertheless, the same agencies worked in Miami to provide "welfare work pending resettlement," supported by both private donations and government funding.[17] Voorhees wrote to President John F. Kennedy in 1961 that "these organizations typify the true warm heart of America. The principal function of the Government is to assist them."[18] Following the Bay of Pigs and Cuban Missile Crisis, return migration grew less attractive for most exiles, and the movement of asylum seekers continued. The refugee movement, while initially thought to be temporary, became permanent.

The Cuban Refugee Program initiated under Eisenhower was significantly expanded under President Kennedy as the number of arrivals increased and permanent resettlement became a more central feature of the program. While initial costs of social assistance to refugees were largely borne by religious charities in Miami, the government channelled increasing sums of money to the cause of the Cuban refugees through the Department of Health, Education, and Welfare (HEW). The Eisenhower administration spent only $1 million on resettlement, while the Kennedy and Johnson administrations spent $214 million between 1961 and 1966.[19] Not all of these funds flowed to the voluntary agencies, but a significant amount was devoted to covering the costs of their services to refugees on behalf of the government.

The groups contracted to implement the resettlement program found Cubans to be increasingly willing to resettle outside of Miami as the prospects for returning home grew dimmer. Church World Service chartered planes to fly several thousand refugees to new destinations around the country, calling them "freedom flights."[20] During the 1960s, it resettled 36,339 Cuban refugees in all fifty states.[21] Catholic Relief Services convened its diocesan directors and outlined a national resettlement strategy that was informed by its DP and Hungarian programs.[22] A Catholic Welfare Bureau was created to foster the creation of local parish subcommittees to focus on employment, housing, social services, and public communication about refugees, with the intention of helping parishioners to facilitate the rapid settlement of Cubans in their communities.[23] Over the next decade, Catholic Relief Services resettled Cuban refugees in almost every diocese in the United States.[24] George Murray explains some of the motivating factors behind the extensive engagement of Catholic agencies in the resettlement of Cubans as follows: "Cubans, like the Hungarians before them, were of special interest to the Catholic Church. Both groups were largely Catholic and both represented an opportunity to battle Communism."[25]

In 1966 Congress debated the Cuban Status Adjustment Act. It heard testimony from the four main voluntary agencies which implemented the bulk of the program. Catholic Relief Services testified to its role in obtaining jobs and employment for about 70 per cent of Cubans resettled outside of Miami and noted the significance of the United States being a country of first asylum for the first time. It also underscored the religious beliefs that motivated its action, as well as its opposition to the "totalitarian regime" of Communist Cuba.[26] Finally, the cooperation between the government and the religious voluntary agencies was once again emphasized: "Without government support, the various voluntary agencies involved in the program would not have been able to carry out their extensive activities. However[,] we cannot minimize the contributions made by private religious and social agencies, both in funds and personnel."[27]

The Cuban Status Adjustment Act passed with relatively little controversy in Congress, allowing an estimated 200,000 Cuban parolees to apply for permanent resident status. There was little ground on which to oppose the normalization of the parolees because the number of Cuban admissions was so high and relations with the entrenched Castro government had become so adversarial. There were dim prospects of return migration for Cubans in the United States. The primary point of debate was a concern from the State Department that status normalization would signal a de facto acceptance of a Communist Cuba. However, this was insufficiently persuasive to hold back the legislation to allow Cubans who arrived after January 1959 as parolees or visa overstayers to apply for permanent residency and, eventually, American citizenship.[28]

Immigration Reform

As the arrivals of Cubans began to slow down, Congress debated a series of bills to eliminate the national-origins quota system. The members of the American Council of Voluntary Agencies actively lobbied from the outset for the inclusion of refugee quotas in a new system, urging the United States to commit to accepting a "fair share" of refugees and also to increasing its participation in the resettlement of refugees from outside of Europe in cooperation with voluntary agencies.[29] Early on, draft legislation incorporated refugees into a new proposed immigration program that would be managed by arrival class (e.g., family, occupational, refugee) rather than by country of origin.[30] As Emanuel Celler (D-NY), one of the lead proponents of the legislation, argued, the admission of refugees outside of national-origins quotas had already altered immigration to the United States in practice. Because of the large admissions of DPs, Hungarians, and Cubans, by 1963 only about 33 per cent of immigration to the United States occurred under the quota terms of the 1952 Act.[31] Celler declared: "We are not talking about *increased* immigration; we are talking about *equality of opportunity* for all peoples to reach this promised land."[32] Advocates for eliminating the national-origins quotas contended that the system was not only discriminatory but also unworkable in light of the use of executive parole authority to admit refugees.

Catholic and Jewish groups had publicly opposed national-origins quotas in the months and years leading up to their adoption. Protestant groups had likewise done so since at least the end of the Second World War. However, the opening of a political window to achieve legislative change brought these groups into a growing civil-society coalition that supported President Kennedy's and Johnson's proposed measures to reform immigration law.[33] The National Council of Churches passed a resolution in 1965 declaring that the United States should change its immigration law to reflect "insights from Christian faith and the nature of a free society [which] suggest that people should be afforded opportunities to move voluntarily for economic and social reasons."[34] The National Catholic Welfare Conference testified before the House Judiciary Committee, asserting the church's opposition to ethnic, racial, or nationality barriers to immigration. Pope John XXIII's encyclical, *Pacem in Terris* (11 April 1963), was cited in support of this position: "Among the rights of the human person there must be included that by which a man may enter a political community where he hopes he can more fittingly provide a future for himself and his dependents … It is the duty of [the] state to accept such immigrants."[35] These declarations of principle reiterated the long-standing policy view of the major religious groups, publicly aligning them with the civil-society coalition that supported the Democrats' intention to "bring our immigration law into line with the Civil Rights Act of 1964."[36]

Although in retrospect the demise of the national-origins quota system seems almost inevitable, it was caused by the confluence of a number of "order-shattering forces."[37] These include the following: a decline in racialist theories owing to their association with Nazi crimes, a shift of eugenicist lobby groups from sterilization and immigration policy toward population and family policy, a strengthened and skilled executive with greater authority over immigration and refugee admissions, an electoral landslide in 1964 (with partisan gains for Democrats in both Houses of Congress), a foreign-policy environment that exerted pressure to liberalize domestic policies, and shifting domestic alliances that brought unions into a pro-liberalization coalition of civil-society and political actors.[38] The passage of immigration reform was also part of a liberal public-policy agenda that was strongly associated with President Kennedy. Despite publicly advocating the repeal of the 1952 act for many years, Kennedy was unable to achieve immigration reform before he was assassinated in 1963. It was left to President Johnson, who had been a supporter of restrictionist measures as a senator, to take up the cause of immigration reform as part of his civil-rights agenda.[39] The Immigration Reform Act of 1965, also known as the Hart-Celler Act, passed both Houses with cross-party support – after a contentious and perilous journey through Congress.[40]

While the act is most notable for opening up immigration to the rest of the world, it also reserved a percentage of the new regional quotas for the admission of refugees. It set aside 120,000 total migration visas for the Western Hemisphere and 170,000 for the Eastern Hemisphere, annually. A set of preferences was established to prioritize the admission of family members and professionals within the Eastern Hemisphere allocation. The seventh preference of the new system reserved 6 per cent of Eastern Hemisphere migration visas for refugees, or 10,200 visas per year. Refugees were identified as those fleeing repressive Communist or Middle Eastern regimes, and for the first time they were given a formal policy pathway in law. This was, more or less, an attempt by Congress to regain control over refugee admissions and rein in the use of executive parole authority to admit large numbers of refugees without congressional approval.

In some respects, the 1965 act was a victory for the religious and voluntary agencies, which had long sought the removal of national-origins quotas and a legislative commitment to the ongoing resettlement of refugees abroad. The groups remained closely connected with the policy debate leading up to its passage. They were part of the civil-rights coalition that advanced progressive politics during the 1960s and that helped frame immigration reform as another step in the process of eradicating racial discrimination.[41] They were also in regular contact with Abba Schwartz, a senior official in the State Department appointed by Kennedy to develop an early immigration reform proposal. Schwartz had himself been involved in refugee relief and resettlement during and after the war, but as a "compulsive insider" he retained close relationships with restrictionists like Francis Walter.[42] Soon after President Johnson was sworn into office, Schwartz urged him to convene a special White House meeting with key members of Congress and religious and voluntary agency officials to consult about the immigration-reform agenda.[43] The National Catholic Welfare Conference, HIAS, and CWS all testified in support of Johnson's immigration-reform proposals before the congressional committees in which they were debated.[44]

The creation of a quota for refugee admissions had been a legislative goal of the religious groups for more than a decade. Its inclusion in the 1965 act, therefore, was a significant achievement. Refugees admitted under the act would be given "conditional entry" rather than a visa, allowing them to become permanent residents after two years in the United States. This was an improvement over the 1960 Fair Share Act, which committed the United States to take 25 per cent of refugees resettled outside of its borders through the attorney general's parole authority. For the first time, under the 1965 act, refugees could be admitted with a direct path to permanent status and citizenship without having to wait for status adjustment through legislative action.

However, the definition of a refugee contained in the 1965 act remained focused on those fleeing persecution in Communist or Middle Eastern countries. As Bon Tempo remarks, the law "consolidated and borrowed from, more than broke with, the previous fifteen years of American refugee policies and laws."[45] It repeated the definition of a refugee contained in 1953 and 1957 legislation – this, despite a growing debate over how to define a refugee in view of the changing causes of forced migration. Edward Swanstrom, head of Catholic Relief Services, advocated a very broad definition of a refugee as one who was unable to earn a livelihood in his or her country of origin. Initial proposals authored by Schwartz in 1963 proposed a definition of a refugee as including those who were uprooted by "natural calamity" or "military operations."[46] However, these broader definitions of a refugee were rejected by restrictionists, whose support was needed to pass immigration reform. Michael A. Feighan (D-OH), chair of the House Immigration Subcommittee and a key architect of the act, insisted that it was the "conspiracy of communism" that produced most refugees – a narrative that he used to win the support of more conservative legislators and interest groups.[47]

Ironically, the passage of the 1965 act was ultimately secured by Feighan's appeal to restrictionist groups and legislators, who were finally won over by the argument that the 1952 act was ineffective at controlling immigration.[48] The reason it was ineffective was owing to the parole authority it granted the attorney general to admit refugees at the discretion of the executive and the limits it placed on family reunification from European countries. The appeal of the 1965 act to restrictionist groups was the constraint it would place on the use of parole authority, as well as the priority it would grant to family reunification – which was intended to maintain the racial and demographic composition of the country, not through quotas but through other means. Although the act retained the executive's parole authority, its intention in setting out a ceiling on refugee admission was to limit its use. The Senate Judiciary Committee Report was explicit in underlining that the parole provision of the 1965 act was to be used only in "emergency, individual, and isolated situations" and was "not for the immigration of classes and groups outside the limit of the law."[49]

President Johnson immediately set aside the idea that the Hart-Celler Act would alter the use of executive parole. In the signing ceremony of the act, beneath the shadow of the Statue of Liberty in New York, he gave his direction to the attorney general to parole all Cubans who fled to the United States.[50] Later that day, he signed a bill into law that authorized a $12.6-million program to help Cuban escapees. Soon after, the United States offered free flights to Cubans seeking to come to the United States.[51] In the year after the passage of the 1965 act, Johnson admitted another 45,000 Cubans with executive parole. And so, although the new act achieved far-reaching changes to immigration law, its inclusion of new quotas for refugees initially did nothing to alter the practice of using executive parole to admit large numbers on a temporary basis. Indeed, executive parole would continue to be employed to admit Cubans, Czechoslovakians, Ugandan Asians, Soviet Jews, and Indochinese refugees in the years ahead. However, President Richard Nixon and his attorney general would be more circumspect about using parole authority unilaterally.

Post-1965 Refugee Policy and Human Rights

Between 1965 and 1972, about 68,000 refugees were admitted to the United States under the "seventh preference" of the 1965 act.[52] These were in addition to the continued arrival of Cubans who were paroled by the attorney general. No single group dominated admissions until the 1968 Soviet occupation of Czechoslovakia prompted the flight of some 80,000 Czechoslovakian nationals. The United States did not initiate a dedicated program for them, as it had in the case of the Hungarians and Cubans, but the voluntary agencies created their own pathways to arrival and resettlement within the framework of the 1965 law. Some arrived as refugees, and many others came as immigrants. Loescher and Scanlan conclude that, unlike the Hungarians, "their resettlement went virtually unnoticed."[53]

They may have been unnoticed by the general public, but the arrival of Czechoslovakian refugees initiated an informal practice of consultation between the attorney general and ranking members of the Judiciary Committees of the House and Senate that became more routinized in the years ahead, and it helped stimulate the next round of refugee-reform proposals within Congress.[54] By early 1970, the seventh- preference allocation had already been used up by Czechoslovakian and Polish refugees, and every member of the House Judiciary Committee proceeded to approach the attorney general to ask him to use his parole authority to increase the numbers. President Nixon's attorney general, John Mitchell, was reluctant to use his authority, but he finally agreed, advising the committee (according to Congressman Peter Rodino [D-NJ]) "that legislation in the refugee field was urgently needed and that the general parole authority would be invoked for refugees only temporarily."[55] The parole of additional Czechoslovakians by Attorney General Mitchell began a process of consultation between the executive and Congress before the initiation of a refugee-parole program. Although the terms of this consultation were contested in other cases presented during the 1970s, the practice was honoured until it became more clearly codified in the 1980 Refugee Act.

The question of who was responsible for authorizing the admission of refugees continued to be a major focus of political debate into the 1970s. As Gary Freeman and Katherine Betts have argued, "the predominant motif of contemporary immigration policymaking has been the struggle between the executive and legislative branches of Government."[56] Within this context, religious groups increasingly focused their lobbying efforts on sympathetic members of Congress who sought to reform U.S. refugee policy. As Loescher and Scanlan observe, "most of the pressure to offer protection to refugees who fled authoritarian states and who did not serve larger US foreign policy interests originated from an emerging coalition of human rights organizations, churches, ethnic groups, and activist lawyers, in alliance with members of Congress concerned about human rights violations abroad."[57] Human rights became a new mantra for refugee advocates within a context coloured by the political realism of Henry Kissinger and his presidents. Congress grew increasingly receptive to lobbying by Jewish and Christian groups, who sought to draw attention to the need for U.S. refugee policy to be responsive to cases of state-sponsored human rights abuses.

Although the language of human rights had been threaded consistently through the personalist discourse of ecumenical Christian, Catholic, and Jewish groups since the end of the Second World War, it had virtually disappeared from the agenda of political decision makers during the 1950s and 1960s.[58] In the early 1970s, human rights made a resurgence through an unexpected alliance between the liberal left and a new movement of neo-conservatives who viewed the concept as an ideological tool to criticize Communism and autocracy.[59] What Jan Eckl and Samuel Moyn term "the breakthrough" of human rights during this period was generated by a number of conditions: the rapid growth of grassroots activism through Amnesty International (and later, Human Rights Watch and Lawyers Committee for Human Rights), an embrace by political actors on the left of a broader social-welfare agenda that could build upon civil rights, and a rejection by political actors on the right of Nixon and Kissinger's foreign policy, which involved uncompromising alliances with political strongmen.[60] Appeals to human rights featured prominently in refugee advocacy for both Soviet Jews and Chileans after the 1973 Pinochet coup.[61]

The Kremlin either prohibited or obstructed the emigration of Soviet Jews, and Congress faced growing pressure in the 1960s and 1970s to create opportunities for their resettlement in the United States. Jewish groups had lobbied the U.S. government – without much effect – to urge the Soviets to make a change in policy during the 1960s. The security achievements of détente were seen as too much to risk by pushing for the rights of a religious minority.[62] As Kissinger remarked dismissively to President Nixon: "Let's face it: The emigration of Jews from the Soviet Union is not an objective of American foreign policy. And if they put Jews into gas chambers in the Soviet Union, it is not an American concern. It is a humanitarian concern."[63] The Soviets relented to pressure from the United States in 1972 (led by Congress, not the executive branch) by allowing 35,000 Jews to emigrate to Israel, but then they immediately proceeded to restrict emigration further by instituting an expensive new departure tax on Jews.[64]

An increasingly powerful American Jewish lobby was at the forefront of advancing the cause of Soviet Jews.[65] Michael Barnett claims that the early 1970s marked a turning point for a range of new Jewish political advocacy groups, which became "more self-confident, assertive, and prepared to defend [their] interests."[66] Over time, the issue of the Soviet Jews also engaged the interest and support of the members of the U.S. refugee policy community, in addition to HIAS.

Christian and Jewish leaders designated 30 April 1972 as National Solidarity Day for Soviet Jews.[67] Earlier that month, six of the leading refugee agencies submitted an "urgent recommendation" to Attorney General Richard Kleindienst to create a provision for the parole of Soviet Jews in the United States.[68] Senator Ted Kennedy, a leading member of an emerging human rights coalition in Congress, took up their cause and pushed for a response from the Nixon administration.[69] The attorney general had promised in September 1971 to use the parole provision "should large numbers of Soviet Jews want to come to the US."[70] He finally agreed to parole 200 refugees in 1972.[71]

As the United States began to open up parole admissions to Soviet Jews, Russia continued to block their emigration. What ultimately triggered a change in Soviet emigration practices, however, was the tactical use of trade negotiations to extract concessions on emigration permits from the Soviets.[72] Congress attached an amendment to an East-West trade bill with Russia that made favourable trade terms conditional on Russia lifting emigration restrictions. The use of this tactic followed the imposition of departure taxes on Soviet Jews seeking to leave Russia in 1972. As U.S.-Soviet relations deteriorated in the wake of the ensuing trade dispute, Jews fled Russia when they were able to do so. After the Yom Kippur War in Israel in 1973, more of these emigrants sought admission to the United States. The numbers grew as large as 50,000 a year in the late 1970s, putting considerable pressure on the resources of the voluntary agencies that took responsibility for their resettlement. Nevertheless, there was virtually no public opposition to their arrival.[73]

Just as the issue of the Soviet Jews brought a range of Jewish groups into more direct opposition with the interests of the U.S. government, the overthrow of the socialist government of Salvador Allende in Chile stimulated Christian groups to push for the admission of refugees from that country.[74] The United States had encouraged the coup by General Augusto Pinochet, yet there was no interest on the part of the administration in taking any of the estimated 12,000 refugees who fled the country. The two issues of Soviet Jews and Chileans were also connected by the use of human rights language (rather than Cold War rationales) by political advocates.[75] Christian groups and human rights organizations like Amnesty International sought out allies in Congress, including Senator Kennedy. In September 1973, weeks after the coup, Kennedy urged the Nixon government to "provide asylum and resettlement opportunities to a reasonable number of political refugees from

Chile" under the parole authority of the executive.[76] A year later, Church World Service continued to press the administration to admit Chilean refugees, calling its response "inadequate" and reiterating that it "stands ready to resettle, through the churches, any or all of this group that are admitted to the US."[77] The government responded to these appeals by insisting that a parole program was not warranted but that Chileans who were present in the United States could always apply for political asylum if they feared persecution upon their return.[78] In 1973 the United States admitted only nineteen refugees from Chile – primarily owing to the administration's anti-Communism.[79] It was not until the Ford administration, in 1975, that a small parole program was set up for some four hundred cases.[80]

By the early 1970s, there was a growing appetite within Congress to pursue comprehensive reform to the law and policy governing refugee admissions. The human rights revolution was disrupting the Cold War consensus on refugees, and, as Bon Tempo notes, "Congress would continue to reassert its voice in refugee policymaking through the second half of the 1970s."[81] The Democrat-controlled Congress (which held majorities in both Houses from 1959 to 1981) was increasingly interested in amending a refugee policy regime that held a narrow definition of refugees and left most admissions to the discretion of the executive. This created an opening for religious groups to press the case for reform and make permanent the features of the refugee program they had helped to construct in the wake of the Second World War.

CANADA

After the conclusion of World Refugee Year, interest among Canada's religious groups in private sponsorship and refugee policy rapidly dissipated. This was due in large part to the increasingly antagonistic relationship between the groups and the government that developed over a divergence in core beliefs about refugee resettlement and the roles and responsibilities of the actors involved. Religious groups wanted to select refugees based on humanitarian and "moral" criteria, whereas the immigration bureaucrats sought readily employable workers. After World Refugee Year, Minister Fairclough was reported to be "suspicious and wary" of the groups, viewing them as useful sources of information but undesirable partners in refugee programs.[82] One expression of this fractured relationship was the steps taken by government officials to close down the Approved Church Program in 1958. In its place, a private-sponsorship program was initiated, shifting more of the costs of resettlement onto sponsoring agencies that selected refugees who did not meet the government's "employability" criteria.[83] As the department described in one memo, the deliberation over World Refugee Year led to "new working procedures" in the relationship between the government and recognized voluntary agencies: "Private sponsorship will be reserved for those refugees who ... cannot qualify for admission to Canada without the guarantees of necessary care and assistance provided by sponsoring individuals or private agencies."[84] A consequence of these shifting arrangements was the waning enthusiasm of church and voluntary groups for refugee sponsorship.[85]

In the early 1960s, it became clear that the religious groups, which had done so much in response to the displaced-persons and Hungarian refugee crises, were disengaging from government cooperation on refugee resettlement. The acrimonious debate over the terms of the Approved Church Program had created a "climate of distrust" between religious groups and the government.[86] "As a result," concludes Hawkins, "the churches continued on their separate ways, individually ... developing their own activities for immigrants in Canada."[87] Their issue network practically disintegrated. Christian groups virtually disappeared from the refugee scene in the early 1960s, aside from some engagement with lobbying for the Canadian government to resettle Chinese refugees from Hong Kong.[88] The Canadian Jewish Congress remained independently active through a small special program in 1966 targeting a few hundred Jews from North Africa and later through advocacy for Soviet Jews.

In the meantime, Canada significantly modulated its participation in refugee affairs. The government maintained a modest refugee-resettlement program in cooperation with the UNHCR which took in around 2,000 refugees a year – those who could show "reasonable prospects of employment."[89] Those who could not show their relevance to labour-market needs were eligible for private sponsorship, but these offers of assistance were no longer forthcoming. Prime Minister Diefenbaker authorized the first program for non-Europeans: 100 Chinese refugee families from Hong Kong were permitted to immigrate to Canada (far short of 10,000 sought by the Canadian Council of Churches).[90] In 1962 Canada pulled out of the Intergovernmental Committee for European Migration, which had coordinated the movement of refugees from Europe. Canada also opposed international funding of UNHCR refugee-maintenance programs in Asia and Africa, saying, "Continuing responsibility for refugee care must rest with the host governments."[91] Canada's participation in large-scale resettlement programs appeared to be a thing of the past now that most of the European refugee camps had closed. Overtures from the United Church and the Anglican Church to resettle a few hundred Chinese refugee families from Hong Kong were slow-walked or disregarded by immigration officials.[92]

The White Paper

By 1963, however, a sluggish Canadian economy was recovering and entering into a sustained period of growth and low unemployment. The Liberal Party formed a government under Prime Minister Pearson that year and immediately showed an interest in immigration reform, which had already been initiated within the bureaucracy. In 1962 Minister Fairclough had eliminated most of the regulations that permitted racial discrimination in immigration policy. The number of visa offices outside of Europe was increased. The recovery from recession stimulated a demand for workers, and immigration once again expanded considerably during this period (tripling in number from 1962 to 1967).[93] Yet, despite the expansion in immigration, refugee admissions were limited to just a few thousand each year.[94] In 1964 the combination of a strong economy and rising immigration led the Liberals to launch a policy review intended to generate new approaches to matching immigration with Canada's long-term economic interests.

The intentions of the Liberal government were made clear by Minister René Tremblay, who announced in August 1964 that he would undertake "detailed studies of the whole field" of immigration and then present a revised Immigration Act to Parliament.[95] Although the plans for a revised act would have to wait more than a decade, Tremblay helped initiate an extended debate over Canada's immigration and refugee policy. Prime Minister Pearson announced in December 1964 that the government would prepare a White Paper on immigration, an official policy statement (different from the later Green Paper, which was a research brief intended to present policy options). The following year he created a new Department of Manpower and Immigration. The new department assumed the responsibilities of the now defunct Department of Citizenship and Immigration, with the intention of aligning immigration and labour policies.[96] In practice, this meant that the responsibilities of the Immigration Division became confined to the selection of immigrants and enforcement of regulations, with an emphasis on "[encouraging and assisting] the movement to Canada of immigrants who will be able to establish themselves economically and socially with little difficulty for themselves or the Canadian community."[97] This emphasis was also extended to refugees, which had been a core objection of the religious groups during the 1950s.

In 1966 the Pearson government released its White Paper on Immigration, drafted by the Department of Manpower and Immigration. The White Paper did not give much detailed attention to refugee policy, aside from noting that there was a need to formalize Canada's approach to the resettlement of refugees. However, the internal documents contributing to its development reveal a stronger emphasis on the government managing the process of refugee resettlement. A memo to cabinet on refugee issues in the draft White Paper revealed an awareness within the department of the need to broaden refugee admissions beyond Europe and a desire to establish an annual quota tied to the UNHCR's caseload of refugees.[98] It also recommended ratifying the UN Refugee Convention and ending the policy of not deporting migrants to Communist countries.

Another preparatory paper disclosed hostility toward the close involvement of religious and voluntary groups in refugee resettlement, insisting that all immigration is "largely the private preserve of government."[99] It observed, wrongly, that in the past voluntary agencies "have played a small part" in immigration.[100] The paper speculated that "an informed public would tend to inhibit the activities of ethnic or religious groups, which seem able to secure immigration concessions by ill-founded claims of discrimination or by political pressure."[101] The conviction of immigration officials that religious groups should be excluded from the implementation of refugee policy was reflected in the White Paper tabled a year later. It stated: "If Canada is to accept its fair share of international responsibility for refugees, including the sick and handicapped, more formal arrangements than now exist are required including the annual appropriation of funds on a continuing basis."[102] Until this point, the "sick and handicapped" had primarily arrived under sponsorship, and the reference to "more formal arrangements" can only be read as expressing the preference of the government to assume full control over resettlement programs. It is no surprise, then, that Joseph Kage, the national executive vice-president of JIAS, felt compelled to urge that the White Paper be modified to include recognition of "sponsorship or co-sponsorship of deserving cases of refugees."[103]

During the 1960s, religious groups remained engaged with the changes in immigration and refugee policy, but they were generally on the periphery of the process. Eighteen religious groups formed a National Interfaith Immigration Committee in 1967 to serve as a point of contact with government visa officers. They played a part that had long been imagined for them by immigration officials, who valued the role of religious groups in "reception and integration" but wanted them removed from "selection and movement processes."[104] The committee received lists of all arriving immigrants and refugees from the government, and these were sent to local communities, which would in turn arrange visits with newcomers and provide them with information about social services and religious activities.[105] A 1970 Department of Manpower and Immigration report indicates that the refugee program had been "broadened and modified" and that the selection of refugees would take into consideration assistance from Canadian groups. In this regard, it notes that visa offers could seek assistance from the Interfaith Immigration Committee.[106] The committee, however, primarily served as a mechanism to connect refugees with community support and did not engage with refugee sponsorship.[107]

The White Paper expressed a significant shift in government perspective toward refugees, which was made more concrete with Canada's accession to the 1951 UN Convention Relating to the Status of Refugees and its 1967 Protocol. Canada joined in 1969, the same year the minister responsible said to the House of Commons Standing Committee on Labour, Manpower and Immigration: "Greater attention will be given to acceptance of refugees for resettlement in Canada from other parts of the world."[108] This change in refugee policy lagged behind the removal of racial and geographic restrictions on general immigration, which began in 1962 and was completed in 1967. Notwithstanding these progressive changes to government refugee policy, however, the total number of refugees resettled in Canada was the lowest in the 1960s of any decade since the Second World War.[109]

Czechoslovakians, Ugandans, and Chileans

The primary exception to Canada's refugee austerity during that decade was the 1968 program to resettle about 11,000 refugees from Czechoslovakia. In August 1968 the Soviet Union invaded Czechoslovakia and ended the period of relative freedom of thought, expression, and association known as the Prague Spring. In an echo of the Hungarian crackdown a decade earlier, about 27,000 people fled the country immediately following the Soviet invasion. As Troper observes, "this time there was no government stalling. Moved by a mixture of humanitarianism, Cold War posturing, and economic incentive, Ottawa moved quickly to its share of the new homeless."[110] Unlike the Hungarian program, which developed in response to public pressure and cooperation with religious groups, the Czechoslovakian movement was virtually entirely government-led.

The characteristics of the resettlement program reflected government priorities, with humanitarianism a rhetorical fig leaf to cover more naked economic interests. It was a pragmatic resettlement program that aligned with the core objectives of Canada's immigration policy. Madokoro writes, "Canadian officials were concerned less with Soviet behaviour and more how they could secure skilled migrants for themselves."[111] Canada sought to maintain positive relations with the Soviet Union within the context of détente, and its program to resettle Prague Spring refugees was presented as a "humanitarian, non-aggressive approach."[112] In practice, officials saw the refugees as "good material" and "high quality" workers, and they adopted a number of measures intended to secure "the best migrants" with competitive resettlement enticements.[113]

A similar logic dictated the Canadian resettlement of Ugandan Asians in 1972. About 7,000 Ugandan Asians (mostly Muslim Ismailis) were admitted to Canada in one of the country's first non-European resettlement programs, following an order by President Idi Amin that gave Asians ninety days to leave the country. Britain's Conservative government, facing great domestic opposition to the admission of the Ugandan Asians, exerted pressure on Canada to accept a portion of these refugees.[114] Australia had refused similar requests, and Canada at first lacked a clear plan. Finally, several weeks after Amin's order, cabinet directed immigration officials to select up to 3,000 people from Uganda who met the ordinary criteria under the new immigration-points system.[115] As the *Globe and Mail* pointed out at the time: "The government appears to be bidding for the cream of the crop."[116] As the situation deteriorated in Uganda, however, the focus turned to the admission of stateless people – Asians with only a Ugandan passport who were threatened with the loss of their citizenship. Canada admitted about 5,000 in the first two months and accepted another 2,000 from temporary camps in Europe the following year.[117] The Ugandan refugees, whether admitted under the points system or refugee protocols, were among the most highly educated populations to be resettled in Canada. Within a year, only a handful still required government assistance.[118] Voluntary groups were involved only marginally, if at all.[119]

Canada's refugee-resettlement programs during the 1960s reflected the disengagement of religious and voluntary groups in a number of respects. First, the total numbers of refugees admitted were significantly lower than what Canada had accepted in the decades previous and in those to come. Civil-society pressure was not a significant factor in either of the two major programs discussed above. Where religious groups were active in lobbying, they were relatively ineffective compared to their role in past programs. As a result, the government's actions were primarily undertaken with an eye to its foreign-policy priorities and its perception of the country's long-term economic interests. Notwithstanding more altruistic and innovative actions undertaken by bureaucrats, as noted by Madokoro and Molloy, the primary policy directives from cabinet reflected more a more clearly strategic orientation that hardly differentiated refugees from economically desirable immigrants.[120]

In 1973, however, the tide of disengagement reversed as a new coalition of Christian groups mobilized on behalf of Chilean refugees in the wake of General Pinochet's military coup against Salvador Allende's socialist government. Social ties to Central and South American churches reinforced a sense of concern and solidarity with these refugees among Canada's Catholic and Protestant churches.[121] Days after the coup, the leadership of the Anglican, United, and Catholic churches sent a joint letter to the Canadian government protesting the military takeover and calling on Ottawa "to offer safe conduct and assistance to [non-Chileans living in Chile] and any other Chilean who may wish to come to Canada."[122] Two weeks later, a senior delegation from these three (the largest) Christian denominations met with the minister of external affairs to reiterate the same. The response of the Canadian government was initially limited to a declaration that Canada would consider all applications for immigration from Chile. Its position was not helped by a leaked telex from the ambassador to Chile which revealed his sympathy for the authoritarian forces that overthrew Allende: "In overthrowing the Allende government," he wrote, "Chile's military and police have accepted an exceedingly difficult and thankless task."[123] The telex set off a firestorm of public criticism, led by an increasingly politicized coalition of church leaders, supported by university, labour, and human rights groups.

The most vociferous church group advocating the admission of Chilean refugees to Canada was the Inter-Church Committee on Human Rights in Latin America, affiliated with the ecumenical Canadian Council of Churches.[124] The Inter-Church Committee broke from the cooperative approach adopted by the National Interfaith Immigration Committee, which in turn criticized its adversarial tactics. Adopting a more "confrontational approach," the Inter-Church Committee sought to pressure the Canadian government to accept Chileans into the embassy in Santiago and then resettle them in Canada.[125] They initiated letter-writing campaigns, sought media publicity, and tried to openly discredit government statements. The group prepared extensive political briefs, aided by on-the-ground reporting facilitated by the World Council of Churches, and presented them to the government and the media with the aim of contradicting official claims that Canada was doing all it could to protect Chileans persecuted by Pinochet's forces.

The Inter-Church Committee argued for the resettlement of persecuted Chileans in Canada. However, a complicating factor for Canadian authorities was that the practice of seeking asylum in a foreign embassy, while a shared norm across Latin America, was not recognized in Canadian law or policy: a refugee had to be outside of his or her country of origin. A series of telexes between Ottawa and Santiago in October and November 1973 reflect an evolving government position on the recognition of political asylum. An early telex instructed the embassy as follows: "Before agreeing to grant shelter to further applicants you should make it very clear that our protection cannot be expected to be more than temporary ... Canada, like other Western countries, does not have a doctrine of [non-territorial] political asylum as Latin American countries do."[126] However, in response to the "sharply divided" and "politically polarized" positions of the churches and Canadian government, the External Affairs Department eventually recommended that the embassy in Santiago work with church authorities to help between 300 and 1,000 refugees escape.[127] In practice, the arrival of Chileans proceeded slowly – especially compared to the recent emergency action undertaken in Uganda.

Around one hundred Chileans had arrived by the end of 1973.[128] Several church-led fact-finding trips to Latin America followed, along with meetings in Ottawa between church leaders and senior officials in the departments of Manpower and Immigration and External Affairs.[129] Several months after the coup, the Canadian Council of Churches began to push for an expansion of the Special Program for Refugees from Chile to authorize the resettlement of between 5,000 and 10,000 refugees.[130]

Persistent pressure by the Canadian Council of Churches and its related agencies was instrumental in the eventual resettlement of some 7,000 Chileans in Canada. Several Conservative and New Democrat members of Parliament and a number of sympathetic bureaucrats supported the CCC. Eventually, other civil-society groups joined their advocacy for an expanded refugee program for Chileans.[131] As one senior immigration official recalls, this "assertive refugee advocacy community" generated "continuous criticism" of government policy as new approaches were in the process of being developed.[132] Eventually, Chileans were resettled through a number of separate schemes. The first was conventional resettlement from neighbouring countries, with the support of the UNHCR. The second was the application of a new "Oppressed Minority" policy that had been pioneered in the case of the Ugandan Asians to extract refugees directly from their country of origin. A third was a related political-prisoners program that targeted those who had been imprisoned and released by the military regime. Although private sponsorship was not used, World Council of Churches networks in Chile facilitated the movement in country, and Canadian churches assisted with orientation and settlement in Canada.[133] Despite the repeated efforts of immigration officials to remove religious groups from the process of identifying, selecting, and transporting refugees from overseas in the 1950s, they were once again dependent on these networks to carry out a resettlement program.

The mobilization of religious groups in response to the coup in Chile reformed issue networks that had become weakened during the 1960s. They also reignited a political discourse about the role of voluntary groups in refugee resettlement in Canada. As debate over the Chilean program was wrapping up, Parliament was presented with a new Green Paper on immigration policy that was intended to inform major legislative change. The role of voluntary groups and private sponsorship arose as a key question in this period of public debate. Although the Canadian Jewish Congress was one of the main advocates of including private sponsorship in the new legislation, the experience of the Chilean program was also significant.

Several retired civil servants describe the significance of the Chilean program for the development of private sponsorship as follows:

> The Chilean refugee crisis ... brought into existence a new community of Canadian refugee advocates who were intensely concerned about human rights violations in Chile (and elsewhere) and deeply suspicious of government action and motivation. In the absence of a sponsorship program, the only option was to demonstrate, organize letter-writing campaigns, and lobby the government to alter selection criteria, speed up processing, and expand the numbers to be admitted. The prolonged and intensive controversy accompanying Canada's response to the Chilean refugees led policy-makers in Ottawa to consider reintroducing a refugee sponsorship option to channel public concern into direct action.[134]

These recollections are corroborated by more oblique references in later internal memos to the need to take steps to channel the interest of religious groups in refugee policy because their relationship with the government "has not a/lways been as productive and mutually beneficial as [it] should be."[135]

Between 1960 and 1973, the issue network connecting religious groups and immigration officials went through a period of disintegration and reconstruction. It collapsed because of divergent beliefs about the purpose of refugee policy and the roles to be played by religious groups. And, in this context, refugee resettlement became more anemic, despite a growing economy, low unemployment, and increasing immigration. With the exception of the Czechoslovakian program in 1967 – which was effectively carried out within the parameters of immigration policy – relatively few refugees were resettled in Canada. This changed with the public debate over Chilean refugees, which was driven by church and solidarity groups. The resettlement of Chileans in 1973 improved the relationship between religious groups and immigration officials (though the relationship remained quite adversarial) and laid the groundwork for the revitalization and formalization of the private-sponsorship program in the years immediately ahead.

CONCLUSION

The period between 1960 and the early 1970s set the stage for major refugee policy reform in the decade to come. The refugee problem was now seen as a permanent international problem and not an issue confined to post-war Europe. After World Refugee Year focused on "clearing the camps" in Europe, it became evident that other global disruptions were pushing people across borders – and some of these people sought resettlement in third countries. The recognition of the global aspect of the refugee problem in Canada and the United States was also connected to the internationalization of immigration policy through the dismantling of racial barriers to entry. In the 1960s, both countries began to admit immigrants from any country in the world without legal obstacles. The same thinking also was applied then to the admission of refugees.

Within this emerging global context for refugee resettlement, relationships between religious groups and the government were reconfigured in ways that would determine the shape of major legislative change. In the United States, the Cuban refugee arrivals produced a policy response that replicated in its resettlement component the Hungarian program from a half-decade before. The position of religious groups as embedded insiders within a refugee policy community continued to be instrumental in the government's response to Cuban arrivals. Catholic, Protestant, and Jewish groups had the administrative capacity and national networks capable of implementing the government-subsidized resettlement program.

Although these groups worked with executive agencies to carry out refugee resettlement, they increasingly aligned themselves with members of Congress who resisted the political realism of the Nixon administration. Advocacy for the resettlement of Soviet Jews and Chileans fleeing Pinochet became a central preoccupation for many of these groups in the early 1970s. In both cases, the groups' views ran counter to the foreign-policy objectives outlined by Nixon and Kissinger, and the White House resisted resettlement as a policy response to the two issues. However, liberal Democrats and a new neo-conservative wing of the Republican Party in Congress embraced the language of human rights that was increasingly used to advocate for refugees abroad. Frustration within Congress grew over the unilateral executive parole authority over refugee resettlement.

In the United States, therefore, relationships between religious groups and the government became structured along two axes. Along one axis, these groups were embedded within a refugee policy community that was instrumental in the implementation of refugee-resettlement programs. They shared core beliefs and policy goals with the agencies with which they cooperated to carry out resettlement, and by the 1970s they had become essential components of the administrative infrastructure of refugee programs. Along the other axis, they were increasingly engaged with lobbying and working alongside members of Congress who advocated human rights and a more formalized and equitable refugee-resettlement system. They were positioned to play a key role in the process of legislative reform during the next decade that would include the last parole program for Indochinese refugees and the creation of the landmark 1980 Refugee Act.

In Canada, religious groups that had played key roles in the postwar refugee resettlement programs were pushed to the margins by an immigration bureaucracy with which they had developed a reluctant partnership. Despite forging cooperative relations with the Department of Citizenship and Immigration in the context of the Approved Church Program and other early models of private sponsorship, they were also seen as a nuisance to government policymaking and implementation. Immigration bureaucrats had always sought to define their role as external to the core government interests of selecting refugees who meet labour-market needs in Canada. The continued focus of religious groups on facilitating the admission of humanitarian cases irritated the immigration gatekeepers, who developed a clearer policy of private sponsorship to ensure that the excess costs associated with such cases would be borne primarily – if not exclusively – by sponsoring groups.

By the 1960s, religious groups had largely disengaged from participation in the private sponsorship of refugees. Even when they persisted with private-sponsorship proposals, as in the case of Chinese refugees, they faced obstruction from bureaucrats. During this decade, they were outsiders to the policy process and played virtually no role in the major refugee programs of the period, outside of some assistance with local settlement through the National Interfaith Immigration Committee. The Czechoslovakian and Ugandan programs were both informed by foreign-policy imperatives and the pursuit of long-term national economic interests. Canada's response to both refugee crises and the mode of its selection of refugees was, at least at the level of policy, significantly motivated by the prospect of attracting skilled immigrants at a time of "brain drain" to the United States and increasing difficulty in attracting Europeans.

By the 1970s, religious groups had become external to the policy process in at least two ways. In the first place, they participated in a subordinate relationship with the Department of Manpower and Immigration through the formation of the National Interfaith Immigration Committee. The committee primarily served as a mechanism for the government to convey information about newcomers so that local religious bodies could reach out to them with settlement assistance and invitations to join religious services. In addition to its membership on this committee, the Canadian Jewish Congress also carried out some small refugee-sponsorship programs for North African and Soviet Jews. A second form of engagement with the government emerged through outsider lobbying, where a coalition "activates its networks to signal to decision-makers its intensity of concern."[136] The Canadian Council of Churches and its agencies led a critical public campaign against government policy toward Chilean refugees and asylum seekers, which produced a reversal of official policy. In the early 1970s, it was clear that religious groups could not be neglected entirely in the process of reforming immigration and refugee policy that would eventually produce the 1976 Immigration Act.[137]

Legislators in both the United States and Canada had been attempting to develop and pass far-reaching immigration and refugee policy reform since at least the 1960s, and by the mid- to late 1970s they were successful. Both legislatures enacted significant refugee laws with broad bipartisan support, leading to annual refugee-resettlement quotas that would be met through cooperation with religious and other voluntary groups. The next chapter traces the evolution of this policy process alongside major Indochinese refugee resettlement programs. In the United States, the scale of the Indochinese program, undertaken using executive parole, helped focus attention and consolidate congressional support for an act that would regularize ad hoc, executive-driven refugee programs. In Canada, the passage of the 1976 Immigrant Act left a lot unspecified at the level of implementation, and it was through the Indochinese program that the provisions of the act became further specified in practice – particularly in relation to the new private-sponsorship regulations.

5

Coming Full Circle

Indochina, Legislative Reform, and the Post-War Legacy

The debates over refugee legislation in the 1970s were propelled by unsustainable contradictions and tensions between existing statutes and what the American and Canadian governments were doing. The law had to catch up with government practice. Accordingly, the law was amended to provide a more stable framework for the ongoing practice of refugee resettlement. Legislators were also influenced by an evolving crisis in Indochina, as a consequence of an international conflict that displaced hundreds of thousands of people from the region.

In the United States, the demand for refugee resettlement from Indochina – especially from U.S.-allied South Vietnam – was met with a massive program of executive parole, carried out in partnership with religious and voluntary groups. The magnitude of this program reinforced a growing tide of discontent within Congress at the contradictions between immigration law and well-established practices of refugee resettlement.[1] It erased any question of the need to clarify, regularize, and make permanent the entire process and authority for resettlement of refugees from abroad.

For Canada, the change to refugee law was accomplished together with major immigration reform in 1976. This reform included a provision for private sponsorship, which was recognized by lawmakers as an historical aspect of Canada's refugee-resettlement programs. At that time, Canada's commitment to resettling refugees from Indochina was comparatively small. However, as the act came into effect in 1978, the "boat people" crisis began to impress itself more forcefully onto the public consciousness – especially following the *Hai Hong* incident in November of that year.[2] The mobilization of Canadian religious groups and civil-society coalitions in response to this crisis led to negotiations over the implementation of previously undefined private-sponsorship provisions of the new legislation.[3] The first major sponsorship agreements were signed with a number of Canada's religious bodies, around which Canada proceeded to structure its private-public partnership to resettle 60,000 Indochinese refugees.[4]

UNITED STATES

The conditions leading to the passage of the 1980 Refugee Act were created by repeated conflict between the executive branch and Congress over the deviation of refugee-admissions procedure from legal statutes – conditions that were amplified in the context of the massive Indochinese resettlement program.[5] In one influential article, Arnold Leibowitz contends, "It was the 1965 amendments to the Immigration and Nationality Act and the very broad use of executive parole authority that led to the Refugee Act of 1980."[6] This statement, taken literally, exaggerates the causal influence of the repeated use of executive parole by several administrations. The leadership of Senator Ted Kennedy, an enduring Democratic majority in both Houses of Congress, and a favourable foreign-policy environment also helped set the stage for legislative reform in the late 1970s.[7]

Although the conditions for reform were set by these interlocking variables, the major aspects of the legislation had already been formed along a developmental pathway that reached back to the end of the Second World War. As Deborah Anker and Michael Posner conclude, the Refugee Act was "the product of years of debate and compromise," in which the religious and voluntary groups were major actors.[8] Other areas of reform had been raised within the refugee policy community since the end of World Refugee Year. The American Council of Voluntary Agencies repeated a set of reform principles in testimony before congressional committees: establish a system of interdepartmental coordination on refugees, create a regular commitment to resettling refugees, accept refugees from outside of Europe, and formalize the partnership with voluntary agencies.[9] These were all included in the 1980 Refugee Act. The perspectives and preferences of the voluntary agencies carried special weight because of the channels for lobbying open to them by virtue of their established cooperation with refugee resettlement.

Debate in Congress over new refugee legislation primarily occurred between 1976 and 1980. This debate transpired simultaneously with the mobilization of the government and voluntary agencies to resettle what was initially estimated to be 130,000 Vietnamese and Cambodian refugees.[10] The conjuncture of these two processes was significant for at least two reasons: it foregrounded the conflicts over the requisite political authority to admit refugees, and it also moved the religious and voluntary groups into the centre of policy discourse. Refugee-advocacy groups grew in size and resources during the 1970s, largely because of the scale of their operations during the Indochinese refugee crisis.[11] As Bon Tempo observes, "the National Catholic Welfare Conference, the Hebrew Immigrant Aid Society, and Church World Service – staffed with policy experts and veterans of previous refugee programs – argued vociferously for an expansion of admissions and government spending on resettlement activities."[12] These groups were already embedded within a refugee policy community and closely aligned with members of Congress who took up human rights and immigration issues. The scale of the Indochinese program made it readily apparent to policymakers what a critical role religious and voluntary groups played in the apparatus of refugee resettlement, and it also helped further mobilize and invigorate their engagement on legislative issues.

The Indochinese Program

The capture of Saigon by the North Vietnamese in April 1975 led the U.S. government to launch a major evacuation of Vietnamese (and some Cambodian) refugees. The United States had not anticipated resettling refugees. Less than two years prior, Congress was assured that refugees from Vietnam were not expected to come to the United States: "It would be our opinion," a senior official declared, "that they could be resettled in their own country."[13] In early 1975 U.S. officials asked Southeast Asian countries about their willingness to accept Vietnamese refugees in the eventuality of a Communist victory.[14] The unexpectedly swift capture of Saigon, however, generated a refugee emergency for which the U.S. government was unprepared. The first movement of refugees included about 130,000 people, who were first relocated in April 1975 to American military installations in Guam. Efforts to "internationalize" the crisis through burden sharing were unsuccessful; U.S. allies initially accepted only nominal numbers of refugees. The federal government was left with an unexpected, unwanted responsibility, and it turned to the religious and voluntary groups for their help to resolve the problem.

As the crisis unfolded, Henry Kissinger, President Ford's secretary of state, recommended the creation of a President's Committee – such as the one established during the Hungarian refugee crisis – to coordinate within and between the government and voluntary agencies the resettlement of the evacuated refugees throughout the United States.[15] The plan developed for the Indochinese was effectively a blueprint of the Hungarian program: a president's special representative was appointed and a special inter-agency task force was created with reference material that included detailed procedures developed during the Hungarian resettlement program.[16] The background papers for the task force described guiding principles that included "maximum dependence on voluntary agencies and private resources."[17] In the scheme of coordination the plan detailed, the military and foreign-affairs agencies led the process of evacuation and reception, with voluntary agencies designated to assume most of the responsibility for resettlement. As an interim report indicated: "The voluntary agencies were the prime movers and the first recourse of resettlement. The nine voluntary agencies initially called upon by the Task Force to take first line responsibility for resettlement of the Indochina refugees all had proved their effectiveness in earlier refugee programs, those having their roots in World War II and the more recent Hungarian and Cuban programs."[18] The president's inter-agency task force was soon complemented by a Presidential Advisory Committee on Refugees, composed of representatives of the seven major religious and voluntary groups.

The scale of the program initiated by the government could not be implemented by the voluntary agencies without a major infusion of federal funding. In May 1975 Congress passed the Indochina Migration and Refugee Assistance Act, which authorized funds for a two-year reception and resettlement program.[19] The government was not in a position to make many demands of the voluntary agencies, whose staff, expertise, and organizational capacity were badly needed to implement the emergency program. The inter-agency task force expressed a sense of urgency to move the refugees out of temporary camps and exerted a great deal of pressure on the voluntary agencies to expedite a program for distributed resettlement across the country.[20] Whereas these groups had been able to negotiate a federal grant of $60 per refugee in the case of the Cuban resettlement program in the early 1960s, they used their leverage to secure a per-capita grant of $500 per refugee to implement the Indochinese program.[21] A direct result was the growth of the leading voluntary agencies, which now offered a range of funded "core services" in addition to matching refugees with local community groups, churches, and social agencies.[22] A new evangelical Christian organization, World Relief, also joined the long-standing groups, including the United States Catholic Conference, Church World Service, HIAS, and the International Rescue Committee.[23]

The implementation of the Vietnamese program came under scrutiny by the Senate Judiciary Committee, chaired by Senator Ted Kennedy. An early evaluation of the resettlement program noted the shortcomings of the Republican Ford administration in supporting the work of the voluntary agencies and a general failure in operational planning. "Despite the repeatedly stated plan of the Administration to 'depend' upon the voluntary agencies, there has been a basic failure to consult, involve, and support their activities," the study reported.[24] Indeed, the dependence on voluntary agencies to sustain the resettlement program expressed itself in the demands placed by the State Department on the groups. In July 1975 it sent a telegram requiring that all voluntary agencies increase staffing and that existing staff work fourteen-hour days, seven days a week.[25] Between May and December 1975, 115,000 Indochinese refugees were admitted under the auspices of the leading religious and voluntary groups.[26] It was one of the largest groups of immigrants to enter the United States in such a short period of time.[27] It was also expected to be the conclusion of the resettlement program for Vietnamese refugees in the United States.

Between 1976 and 1978, American interest in and commitment to the resettlement of refugees from Indochina diminished considerably, aside from a few comparatively small parole programs.[28] By the fall of 1977, the departures of boats carrying Vietnamese refugees to other Southeast Asian countries were becoming more frequent. Some of these voyages ended tragically. The Carter administration, elected the previous year, resisted opening up another large refugee program despite the increasingly critical news coverage of deaths at sea.

Within the refugee policy community that connected State Department officials with the religious and voluntary groups, plans developed to forge a civil-society-led commission to pressure the government to expand the parole program for boat people.[29] The idea of a commission originated in a phone call from Shepard Lowman, a division chief at the State Department, to Leo Cherne, head of the

International Rescue Committee – the leading non-sectarian voluntary group.[30] Cherne swiftly assumed the leadership of a civil-society coalition that explicitly modelled itself on the influential Citizens Committee on Displaced Persons, which formed at the instigation of Jewish groups in the wake of the Second World War.[31]

The Citizens Commission on Indochinese Refugees was created with the support of a handful of prominent Americans, including former government officials, Jewish and Catholic theologians, and leaders of the civil-rights movement.[32] Its supporters included the National Council of Jewish Women, the American Council of Voluntary Agencies, the U.S. Catholic Conference, the American Jewish Committee, and the Anti-Defamation League.[33] They courted the support of labour and African American leaders as well as important constituencies of the governing Democratic Party (by 1977, the Democrats controlled both Houses of Congress as well as the White House). The commission focused on securing media coverage aimed at shifting elite opinion about initiating another parole program for Indochinese refugees. Religious publications like the Catholic magazine *America* and the Protestant weekly *Christian Century* ran favourable articles urging the government to act because "the suffering of the boat people is an outrage to our common humanity."[34] A manifesto signed by eighty-five African American leaders was published in the *New York Times* and covered by other papers. Lobbying also targeted influential people in the Carter White House, Congress, and the State Department.[35] The *Wall Street Journal* noted that the actions of the Citizens Commission "played a significant part in finally forming an administration policy."[36]

In early 1978 the lobbying effort appeared to be gaining traction. Members of the ACVA's Migration and Refugee Affairs Committee met with a representative of the National Security Council (NSC) to deliberate on strategy regarding a possible U.S. parole program.[37] They assured Dr Jessica Tuchman, the director of global issues at the NSC, that they would find jobs and housing for refugees and mobilize "widespread support of initiatives which might be taken by the White House."[38] On 30 March 1978 President Carter approved a new parole program to admit 25,000 Indochinese refugees over the following year.[39]

In subsequent months, the rate of refugee-boat departures from Vietnam increased significantly – in part because of the increasingly well-organized activities of traffickers.[40] By late 1978, almost 100,000 boat people from Vietnam and Cambodia had arrived in other parts of Southeast Asia, and some 38,000 of these had been resettled in the United States (21,000), Australia (10,000), and France (3,000).[41] As the rate of arrivals continued to increase and Southeast Asian countries prevented boats from landing, the number of deaths at sea increased. Jewish, Catholic, and Protestant groups led a public outcry at the humanitarian disaster unfolding in the region. As Loescher and Scanlan note, "the memory of America's failure to help Jews in the 1930s was instrumental in the demands made in Congress to resettle Indochinese refugees."[42] A series of United States-led international negotiations followed in 1979, aimed at generating increased funding contributions for the UNHCR and broad acceptance of the principle of "non-refoulement" by Southeast Asian countries, in exchange for commitment to resettlement in third countries.[43] The United States proceeded to double its parole program so that it would accept up to 14,000 refugees a month.[44] Although public pressure helped increase the total number of refugees admitted, they were admitted through established systems of resettlement with the cooperation of religious and voluntary groups.

Deliberation over the launch of this parole program generated conflicting reactions within government, as captured in a memo from Zbigniew Brzezinski, the national security adviser to President Carter, in advance of the program announcement.[45] The State Department was in favour of a regular and ordinary way to resettle the boat people, which could be achieved with a larger parole program. The Justice Department opposed the use of parole, noting that the 1965 Immigration and Nationality Act was not meant to be employed to admit large numbers of refugees and that there had been increasing congressional criticism of the use of parole power in these situations, which it regarded as valid. Brzezinski, however, held that the issue of the boat people "raises not only moral problems but has become also politically urgent ... The *New York Times* is attacking us editorially for inaction and the Congress is proceeding with [critical] hearings."[46] He recommended approving the program. Following President Carter's announcement, Brzezinski communicated to members of the president's cabinet a new policy framework aimed at contributing to the refugee legislation that was being debated in Congress. The secretary of state, Cyrus Vance, took this as an indication that the president would pursue changes to the Immigration and Nationality Act to enable the United States to admit larger numbers of refugees than could be achieved through repeated debates over parole.[47] This fractious debate over the 1978 boat-people parole program influenced the White House in its decision to support refugee legislation that was moving through Congress.[48]

The 1980 Refugee Act

In March 1978 Senator Ted Kennedy introduced major legislation in the Senate to reform U.S. refugee law.[49] The members of the refugee policy community were closely involved in the entire legislative process. An inter-office memo of the United States Catholic Conference noted that Kennedy intended to rewrite refugee law and that "it will be necessary for the Catholic Church to maintain a direct presence in these discussions."[50] Ingrid Walter, chairman of the ACVA, was among the first to testify before the Senate Judiciary Committee, along with Bishop Swanstrom, former executive director of Catholic Relief Services. In his testimony before the Senate committee, Swanstrom asserted that the religious and voluntary groups were largely responsible for changing public opinion related to refugees and mobilizing support for past major revisions to immigration and refugee law. He declared his "wholehearted support" for the bill, endorsed the admission of 50,000 refugees per year, applauded the adoption of the UN definition of a refugee, urged a clear framework for working with voluntary groups, and expressed his confidence that the voluntary structures and churches are capable and willing "to support the newcomers upon their arrival to our shores."[51]

The Senate passed Kennedy's bill unanimously, but it faced more opposition in the House.[52] The Senate Judiciary Committee's counsel for immigration and refugee affairs wrote to the chairman of the ACVA seeking the support of the voluntary agencies for passage of the legislation: "We will need very strong and high-level support to assure the passage of this important reform legislation ... I would hope that all the agencies associated with the American Council of Voluntary Agencies – not just the migration and refugee agencies – will have their top leadership and Board Members write every member of Congress in support of the bill. We need to develop over the coming weeks a small ground swell that will convince members of Congress that there is, in fact, public support for the legislation."[53] The ACVA's response included a letter fully endorsing the Refugee Bill signed by all forty-five of its members. The groups described the bill as "the most significant piece of refugee legislation of many years."[54] Kennedy sought to amplify these endorsements by entering statements by religious groups into the congressional record, noting that the committee "received communications from every major religious and voluntary agency leader in the country" who were "unanimous in their support" of the proposed legislation.[55]

The voluntary groups wanted a clear framework for their relationship with the government, which had evolved informally over the past several decades. Their operational budgets relied upon government funding that was tied to the scale and pace of resettlement programs. The pressure they faced during the Indochinese program to increase staff and budgets rapidly at the behest of the government could just as quickly be followed by fallow periods characterized by layoffs and the loss of organizational capacity. Therefore, in their testimony before congressional committees and in private lobbying, they emphasized the importance of giving a statutory basis to the established relationship between voluntary groups and the government. The chairman of the ACVA wrote in a letter to senators on behalf of the voluntary groups that the parole system had resulted in funding problems: "For the voluntary agencies it becomes extremely difficult to plan and carry out effective resettlement programs. It is impossible for us to determine how many refugees will be admitted in a given period of time, the rate of admission and the government funding which will be available to assist us in the resettlement process. Thus inhibited, it is not always possible to marshal and utilize the vast resources of the private sector which will ultimately determine the success of failure of any resettlement program."[56] Archbishop John Quinn, president of the U.S. Catholic Conference, was more direct in his remarks to Senator Kennedy: "Over the years the voluntary agencies have labored under severe handicaps, both in maintaining their structures in the field and in continuing their service of resettling refugees, because of a lack of proper government programs to assist the agencies in this humanitarian effort ... Authorization for funding and support services ... should go a long way to help the voluntary agencies, in cooperation with public agencies, to provide services which meet the needs of refugees."[57] As the proposed legislation moved through the House, the voluntary groups lobbied in support of it and for a continuing statutory basis for their government-funded programs to resettle refugees.[58]

The issue of government funding for a regular refugee-resettlement program was also the main obstacle to the passage of the legislation. The primary opposition came from House Republicans, who objected to the authorization of public assistance for refugee resettlement through grants provided to voluntary agencies and states.[59] Fiscal conservatives expressed reservations about legislation that would turn immigration into an area of redistributive policy.[60] The Indochinese program had brought in about 300,000 refugees between 1975 and 1979, and the new legislation proposed regularizing the admission of 50,000 refugees a year, with guaranteed per-capita support to the groups and agencies that would support their resettlement. Although this would effectively retain the existing system of refugee resettlement, albeit with annual quotas, conservatives were reluctant to endorse a universal refugee program with guaranteed public assistance.[61] However, Republicans were in a minority in the House, and they lacked a strong constituency for their position. Furthermore, restrictionists were not well organized in the 1970s, and so the primary interest groups engaged with the refugee legislation were supportive of its passage.[62] After passing the Senate 85–0, the bill was approved in the House by a vote of 328–47 in December 1979.[63] The Refugee Act was signed into law by President Carter on 17 March 1980.

The Refugee Act of 1980 marked the culmination of an evolving policy over the past several decades which had advanced through repeated negotiations between religious and voluntary groups and members of Congress and the White House. In his announcement of the legislation, Kennedy declared that it would ensure greater equity in the treatment of refugees, rationalize how the United States responds to refugee emergencies, and assure "full and adequate federal support for the resettlement efforts of state, local, and voluntary agencies."[64] The legislation accomplished a number of basic objectives. It redefined a refugee along the more universal lines of the United Nations definition. It increased the annual regular-refugee admission to at least 50,000 per year. It replaced the use of parole authority with new statutory language that gave more authority to Congress. The law also established increased federal support for recognized voluntary agencies carrying out resettlement programs. It authorized the creation of a U.S. coordinator for refugee affairs at the rank of ambassador. In addition, it finally divorced the definition of a refugee from that of an immigrant, and it also made clear the distinction between a refugee (found outside the country) and an asylum seeker (present within it).

No sooner had the 1980 Refugee Act been passed than a new debate over humanitarian obligations took hold. The act established a basic procedure for the allowance of asylum claims for those who were physically present in the United States. Within a month of the passage of the act, Castro expelled more than 125,000 Cubans in what became known as the Mariel boatlift. The subsequent three decades of refugee policy debates would be consumed with the issue of asylum seekers, deportation, and the sanctuary movement.[65] The legislative and policy framework for refugee resettlement, however, was basically locked in.

Although the Refugee Act was not considered a major piece of legislation at the time, it crystallized an evolving refugee policy framework that developed during the post-war period. From a policy of refugee deterrence after the Second World War, the United States – with a strong congressional vote and support from the White House – created a global program of annual refugee resettlement that continues to be the largest in the world. Doris M. Meissner writes that "the Refugee Act of 1980 was born of a deeply held consensus that our humanitarian and foreign policy interests call for an orderly and generous system of refugee resettlement in this country."[66]

This consensus was hard won. It was the product of an evolving policy framework that developed through iterative negotiation between members of a refugee policy community, including religious and voluntary groups and political decision makers. The passage of the 1980 Refugee Act was a signature achievement for those groups that first took up the cause of refugee resettlement in the post-war period and continued to persist in advancing it in cooperation with government agencies. By 1980, the refugee policy debate was no longer a matter of whether to open the gates or to keep them shut but about whom to admit.

CANADA

The 1976 Immigration Act

Just as in the United States, the policy process leading to legislative reform in Canada was propelled by the dissatisfaction of legislators with a growing disjuncture between law and practice. The primary impetus for reform came from the Liberal minister of manpower and immigration, Robert Andras, and his deputy minister, Allan Gotlieb.[67] Andras was a new minister when the 1973 Chilean coup and subsequent refugee controversy unfolded. He noted that, when reviewing the existing Immigration Act within this context, he found it to be "very, very much out of date": "It had only been amended three times since Confederation, and was in the language of the turn of the century, designed to deal with the slow, casual immigration movement by boat, or dog team, or whatever travel was available in the early 1900s. I found it was discriminatory and had some extraordinarily disgusting clauses in it, about which, thank goodness, current practices did not conform ... Mainly, the Act empowered the government to act under regulation and directives."[68] The government had historically been reluctant to open up immigration and refugee policy to public debate for fear of igniting a popular backlash, with the result that reform to this point had been primarily accomplished through policy regulation rather than legislation.[69] Most deliberation over shifting refugee policy had occurred within the government and in small meetings between government officials and representatives of organized groups. Therefore, as Andras observed, immigration and refugee policy was in many respects in tension or outright contradiction with the law. The conclusion drawn by Andras and Gottlieb was that regulatory policy had developed without adequate political or public deliberation on a coherent framework.

Andras commissioned an immigration and population study through a series of research reports, which were collectively published as a Green Paper. As he put it, the reports sought to inform answers to the following question: "In terms of the national interest of Canada, why do we have immigration?"[70] This policy review was carried out between September 1973 and the fall of 1974. Whereas the 1966 White Paper on Immigration was a government position statement, the stated purpose of the 1974 Green Paper was to present the government with policy options for immigration reform. Another difference between the two papers was the context in which they were produced: the White Paper was written within the context of an expanding economy, whereas the Green Paper was authored at a time of high unemployment, high inflation, and concern about the changing racial composition of immigration.[71] The Green Paper was finally tabled before cabinet in October 1974, and it presented a number of policy options for immigration reform: a responsive system with no annual limit; a focus on employability, with more restrictions on family reunification; annual visa targets on a regional or country basis; and a global annual ceiling on immigration.

There was more consensus on what the Green Paper had to say on refugees than on other aspects of immigration policy. If anything, the view of refugees and the narrative it presented of Canadian responses to them was too romantic, glossing over the role of racial bias and labour-market preferences in the past selection process for refugees.[72] On immigration, however, the paper was less sanguine. It primarily focused on the negative effects of immigration in the context of a stagnant economy and perceived racial tensions.[73] Critics viewed the analysis and policy options presented within the Green Paper as restrictionist in tone and substance.[74]

The government initially proposed a small national conference on the paper; however, critical reactions from the public and from within the Liberal caucus led Prime Minister Pierre Trudeau to call for a series of public hearings.[75] Minister Andras embraced the notion of Canada-wide hearings, declaring: "We're going to have a dog and pony show. We'll take this across the country and talk it out."[76] The Department of Manpower and Immigration funded a series of open meetings to debate the contents of the paper, some of which were held by groups like the Canadian Council of Churches (which focused its commentary on expanding refugee admissions).[77] The refugee groups that had mobilized in support of Chilean refugees exploited these new forums to advocate refugee reform.[78] JIAS used the opportunity to propose that the new Immigration Act include provisions for "individuals, or responsible voluntary social agencies to offer sponsorship or co-sponsorship" of "humanitarian immigrants."[79] In February 1975 the government announced the formation of a Special Joint Committee of the Senate and the House of Commons to undertake an extensive series of public consultations. Over 35 weeks, the committee held nearly 50 hearings in 21 cities, receiving 1,200 letters and briefs from individuals and more than 200 from groups.[80]

The final report of the committee expressed the view that Canadian refugee policy was "ad hoc, inconsistent, and undisclosed" and recommended a clear statement on the subject, with a more flexible definition than that of the United Nations and no annual ceiling of admissions.[81] This was more or less consistent with what the Green Paper proposed as an ongoing government commitment to resettling refugees. The Green Paper identified an active refugee policy as one of the four key elements of immigration policy to retain in future legislative reform.[82] On immigration, however, the committee rejected many of the Green Paper's recommendations and instead proposed a universal, merit-based, quota system of immigration, with annual targets for admissions. Ultimately, it was the report of the Special Joint Committee, and not the Green Paper itself, that generated the policy consensus on immigration reform. The 1976 Immigration Act, when tabled before Parliament, included sixty of the sixty-five recommendations made by the committee in its final report.[83]

The Immigration Act of 1976 was passed with near unanimous support in Parliament. It received royal assent in August 1977 and took effect on 10 April 1978. The act described the following main objectives of Canadian immigration policy:

1 promotion of demographic, economic, cultural, and social goals;
2 support for family reunification;
3 the fulfilment of Canada's international obligations under the UN Refugee Convention and the 1967 Protocol;
4 non-discrimination in immigration policy and selection; and
5 cooperation between all levels of government and the voluntary sector in the settlement of immigrants.[84]

Triadafilopoulos notes the remarkable *volte-face* of the Liberal Party, which tabled a Green Paper that was relatively dismal about immigration and then proceeded to marshal a broad-based political consensus in support of an expansionary piece of legislation.[85] Following John Wood, he attributes this turnaround to the surprising mobilization of minority ethnic groups in response to the hearings of the Special Joint Committee, which alerted members of the Liberal Party (and others) to the potential electoral support to be derived from new citizens.[86] As for the refugee provisions of the legislation, religious groups were the most influential advocates for generous refugee policies.[87] They took positions contrary to public opinion at the time, which polling showed to be overwhelmingly against increasing refugee admissions by relaxing the point-system criteria.[88]

The 1976 act affirmed the UN definition of a refugee, which Canada had officially accepted in 1969. It also gave the government the authority to identify "designated classes" of people and "oppressed minorities" as refugees, even if they did not meet the United Nations definition – which had been the de facto process during past refugee movements. It also established private sponsorship in legislation: "I.6.(4.) Any body corporate incorporated by or under any Act of Parliament or the legislature of a province, and any group of Canadian citizens or permanent residents, may, where authorized by the regulations, sponsor the application for admission of [a recognized refugee]."[89] This private-sponsorship provision is unspecific, and lawmakers left it to be elaborated through future policy development. Although private sponsorship was formally introduced as such in 1960 – when the Approved Church Program was ended – it had been little used since. One of the only exceptions was the use of private sponsorship by JIAS of Canada to facilitate the resettlement of Soviet Jews in the late 1960s and early 1970s.[90]

Private sponsorship was included in the 1976 act because it had been established as a practice in Canadian refugee resettlement. The new law was not going to create a policy framework on a blank slate; it looked to the past. As William Janzen notes, "officials who worked in the Immigration Department at that time said they had not known what to expect from the private sponsorship provision. They had just felt that it would be good to have [in] the Act, to be used if necessary."[91] Michael Molloy et al. also point to the controversy faced by the department in the wake of the Chilean coup, which "led policy-makers in Ottawa to consider reintroducing a refugee sponsorship option to channel public concern into direct action."[92]

After the passage of the 1976 act, the Department of Employment and Immigration looked for a test case to develop the new private-sponsorship program. It found one in the Jewish human rights group B'nai Brith's sponsorship of Soviet Jewish refugees.[93] Jack Manion, the deputy minister of employment and immigration, recommended that the private-sponsorship scheme "should rely on national organizations responsible for the identification of needy groups of refugees and displaced persons but that the actual sponsorship should come from local groups providing services directly to the immigrant or refugee."[94] In this pilot program, B'nai Brith's planned sponsorship of some fifty Soviet Jews required their local chapters to arrange accommodation, provide initial food and clothing, and offer reception and resettlement assistance. The program was eventually carried out by JIAS after B'nai Brith backed out, but the experience was sufficiently instructive to be described in an internal departmental memo, "Sponsorship Provisions for Refugee and Humanitarian Cases," which set out its main elements.

Following the program for Soviet Jews, department officials began to meet with religious groups to develop the private-sponsorship program. One of the early meetings was with bishops of the Catholic Church's Migration Commission. The commission was initially reluctant to cooperate with the government, as it had been one of the advocacy groups that campaigned in favour of admitting Chilean refugees. This adversarial history coloured the tone of the first meeting, at which there was resistance to assuming the cost and responsibility of a program that was viewed as a government duty.[95] However, the bishops eventually endorsed the program as a complementary measure to government resettlement efforts. Soon after this initial meeting, the deputy minister wrote to the leaders of the major religious denominations in Canada to outline a process for securing refugee sponsorships.[96] Local Catholic groups responded most positively, as did Mennonite groups, and articles began to appear in church bulletins and newsletters outlining the program.

Private sponsorship did not finally expand in a significant way, however, until the Indochinese boat-people crisis. During this time, public attention became focused on the humanitarian crisis unfolding in Southeast Asia as governments appeared slow to respond. Efforts to publicize the private-sponsorship program through religious-community networks generated more traction within this new context and expanded the program to a scale far beyond what had been initially expected.

The Indochinese Program

Despite the unfolding refugee emergency in Indochina in 1975, Canada remained on the periphery of the international resettlement effort led by the United States. Temporary visitors from Vietnam and Cambodia were permitted to apply for permanent residence, and Canada initially agreed to accept 2,000 refugees from evacuation camps administered by the United States.[97] As the phenomenon of boat people emerged as a humanitarian concern, Canada made further nominal commitments in response to pressure from the United States.[98] The government agreed to accept 180 boat-people refugees in 1976 and 450 in 1977.[99] However, as a memo to the minister of employment and immigration stated, "a major resettlement program ... would not be realistic at this time" because "the present economic situation would impede the successful establishment in this country of large numbers of Vietnamese."[100] Public opinion was also not in favour of a large resettlement program; most Canadians viewed even the modest commitments of the government as too high.[101]

In 1978 the Trudeau government deployed a "metered" approach to resettlement by agreeing to take fifty families per month.[102] Adelman argues that these commitments were "token" responses to American pressure.[103] The Department of Employment and Immigration held that labour-market conditions would not allow a large resettlement program in Canada owing to high unemployment. However, the foreign minister insisted that some commitment on Canada's part was necessary to help convince Congress to support a larger U.S. program, which would in turn "convince smaller countries in the region, such as Singapore, to allow temporary safe haven to the small-boat people."[104] For the time being, Canada's policy was to do as little as possible – just enough to maintain its international standing and keep open the borders of Vietnam's neighbouring countries to the small vessels that were arriving on their shores.

There was some awareness, however, that Canada might have to assume more responsibility for resettlement. This was an uncomfortable position for an Employment and Immigration Department that had historically sought out refugees who were economically desirable. The Indochinese boat people were humanitarian cases, with unknown education and skills, entering into an economy in recession. Officials ascertained that cooperation from religious groups would be a necessary aspect of any large resettlement program. An internal memorandum from the department noted that a further increase in resettlement would need to be "supplemented by help from religious organizations."[105] The department also directed its regional offices to "build cordial working relationships with these groups and organizations" because they were "regarded by senior management as a potentially useful tool to broadening public response to the plight of refugees."[106]

A turning point in Canada's response to Indochinese refugees was the *Hai Hong* incident in November 1978. An overcrowded freighter carrying several thousand refugees was turned away from Indonesia and Malaysia and left to drift off the coast of Port Klang.[107] The boat received food and medical supplies from the UNHCR and became a major international and domestic media story. The Canadian government sought to intervene with Malaysian authorities to pressure them to accept the passengers, but the Malaysians refused out of a stated concern that doing so would incentivize the commercial trafficking of refugees.[108] Furthermore, Malaysia had accepted 35,000 refugees already and appeared to be exploiting the incident to provoke greater assistance from a reluctant international community. There was initially little support for resettlement in Canada.[109] The refugees were described in a *Toronto Star* newspaper editorial as "sick and hapless cargo" who "would find it all but impossible to adjust ... to this different world, culture, and climate."[110]

One of the barriers to Trudeau's Liberal government accepting more refugees was a concern about inflaming anti-immigrant sentiment, especially in Quebec. Therefore, when the Quebec immigration minister agreed to take at least 200 refugees from the *Hai Hong* – as a way to demonstrate the capacity of the separatist Parti Québécois government to operate an independent foreign policy – it opened the door more widely to federal action. Furthermore, pressure from organized groups to "do something" to resolve this particular humanitarian crisis demanded a response, especially on the eve of a federal election. Employment and Immigration Minister Bud Cullen announced in November 1978 that Canada would accept 600 refugees from the ship. This proved to be the beginning of a larger Canadian resettlement effort targeting the boat people – many of whom were marooned in makeshift camps on various islands in Southeast Asia. Public attention had keyed into the refugee crisis, and opinion (which had previously opposed resettlement) responded positively to the *Hai Hong* evacuation and resettlement effort. However, the government remained sensitive to a reactionary swing in public opinion.

What followed the *Hai Hong* incident, however, was only a modest increase in Canada's resettlement commitment. Canada tried to lock arms with other Western countries in refusing to accept a major surge in refugee admissions from Indochina. A confidential internal memo to Canadian foreign missions outlined the government's thinking at the time: "In case of Southern Cross and more particularly Hai Hong, very considerable public and media pressure on Cda made extraordinary measures almost inevitable ... We do not anticipate repeating special measures undertaken for Hai Hong refugees as we believe to do so will encourage the large boat movement and financial exploitation of refugees ... What we have in mind therefore is common stance among major resettlement countries that extraordinary measures not/not be adopted every time intl community confronted with large refugee incident."[111] In December 1978 the Trudeau government committed to resettling 5,000 more refugees in the year to come – in addition to the 9,060 who had arrived between 1975 and 1978.[112] Despite taking a restrained approach to resettlement, the Liberals lost the May 1979 election to the Progressive Conservatives anyway.

Soon after Joe Clark's government came to power, it was exposed to growing domestic and international agitation over the continuing humanitarian disaster in Indochina. The foreign minister, Flora MacDonald, initially floated the idea of an increased commitment to accept 8,000 to 12,000 more refugees and began to urge religious groups to undertake sponsorships.[113] However, a loose coalition of "articulate groups," a critical press, and some municipal leaders promoted a larger commitment.[114] MacDonald, along with Prime Minister Joe Clark and Employment and Immigration Minister Ron Atkey, were gradually convinced of the need for "radical action" by the Canadian government.[115] In July 1979 the United Nations secretary general convened a conference in Geneva to promote international joint action on problems in Southeast Asia. Just before the conference, MacDonald announced a cabinet decision to resettle up to 50,000 Indochinese refugees before the end of 1980.[116] She described the program as "one of partnership between the Canadian Government and private citizens and organizations."[117] It committed to a one-for-one matching scheme, where the government would match private sponsorship up to 50,000 refugees. The proposed scale of the program was a "shock" to the staff of the Employment and Immigration Department, who were charged with admitting 3,000 refugees a month – half of them under the sponsorship of private groups.[118] Despite the general public's reticence to support a large resettlement effort, the efforts of organized groups to pressure the government proved instrumental in achieving the increase in quota.

In her history of Canadian immigration policy, Knowles observes that the variables influencing the large Indochinese admissions were similar to those present in the 1956 Hungarian program – namely, growing international pressure to admit refugees, alongside greater public interest and mobilization by religious and voluntary groups.[119] The continued deterioration of the refugee situation in Southeast Asia, increasing international attention to the crisis at G7 and other meetings, and the progressive mobilization of public opinion and religious groups exerted growing pressure on the new Progressive Conservative government. The *Globe and Mail* and the *Montreal Gazette* ran editorials in June 1979 calling on the new government to take more dramatic action.[120] A social movement to resettle refugees emerged through the organizing of Operation Lifeline and a number of municipal advocacy groups.[121] As Molloy et al. describe, by the time of the Geneva conference, "Canada had the domestic elements in place to welcome a major increase in Indochinese refugee intake."[122] MacDonald looked ahead to the Geneva conference with an awareness of organized domestic pressure to do something and the confidence that "the non-government, community and church sectors ... could effectively partner with the government" to undertake a large resettlement program.[123]

Indeed, the Canadian resettlement program would not have reached anywhere near the scale it did without private sponsorship and the collaboration between bureaucrats and religious groups that preceded the July 1979 announcement. The 1976 Immigration Act came into force in April 1978, creating private sponsorship as a formal refugee program in law. However, it took the initiative of the Mennonite Central Committee of Canada, meeting with senior immigration senior officials in January 1979, to create the policy framework to implement private sponsorship on a larger scale. This first meeting took place seven months before Canada's massive expansion of refugee resettlement. William Janzen, the MCCC representative in Ottawa, recalls this meeting as follows:

> I had been instructed by colleagues in MCCC's Winnipeg head office to arrange a meeting with senior Immigration officials to look for better mechanisms for bringing in refugees from Southeast Asia, whose tragic situation was filling the news at the time. The officials were most open. The meeting took place on January 9, 1979. The Assistant Deputy Minister, Cal Best, chaired it ... In that meeting we sketched the outline of an agreement. Gordon Barnett and I were then asked to write it up. We met three or four times within the next few weeks, always checking with our respective colleagues. But things came together relatively quickly. The agreement was formally approved by the MCCC Executive Committee in a telephone conference on February 14 and signed in the Winnipeg MCCC offices on March 5.[124]

The lead negotiator for the Canadian government, Gordon Barnett, recalls their approach to discussions with Janzen and the MCCC:

> Initially, the Department intended to negotiate an agreement which would assign all responsibility for the sponsored refugees to the sponsor ... As negotiations progressed and the goodwill of the [MCCC] became evident this approach changed and both sides readily accepted to do what each would do best ... I thought we should adopt a different, more cooperative approach ... In the end we put together an agreement that had the individual sponsoring groups provide the day-to-day hands-on care, the national organizations would mitigate any unusual costs or difficulties and the Department would provide an overall structure that

included language training and allowances and a willingness to take over from the sponsors any cases that were exceptionally costly or requiring unusual professional services.[125]

The willingness of the government to assume more risk and cost for privately sponsored refugees marked a change from the private sponsorship of the 1960s, which imposed all responsibility on sponsors and led to the disengagement of religious groups from the program.

The result of these negotiations was the creation of "Master Agreements," whereby a national corporate body could accept responsibility for sponsored refugees, releasing local groups from liabilities required by the government. The Master Agreements resembled earlier arrangements made under the Approved Church Program, although they made available more government-funded services for refugees. These agreements also enabled the program to operate at a larger scale than would have been possible otherwise. After the government signed its Master Agreement with the MCCC on 5 March 1979, it quickly proceeded to sign agreements with four other religious groups before making its July 1979 announcement. After that announcement, eight other national groups signed agreements, alongside twenty-one Roman Catholic dioceses and five Anglican dioceses. All forty Master Agreements signed in 1979 were with religious organizations.[126]

Although the government committed to admitting 50,000 refugees through its matching program, the number of refugees resettled through private sponsorship quickly exceeded 25,000. By January 1980, 5,604 groups had sponsored 31,162 refugees.[127] The government initially sought to retain the 50,000 limit while using the money freed up by extra private sponsorship to fund humanitarian relief programs in Cambodia. Ministers Atkey and MacDonald communicated this decision at a meeting with the major religious groups that were Master Agreement holders, who objected to the redirection of funds away from resettlement and asserted the need for closer consultation on refugee policy in the future.[128] Atkey replied to the criticism by noting that "it would be wrong to disturb that target of 50,000" by claiming that it would undermine public support for the program.[129] Several days later, a broader coalition of groups calling itself the Committee of Organizations Concerned for Refugees held a separate meeting, at which the atmosphere was more charged. Government officials attending the meeting reported to the minister that "a good deal of anger was centred on their perception that the government had struck a partnership with the voluntary sector and then unilaterally altered the terms and conditions."[130] Little more than a week after these meetings – and for reasons unrelated to refugee policy – Joe Clark's government lost the confidence of the House of Commons and a general election was called for February 1980.

Trudeau's Liberal Party won the election and assumed office in March 1980. During the time in which Parliament was not in session, the Employment and Immigration Department continued to deliberate on the question of whether or not to recommend an increase in the refugee quota. The dilemma was presented as a question of domestic politics – whether to respond to public opinion (which did not favour further increases in resettlement) or to sponsorship groups. An internal discussion paper notes: "The 50,000 figure remains a potent symbol for those opposed to the movement, and a decision to increase the program substantially, particularly in the absence of a new crisis, is likely to prove controversial and divisive, possibly threatening the long-term success of this major program."[131] This problem was inherited by Lloyd Axworthy, who was appointed employment and immigration minister on 3 March 1980.

Axworthy was immediately pressured to increase the 50,000 quota. The main point of contention was what sponsoring groups perceived to be a violation of the matching principle, what was later termed "additionality" – the notion that private sponsorship would add to, and not replace, government resettlement programs. The Indochinese program, as it was approved, envisioned a one-for-one matching scheme up to 50,000 refugees. Since private sponsors had supported more than half of that number, they sought a commensurate increase in the government commitment. Operation Lifeline, the United Church, World Relief, the Anglican Church, and the Canadian Council of Churches wrote jointly to urge Axworthy to increase the number of government-sponsored refugees beyond the 50,000 mark in order to uphold the matching principle: "Continuing the previous policy without change or any new program would alienate churches, private sponsorship organizations and the sponsors themselves who are still upset at what they view as reneging on the matching formula."[132] Several weeks later, Axworthy announced that the government would increase the total number of government-sponsored refugees by 10,000, bringing the total target for 1979–80 up to 60,000.[133]

The sixty-thousandth refugee arrived at Longue Point, Quebec, on 8 December 1960, sponsored by a church in Goderich, Ontario. By the conclusion of the program, private sponsorship had accounted for 32,281 refugee admissions (53.8 per cent), government-assisted refugees numbered 25,978 (44.2 per cent), and family sponsorship made up the balance of 1,790 (3 per cent).[134] The total number of admissions was 60,049, making the Indochinese program the largest special-refugee movement since the displaced-persons movement after the Second World War. Religious groups were singled out by Axworthy in his report on the Indochinese program, noting that "no account of the program would be complete without acknowledging the leadership role provided by the churches of Canada in mobilizing their congregations to welcome and support the refugees."[135]

Private sponsorship during the Indochinese crisis was organized along two lines, following the 1976 act and associated regulations – organized groups that were affiliated with a Master Agreement holder and groups of five or more private citizens. Of the roughly 7,000 sponsorship groups, about 70 per cent of sponsors were organized groups, and 30 per cent were citizen groups. Ninety-nine per cent of organized groups were affiliated with churches and synagogues, whereas most citizen groups were classified by the government as "secular."[136] In the wake of the Indochinese crisis, notwithstanding the important role played by citizen mobilization outside of religious structures, the organized groups established a tighter policy network that become more closely connected with government decision making. The Employment and Immigration Department began at this time to introduce annual planning into its refugee-resettlement program – alongside planning of immigration levels.[137] This process engaged the leaders of the major sponsorship groups in a number of "extensive consultations," including "face to face discussions and written exchanges."[138] The reinvigoration of private sponsorship also had the effect of rebuilding the issue network connecting religious groups and immigration officials.

Although the landmark Immigration Act was passed in 1976, its full implications for refugee resettlement were not realized until the conclusion of the Indochinese program that saw private sponsorship more fully elaborated and exploited. What the legislation produced as a placeholder for cooperation between the government and private groups was refined through negotiations between senior bureaucrats and organized religious groups. This was a well-established pattern in Canadian refugee policymaking: political leaders made broad commitments in response to lobbying and other domestic and international sources of pressure, and these commitments provided a framework for practical deliberation between civil servants and organized groups. As civil servants who observed these negotiations up close have noted in published recollections, the "emergence of a forceful advocacy community" often "pushed us in the direction we wished to go."[139]

Yet the sentiment of common cause between bureaucrats and voluntary groups was an exception largely confined to the Indochinese program. For most of the preceding decades, the relationship of bureaucrats to refugee groups could be characterized as a reluctant partnership. Political leaders were sensitive to the pressure that organized groups could generate through their constituencies and media, but bureaucrats often saw them as naive, inexpert, or hostile – and sometimes all three – in relation to their policy goals. However, when it came to implementing the private-sponsorship provisions of the 1976 act, cooperation came more easily. Molloy and Madokoro contend that policy innovation was "driven" by civil servants during the late 1970s, and this may be overstating their singular role.[140] The way in which the 1976 act reframed an active refugee policy aligned the government position more closely with organized groups and enabled a cooperative relationship within the framework of private sponsorship. Cooperation was also supported by a shared view of the refugee as an individual in need of humanitarian protection, which was a significant change from the more pragmatic view of immigration officials in the past.

CONCLUSION

In the United States and Canada, refugee reform in the late 1970s confirmed in law what became established in practice following the Second World War. The 1980 Refugee Act in the United States affirmed in statute what had developed over decades of policy feedback: a regime of cooperation with a small number of religious and voluntary groups, the identities of which were virtually unchanged since the 1940s. These groups had long since forged a policy community that was connected to the State Department and influential members of Congress. With each refugee crisis, an increasingly capable and well-resourced coalition pushed decision makers to replicate past programs, presenting their national networks and experience as a means by which resettlement could be carried out in ways that could minimize public backlash. The expertise, capability for public mobilization, and national networks of these groups made them essential partners of and advisers to administrations that could be persuaded to resettle refugees. However, they were vulnerable to the resource disruptions caused by waxing and waning federal funds that followed large parole programs. The 1980 Refugee Act not only formalized their role in U.S. refugee programs; it also established an annual commitment to resettlement that put them on firmer financial footing.

In Canada, by contrast, the 1976 Immigration Act created private sponsorship as a placeholder for what had become a negotiated practice of complementary responsibility for refugee resettlement. The precise meaning of private sponsorship awaited further deliberation between bureaucrats and religious groups, led initially by the Mennonite Central Committee of Canada. In substance, private sponsorship came to resemble the Approved Church Program of the 1950s, which itself built on the church-sponsorship program and the close-relatives scheme to resettle displaced people. Bureaucrats had repeatedly tried to exclude groups from an active role in resettlement, especially at the point of selection, but their ministers were unwilling to alienate these willing protagonists. Private sponsorship was the product of these negotiations, a kind of division of labour through complementary efforts that would allow the government to do its part while creating a framework for groups to select, sponsor, and settle recognized refugees.

Conclusion

I have argued that the origins of refugee-resettlement policy in the United States and Canada can be traced to the structured interactions between religious groups and policymakers in the wake of the Second World War, during a critical juncture that stretched from roughly 1945 to 1951. Ruth and David Collier describe critical junctures as "moments of relative structural indeterminism when willful actors shape outcomes in a more voluntaristic fashion than normal circumstances permit ... these choices demonstrate the power of agency by revealing how long-term development patterns can hinge on distant actor decisions of the past."[1] The normal political, institutional, and ideological constraints on decision making are somewhat relaxed, allowing for creative responses and the introduction of new actors and ideas into the policymaking arena. The choices made during these periods can have significant consequences farther down the road, however, by locking in particular arrangements or practices. The structures of resettlement created in the post-war period to facilitate the arrival of displaced people became path dependent over subsequent decades, as policy networks connecting religious groups and decision makers produced positive feedback effects. To understand the policy framework and institutions responsible for refugee resettlement in the United States and Canada today, we also need to understand the choices made during the post-war period.

In the United States, Protestant, Catholic, and Jewish groups mobilized independently and in coalition to influence the policy process leading to the resettlement of displaced people. The promise of their cooperative role as implementing agencies of the government's resettlement program was politically crucial for the passage of early legislation that admitted European refugees. They consolidated their position in the context of the Hungarian and Cuban refugee programs, securing a national role for a small handful of voluntary groups within the architecture of U.S. refugee resettlement. The 1980 Refugee Act finally incorporated into law their cooperative relationship with the U.S. government agencies responsible for refugee resettlement. At each step in the development of law and policy, these core groups exerted an upward pressure on refugee levels, which they supported by maintaining international structures connected to grassroots constituencies that were capable of managing the complex process of refugee settlement and integration.

In Canada, the path was rockier, and the relationship between decision makers and religious groups more reluctant and tenuous. A number of enterprising Jewish, Protestant, and Catholic groups negotiated roles in the failing family-reunification program developed by the Canadian government to resettle post-war refugees with close relatives in Canada. This program was converted into a church-sponsorship plan, consolidated into an Approved Church Program, terminated in 1958, and then resurrected as a private-sponsorship scheme in 1960. Lack of agreement over the financial terms of sponsorship, criteria of selection, and the duration of liability for the welfare of refugees led the issue network connecting groups and decision makers to break down during the 1960s. However, the concept of private sponsorship was retained and continued to be promoted by legislators in the 1970s, when it was incorporated into the 1976 Immigration Act and then hammered out into regulations through direct negotiation with the Mennonite Central Committee of Canada leading up to the landmark Indochinese program. This massive resettlement scheme extended the policy framework to include dozens of other religious groups and small voluntary organizations.

The complex dynamics of negotiation, public pressure, and cooperation that developed between religious groups and decision makers in the 1940s and early 1950s produced institutional structures for managing the resettlement of refugees at a relatively large scale. In the United States, the comparatively high total number of displaced people resettled in the post-war period can be directly traced to advocacy by and cooperation with religious and voluntary groups, which worked through the Citizens Committee on Displaced Persons and the American Council of Voluntary Agencies. In Canada, the primary resettlement program developed by the government was an economic-migration plan co-managed by Canadian industries and railroads. To the extent that displaced people were resettled on humanitarian terms, they primarily arrived under the sponsorship of a religious group. The engagement of religious groups with the refugee policy process during the post-war period, and their subsequent cooperation with the U.S. and Canadian governments to resettle refugees, created domestic institutional capacity for the continued admission of relatively large numbers of refugees.

What would have happened if religious groups *had not* intervened in the policy process during the post-war period? Giovanni Capoccia and R.D. Kelemen note that well-constructed counterfactuals can help to assess the causal impact of specific factors on historical outcomes.[2] Effective counterfactuals should consider policy choices that were actually on the table during the critical juncture and that would have led in logically different directions. In both cases, there were clear policy alternatives to cooperation with religious groups.

In the United States, the alternative was a dramatically smaller resettlement program designed to exclude particular racial and religious groups. Indeed, the original 1948 Displaced Persons Act (before it was expanded in response to CCDP lobbying) was called "flagrantly discriminatory" by President Truman because of qualification criteria that were intended to discriminate against Jews and reduce overall numbers. Absent the engagement of religious groups with the policy and legislative process, in all likelihood a U.S. resettlement program would have been minimal, discriminatory, and temporary. The U.S. approach to refugees would primarily have focused on relief and humanitarian aid overseas, with a select few political asylum seekers admitted during the Cold War. Indeed, some scholars today have argued for the resurrection of this approach to refugee admissions – contending that the rise of the humanitarian conception of the refugee has distorted the structure and priorities of immigration and refugee policy.[3]

In Canada, the counterfactual is equally clear: the primary resettlement plan was a Bulk Labour Program intended to select workers for the Canadian economy. If religious groups had not intervened to help implement the Close Relatives Program, convert it into a church-sponsorship program, and finally create a system of private sponsorship, resettlement in Canada would have been primarily been driven by economic interests. Indeed, this hypothesis is supported by the direction of refugee policy during the 1960s, when religious groups largely disengaged from private sponsorship. The Czechoslovakian and Ugandan programs, notwithstanding their humanitarian merits, were principally motivated by foreign policy and designed around the acquisition of "good material" for the Canadian economy.[4] Without the engagement of religious groups with refugee policy in the post-war period, Canadian refugee policy would almost certainly have continued to be economic migration by another name.

FUTURE IMPLICATIONS

In both countries, the policy nexus between religious groups and government has proved to be durable since the 1940s. However, the success of these groups has contributed to the emergence of issues that put growing pressure on their programs.

In Canada, the private refugee-sponsorship program that initially developed as a family-migration scheme appears to have largely reverted to its original characteristics. A 1990 government review of the program found that, outside of periods of "crisis," the program was primarily used as a tool for family reunification. By 2003, between 95 and 99 per cent of private-sponsorship applications were for extended family or close friends.[5]

In response to these developments, the government created a number of blended models that combined elements of private sponsorship with government-assisted sponsorship. Most of them have required sponsors to sacrifice their authority to "name" refugees in exchange for greater cost-sharing by the government. These programs, however, have been time-bound or small, and private refugee sponsorship is projected to comprise the majority of Canadian resettlement over the foreseeable future.[6] It is reasonable to anticipate that, with the exception of moments of "crisis" like the Indochinese or Syrian programs, most private sponsorship will target family members of Canadians and recently arrived refugees. Whether this pattern will ultimately undermine the program remains to be seen, but it clearly reflects a normative tension between liberal ideals of neutrality and the preferential attachments and intimate ties that have often driven the success of the program since its inception.[7]

Despite the changing characteristics of the program, religious groups continue to play a central role in the field of private refugee sponsorship in Canada. An estimated 90 of the 120 Sponsorship Agreement Holders are affiliated with a religious community.[8] Private sponsorship is an institutional legacy of government cooperation with Canada's religious groups as they existed in the mid- to late twentieth century. The terms of the program were negotiated by groups that had institutional capacity, social networks, community support, and a resource base independent of the government.

The declining resources and active membership of many of the communities that initially forged this partnership raise questions, however, about the future of the program in its current form. The Syrian program renewed a widespread engagement of Canadians with private refugee sponsorship for the first time since the Indochinese movement in the 1970s, such that 25 per cent of Canadians know someone who has been personally involved with sponsorship.[9] This suggests that there exists within the Canadian population a latent interest and capacity to give private sponsorship a broader basis of practical support. However, without the infrastructure of intermediate civil-society institutions – like that provided by religious groups – enabling continuous action and collective learning over time, it is uncertain whether the upsurge in humanitarian concern can be harnessed into something more enduring. In principle, it is possible that the private-sponsorship program could be sustained by a wider circle of secular associations, such as ethnic associations or those with a connection to a particular persecuted group. However, it is just as likely that the future of private refugee sponsorship will hinge on the future role of religion, and religious groups, in Canadian society.

In the United States, the success of religious and voluntary agencies at embedding themselves into the apparatus of refugee resettlement now exposes them to profound organizational challenges when annual admission numbers fluctuate at the behest of the president. The year 2018 marked the lowest levels of refugee admissions since the passage of the 1980 Refugee Act.[10] The United States accepted 24,000 refugees, roughly one-quarter of the numbers admitted during the high point of the Obama administration. Numbers have declined even further in the wake of the coronavirus epidemic, a phenomenon whose full implications for refugee policy are still undisclosed. One of the institutional consequences of a cut to refugee admissions is the reduction in government funding to the nine religious and voluntary groups that implement the program. In the wake of the announcement of reduced resettlement numbers, the CEO of the Jewish agency HIAS remarked, "If no refugees are arriving and if we are not getting funding to employ them, then we have to let them go and we lose our infrastructure to resettle refugees. That's a huge issue."[11] Donald Kerwin, a scholar and lawyer closely connected to the United States Conference of Catholic Bishops, wrote that the recent cuts to the U.S. program have "decimated the community-based resettlement infrastructure built up throughout many decades."[12]

The long-term consequences of these program reductions remain to be seen. Voluntary agencies have long been influential advocates for the admission of refugees to the United States, in part because of their capacity to help to shoulder the practical responsibilities of resettlement. Their role has been discussed and analyzed at length in this book, and it is neatly summarized in the passage below by Norman Zucker and Naomi Zucker, who call these agencies "the cornerstone of resettlement":[13]

> The volag [voluntary agency] is crucial to resettlement. Its services range from governmental and quasi-governmental functions to purely private aid activities. It links the refugee to the various public and private bureaucracies. The volag acts as, or works with, the refugee's sponsor. But the volag goes beyond the crucial issue of sponsorship; the volag is integral to the formulation and execution of refugee policy in general, and resettlement specifically, in general acting at the public's conscience; the private agencies testify before Congress on which, and how many, refugees should be permitted to enter. They also testify on what the refugees' status and benefits should be, and for how long these benefits should continue.[14]

Donald Kerwin's pessimistic expectation that the recent cuts to the program have "decimated" the voluntary agencies suggests that there may be irreparable damage to a policy community that has led to the resettlement of some three million refugees since 1980.

There are some reasons for hope. Despite the federal subsidy of voluntary agencies, these groups also sustain themselves from independent funding sources. One study carried out by the Lutheran Immigration and Refugee Service found that the federal government funded only about 39 per cent of the cost of resettling refugees during their first ninety days in the country.[15] This suggests that resources can be mobilized to sustain infrastructure and operations outside of the per-refugee grant provided to resettlement organizations through the Department of Health and Human Services. Other regional studies have found that pockets of citizens have responded to anti-immigration policies and rhetoric emanating from the capital through constructive actions that express solidarity with foreigners by actively supporting the resettlement program with fundraising and community assistance.[16] The groundswell of grassroots support for refugee resettlement in some parts of the country has animated a policy discourse about incorporating a version of private refugee sponsorship in the United States.[17]

Indeed, the prospects for the resettlement programs in both the United States and Canada may ultimately be dependent on the future vitality and character of associational life. I have argued that the institutions and organizations that can emerge from the life of religious communities provided a key impetus for the rise and development of refugee resettlement in both countries. Their cooperation with each other, and their engagement as intermediaries between the state and their members, generated a core dynamic both to initiate and to perpetuate large-scale programs of resettlement. The reasons and evidence for this have been canvassed above: they help to reframe issues, mobilize resources, facilitate wide-scale political engagement, and influence public opinion. They also serve as mechanisms for collective learning and memory, as systems are developed, processes refined, and lessons are learned over time within structures that endure beyond the changeable interests of politicians. The role that religious groups and other voluntary associations play in creating the culture and practices that sustain democracy needs no further review, certainly not for anyone who has read Alexis de Tocqueville. To de Tocqueville's students, it is also no secret that the fabric of this associational life has frayed in the late twentieth century, eroding the stock of social capital that makes democratic government and its policy decisions effective. It might be reasonably asked what implications this could have for refugee-resettlement programs that have been designed to rely heavily upon the cooperation of civil-society organizations.

Refugee policy is almost always viewed as a matter of foreign policy: a responsibility of states in a community of nations. Indeed, this is a perfectly valid way to view the subject, and one that has generated countless insights into the motivations and actions of states. Shirking and free riding are lamentable features of an international system that presents humanitarian action in a zero-sum relationship, pitting the interests of states against each other. There is little doubt that a refugee regime with more clear and direct mechanisms of enforcement to facilitate a fairer distribution of refugees, within a properly resourced system, is needed. However, democratic states also act on the consent of their citizens, and many democratic states are experiencing citizen revolts against high rates of immigration. To expect these same states to lead an international process resulting in an enforceable compact that requires them to admit more refugees seems politically naive at this juncture in history.[18]

If we are to envision a future in which such a compact appears more achievable, then greater attention is required to the conditions shaping public opinion and public engagement in potential destination states. Furthermore, to create a future in which refugees are uniformly treated with the dignity and respect they are owed, the duty of hospitality and care cannot simply end with states themselves. This duty also needs to be cultivated within communities formed around moral and ethical ideals that call on their members to befriend the foreigner and show kindness to the stranger. The most powerful communities organized around such ideals have always been identified with religion. Indeed, religious communities have been at the centre of a centuries-long process of advancing a transnational global humanitarian ideal.[19] Their role within the political enterprise of refugee resettlement cannot be neglected by policymakers or advocates with impunity.

Notes

INTRODUCTION

1 Loescher and Scanlan, *Calculated Kindness*, 1.
2 Rep. Emanuel Celler to the editor *of Life Magazine*, 24 September 1946, box 15, part 1, Celler Papers, Library of Congress.
3 Skran, *Refugees in Inter-War Europe*, 248.
4 Betts and Loescher, "Introduction: Continuity and Change in Global Refugee Policy"; Miller, "Global Refugee Policy: Varying Perspectives, Unanswered Questions"; Milner, "Introduction: Understanding Global Refugee Policy"; Salehyan, *The Strategic Case for Refugee Resettlement*; Garnier, Jubilut, and Sandvik, *Refugee Resettlement: Power, Politics, and Humanitarian Governance*; Couldrey and Herson, "Resettlement."
5 Between 2003 and 2017, 77 per cent of all resettled refugees came to one of these two countries. The refugees counted here are those whose departure was counted by the UNHCR. Data from UNHCR Resettlement Data Finder: www.rsq.unhcr.org. The arrival of resettled refugees declined precipitously under the Trump administration – an anomaly of U.S. refugee policy since the passage of the 1980 Refugee Act.
6 Shaw, *Britannia's Embrace*, 220.
7 Thompson, *For God and Globe*, 5. See also: Hollinger, *Protestants Abroad*; King, *God's Internationalists*; and Curtis, *Holy Humanitarians*.
8 Skran, *Refugees in Inter-War Europe*, 276.
9 Cameron and Labman, "Private Refugee Sponsorship: An Evolving Framework for Refugee Resettlement."
10 Hyndman, Payne, and Jimenez, "Private Refugee Sponsorship in Canada"; Macklin et al., "A Preliminary Investigation into Private Refugee Sponsors."
11 Lipset, *Continental Divide*, 8.

12 In the early twentieth century Canada was a country characterized by what Peter Beyer calls "denominational establishment," with five Christian denominations claiming over 90 per cent of the population as their adherents. Until the 1960s, "the churches controlled or had a significant presence in the educational system at all levels; they were integral to the hospital sector; their leaders' voices had a hearing in the halls of political power, and the legal regime was imbued with the moral orientations they espoused." Beyer, "Deprivileging Religion," 83.
13 Lipset, *Continental Divide*, 8.
14 During the post-war period, popular agitation blocked a growing role for the church in both public schooling and foreign policy. President Truman was unable to appoint an ambassador to the Vatican owing to Protestant-led opposition. And yet Catholic groups were at the same time successfully building coalitions with Jewish and Protestant counterparts to undertake large-scale resettlement programs in which they played a leading role. Thanks to Gene Zubovich for these observations.
15 Press Release: "Senator Kennedy Hails Final Congressional Action on the Refugee Act of 1980," 4 March 1980, box 36, series "Judiciary Committee, 96th Congress," RG 46, National Archives.
16 Wimmer and Schiller, "Methodological Nationalism."
17 Brown and Scribner, "Unfulfilled Promises, Future Possibilities," 103.
18 Bon Tempo, *Americans at the Gate*, 8.
19 Zucker, "Refugee Resettlement in the United States," 172.
20 Hawkins, *Critical Years in Immigration*, 174. Emphasis in original.
21 Kelley and Trebilcock, *The Making of the Mosaic*, 367.
22 Labman, *At Law's Border*, 269. Emphasis in original. See also Labman, *Crossing Law's Border*.
23 Loescher and Scanlan, *Calculated Kindness*.
24 Zolberg, *A Nation by Design*, 18.
25 Teitelbaum, "Immigration, Refugees, and Foreign Policy," 439.
26 Price, *Rethinking Asylum*.
27 Zolberg, *A Nation by Design*, 18.
28 Loescher and Scanlan, *Calculated Kindness*.
29 Stoessinger, *The Refugee and the World Community*.
30 Gibney, *The Ethics and Politics of Asylum*, 141.
31 Over the period studied in this volume, the name of the federal department responsible for immigration matters changed a few times: Department of Mines and Resources, 1936–50; Department of Citizenship and Immigration, 1950–66; Department of Manpower and Immigration, 1966–77; Department of Employment and Immigration, 1977–91.

32 Anderson, *Canadian Liberalism and the Politics of Border Control*, 144.
33 Madokoro, *Elusive Refuge*.
34 Atkinson, *The Burden of White Supremacy*.
35 Suhrke, "Burden-Sharing During Refugee Emergencies," 400.
36 Ibid., 413.
37 Betts, "North-South Cooperation in the Refugee Regime; Betts, "Institutional Proliferation and the Global Refugee Regime."
38 Anker and Posner, "The Forty Year Crisis," 15.
39 Dirks, *Canada's Refugee Policy*.
40 Memo from R.M. Tait (director, Immigration Policy) to Dep. Min. J.L. Manion, 8 November 1977, file 8620-8, vol. 1815, RG 76, Library and Archives Canada.
41 Hathaway and Neve, "Making International Refugee Law Relevant Again"; Shuck, "Refugee Burden-Sharing."
42 Thielemann and El-Enany, "Refugee Protection as a Collective Action Problem," 209–29.
43 Gibney, *The Ethics and Politics of Asylum*, 107.
44 Adelman, "Canadian Refugee Policy in the Postwar Period: An Analysis."
45 Gilmour, "'The Kind of People Canada Wants.'"
46 Adelman, "Canadian Refugee Policy in the Postwar Period: An Analysis," 190.
47 Loescher and Scanlan, *Calculated Kindness*, 14.
48 Ibid, 13.
49 Soysal, *Limits of Citizenship*.
50 Jacobson, *Rights Across Borders*, 2.
51 Triadafilopoulos, *Becoming Multicultural*, 8.
52 Ibid.
53 Gurowitz, "Mobilizing International Norms."
54 Hansen and King, "Eugenic Ideas, Political Interests, and Policy Variance."
55 Triadafilopoulos, *Becoming Multicultural*.
56 Truman argued that "the behaviors that constitute the process of government cannot be understood apart from the groups, especially the organized and potential interest groups, that are operative at any one point in time." Truman, *The Governmental Process*, 502.
57 Roof, "Interest Groups."
58 Schattschneider, *The Semi-Sovereign People*; Olson, *The Logic of Collective Action*.
59 McFarland, "Neopluralism"; Baumgartner and Jones, *Agendas and Instability*; Baumgartner and Leech, *Basic Interests*.
60 Kingdon, *Agendas, Alternatives, and Public Policies*; Baumgartner and Jones, *Agendas and Instability in American Politics*.

61 Baumgartner and Jones, *Agendas and Instability in American Politics*; Sabatier and Jenkins-Smith, *Policy Change and Learning*.
62 Levi, "A Model, a Method, and a Map," 28.
63 Thelen, "Historical Institutionalism."
64 Since Heclo's initial studies of policy networks, a variety of metaphors and analytical frameworks have been developed to understand the "regularized patterns of interaction between state actors and representatives of societal interests." A key finding of this research has been that the cohesion and stability of a policy network is related to the commonality of core beliefs held between the various actors. Quotation from Skogstad, "Policy Networks and Policy Communities," 205–20, 207–8. See also Sabatier and Jenkins-Smith, *Policy Change and Learning*; Dowding, "Model or Metaphor?"; Kenis and Schneider, "Policy Networks and Policy Analysis"; Heclo, "Issue Networks," 87–107, 115–24.
65 Schmitter, "Still the Century of Corporatism?" 86.
66 Marsh and Rhodes, *Policy Networks in British Government*; Jordan, "Sub-Governments, Policy Communities and Networks."
67 Sabatier and Jenkins-Smith, *Policy Change and Learning*, 72.
68 Heclo, "Issue Networks."
69 Jordan, "Sub-Governments," 329.
70 Hansen, *Citizenship and Immigration in Post-war Britain*, 27.
71 Knowles, *Strangers at Our Gates*, 217–19.
72 John, *Analyzing Public Policy*, 19.
73 Allison, *Essence of Decision*.
74 Schattschneider, *The Semi-Sovereign People*.
75 Baumgartner and Jones, *Agendas and Instability*.
76 This may simply be a reflection of path dependency and the high costs associated with creating a national social infrastructure capable of resettling hundreds, if not thousands, of refugees every year.
77 Riera and Poirier, "'Welcoming the Stranger' and UNHCR's Cooperation with Faith-Based Organisations"; Christine Goodall, "Shouting Towards the Sky."
78 Mavelli and Wilson, *The Refugee Crisis and Religion*.
79 Moyn, *Christian Human Rights*; Duranti, *The Conservative Human Rights Revolution*; Thompson, *For God and Globe*; Inboden, *Religion and American Foreign Policy*; Zubovich, "For Human Rights Abroad, against Jim Crow at Home"; Chamedes, *A Twentieth-Century Crusade*.
80 Gibney and Hansen, "Asylum Policy in the West: Past Trends, Future Possibilities."

81 Abella and Troper, *None Is Too Many*; Zolberg, "The Roots of American Refugee Policy"; Zolberg, *A Nation by Design*; Dirks, *Canada's Refugee Policy*; Madokoro, *Elusive Refuge*.
82 Hampshire, *The Politics of Immigration*.
83 Before the passage of the 1948 DP Act, the War and State Departments of the United States worked with the Catholic Church to promote resettlement programs in Latin and South America: "Both the Intergovernmental Committee for Refugees and the US State Department have been continually urging that representatives from this agency visit the South American countries to assist Catholic groups there to assume the initiative in meeting this problem." See: NCWC, "Report to Board of Trustees – War Relief Services, October 1, 1945–September 30, 1946," 30 September 1946, box 6, series 26, War Relief Services Collection, Center for Migration Studies Archives.
84 Kingdon, *Agendas*.
85 Betts, "Public Goods Theory and the Provision of Refugee Protection."
86 President's Advisory Committee on Refugees, Background Papers, Interagency Task Force, 19 May 1975, file 2, box 2, John Marsh Files, Ford Presidential Library.
87 A notable exception would be the International Rescue Committee, a non-sectarian group that worked alongside leading religious groups in the United States.
88 Nichols, *The Uneasy Alliance*; Moyn, "Personalism"; Moyn, *Christian Human Rights*; Scribner, "'Pilgrims of the Night'"; Lacroix, "Immigration."
89 Casanova, *Public Religions in the Modern World*, 6.
90 Berger, *The Sacred Canopy*.
91 Quotation is from Philpott, "Has the Study of Global Politics Found Religion?" 188.
92 Clark and Wilson, "Incentive Systems"; Wilson, *Political Organizations*; Hildreth, "The Importance of Purposes"; Hertzke, "Lobbying for the Faithful."
93 Levine, "Review: Religion and Politics in Comparative and Historical Perspective," 96.
94 Wilson, *Political Organizations*; Hildreth, "The Importance of Purposes."
95 Rudolph and Piscatori, *Transnational Religion*.
96 Philpott, "Has the Study of Global Politics Found Religion?" 198.
97 Grzymala-Busse, "Weapons of the Meek: How Churches Influence Public Policy."
98 Putnam and Campbell, *American Grace*.

CHAPTER ONE

1 Genizi, *American Apathy*; Genizi, *The Holocaust, Israel, and Canadian Protestant Churches*.
2 Jonah Wise, Joint Distribution Committee, to H.M. Caiserman, Canadian Jewish Congress, 26 August 1938, file 6, box 5, box ZA 1938, Evian Conference, Canadian Jewish Congress Archives.
3 Leonard Dinnerstein, qtd. in Genizi, *American Apathy*, 72.
4 Hawkins, *Canada and Immigration*, 204.
5 Greif, *The Age of the Crisis of Man*; Jacobs, *The Year of Our Lord 1943*.
6 Arendt, *Origins of Totalitarianism*, 290–302.
7 "It was thanks to this event that the rhetoric of 'the human person' as a moral alternative to power politics – and likewise defined against the totalitarian spectre – was matched in some transatlantic Protestant thinking." Moyn, *Christian Human Rights*, 17.
8 Wald, Silverman, and Fridy, "Making Sense of Religion in Political Life."
9 Ibid.
10 Olson, *The Logic of Collective Action*; Salisbury, "An Exchange Theory of Interest Groups."
11 Wilson, *Political Organizations*; Hertzke, "Religious Interest Groups in American Politics."
12 Institutional histories of Church World Service and Catholic World Relief make such claims. See, for example, Fey, *Cooperation in Compassion*; Stenning, *Church World Service*; Egan, *Catholic Relief Services, the Beginning Years*.
13 Barnett, *Empire of Humanity*, 17–18; Stamatov, *The Origins of Global Humanitarianism*.
14 Moyn, "Personalism, Community, and the Origins of Human Rights."
15 Wald, Silverman, and Fridy, "Making Sense of Religion in Political Life," 131.
16 Leech et al., "Drawing Lobbyists to Washington."
17 Ibid., 20. Emphasis in original.
18 Kingdon, *Agendas*.
19 Sauer, "A Matter of Domestic Policy?"
20 Tichenor, *Dividing Lines*, 151.
21 Anker, "U.S. Immigration and Asylum Policy: A Brief Historical Perspective," 74–85, 76.
22 Tichenor, *Dividing Lines*, 161.
23 Wyman, *The Abandonment of the Jews*.
24 Anker, "U.S. Immigration and Asylum Policy," 77.

25 Tichenor, *Dividing Lines*, 166.
26 Ibid.
27 Nichols, *The Uneasy Alliance*, 49.
28 Ibid.
29 Ibid., 50.
30 Bon Tempo, *Americans at the Gate*, 18.
31 Wyman, *Barring the Gates to America*, vi.
32 Ibid., 18.
33 Tichenor, *Dividing Lines*, 167.
34 Ibid.
35 Penkower, "Jewish Organizations and the Creation of the U.S. War Refugee Board."
36 Wyman, *The Abandonment of the Jews*, xx.
37 Skran, *Refugees in Inter-War Europe*, 205.
38 Ibid., 276.
39 Tichenor, *Dividing Lines*, 177.
40 The membership of the Committee on Postwar Immigration Policy included the American Jewish Congress, HIAS, B'nai Brith, the National Catholic Welfare Conference, the Federal Council of Churches, the American Committee for Christian Refugees, the ACLU, the Common Council for American Unity, and the YWCA.
41 Harry S. Truman, "Statement and Directive by the President on Immigration to the United States of Certain Displaced Persons and Refugees in Europe," 22 December 1945, accessed 19 December 2016, www.presidency.ucsb.edu/ws/index.php?pid=12253.
42 Genizi, *American Apathy*, 336.
43 Ibid., 336.
44 Fey, *Cooperation in Compassion*, 18. The committee later changed its name to the American Christian Committee for Refugees (ACCR).
45 Nawyn, *American Protestantism's Response to Germany's Jews and Refugees*, 145.
46 Ibid., 159.
47 Ibid.
48 "ACCGR Purpose and Organization," 1934, file 12 – ACCR, box 3, RG 18, National Council of Churches Archives, Presbyterian Historical Society.
49 "Minutes of the Executive Committee of the American Christian Committee for German Refugees," 1 March 1934, file 12 – ACCR, box 3, RG 18, National Council of Churches Archives, Presbyterian Historical Society.
50 "Minutes of the Executive Committee of the American Christian Committee for German Refugees," 5 November 1934, file 12 – ACCR,

box 3, RG 18, National Council of Churches Archives, Presbyterian Historical Society.
51 Nawyn, *American Protestantism's Response to Germany's Jews and Refugees*, 160.
52 "Minutes of the Executive Committee of the American Christian Committee for German Refugees," 31 March 1946, file 12 – ACCR, box 3, RG 18, National Council of Churches Archives, Presbyterian Historical Society.
53 Moyn, *Christian Human Rights*, 17.
54 J.H. Oldham, "The Function of the Church in Society," prepared for the Universal Christian Council for Life and World Research Department, January 1937, file 2, box 4, series 1, WCC Papers, Burke Library, Columbia University.
55 Ibid.
56 Nurser, "The 'Ecumenical Movement' Churches, 'Global Order,' and Human Rights," 842.
57 Bennett, "Breakthrough in Ecumenical Social Ethics"; Nurser, "The 'Ecumenical Movement.'"
58 "Draft Pamphlet on Service to Refugees, An Account Rendered by the World Council of Churches Department of Inter-Church Aid and Services to Refugees," October 1950, file 4, box 75, series 1, WCC Papers, Burke Library, Columbia University.
59 "Report from Committee IV (d): Christian Reconstruction and Inter-Church Aid," file 5, box 16, series 1, WCC Papers, Burke Library, Columbia University.
60 Samuel McCrea Calvert to Leland Rex Robinson, 19 February 1945, file: DPS, Hungary, World Refugee Year, box 114, RG 8, Church World Service Archives, Presbyterian Historical Society.
61 Ibid.
62 Fey, *Cooperation in Compassion*, 30.
63 "Resolution on Displaced Persons Adopted by the Executive Committee of the Federal Council of Churches," 26 September 1946, file: DPS, box 113, RG 8, Church World Service Archives, Presbyterian Historical Society.
64 "Proposal for Agreement of Joint Service by Church World Service and the American Christian Committee on Refugees," 13 May 1946, file: DPS, box 113, RG 8, Church World Service Archives, Presbyterian Historical Society.
65 Genizi, *America's Fair Share*, 128.
66 "Statement issued by a conference of representatives of the WCC, CWS, Lutheran World Federation, YMCA, and YWCA," file 9, box 18, RG 18, National Council of Churches Archives, Presbyterian Historical Society.

67 Ibid.
68 Church World Service Press Release, 19 January 1948, file 9 – CCDP, box 30, RG 18, National Council of Churches Archives, Presbyterian Historical Society.
69 Ibid.
70 Bennett, "Breakthrough in Ecumenical Social Ethics"; Nurser, "The 'Ecumenical Movement'"; Stenning, *Church World Service*.
71 The United States Displaced Persons Commission, *Memo to America*, 278.
72 Murray, "Welcoming the Stranger," 60.
73 Ibid., 55.
74 Ibid., 59. Father Charles Coughlin (the "radio priest") gained a massive grassroots radio following in the 1930s with his antisemitic, fascist, and anti-refugee views before pressure from both the church hierarchy and the U.S. government forced him off the air. Other influential Catholic periodicals, like *Tablet* and *Ave Maria*, were also hostile to Jews and refugees.
75 Stamatov, *The Origins of Global Humanitarianism*.
76 Norris, "The International Catholic Migration Commission," 122.
77 Ibid.
78 Murray, "Welcoming the Stranger," 49.
79 "NCWC – Annual Report to Board of Trustees – War Relief Services, October 1, 1944–September 30, 1945," 30 September 1945, box 6, series 26, War Relief Services Collection, Center for Migration Studies Archives.
80 Murray, "Welcoming the Stranger," 77.
81 Genizi, *America's Fair Share*, 185.
82 Ibid., 170.
83 Ibid.
84 "The Problem of Displaced Persons," 1947, box 2, series 26, War Relief Services Collection, Center for Migration Studies Archives.
85 Ibid.
86 Ibid.
87 "NCWC – Report to Board of Trustees – War Relief Services, October 1, 1947–September 30, 1948," 30 September 1948, box 6, series 26, War Relief Services Collection, Center for Migration Studies Archives.
88 Ibid.
89 Scribner, "'Pilgrims of the Night,'" 3.
90 Moyn, "Personalism"; Moyn, *Christian Human Rights*.
91 Scribner, "Negotiating Priorities," 5.
92 Loescher and Scanlan, *Calculated Kindness*, 4; Culpepper, *Quiet Politics and Business Power*; Grzymala-Busse, *Nations under God*.
93 Sanua, *Let Us Prove Strong*.

94 Handlin, *A Continuing Task*, 81.
95 Sanua, *Let Us Prove Strong*; Handlin, *A Continuing Task*; Penkower, "Jewish Organizations."
96 Jonah Wise, Joint Distribution Committee, to H.M. Caiserman, Canadian Jewish Congress, 26 August 1938, file 6, box 5, box ZA 1938, Evian Conference, Canadian Jewish Congress Archives. Emphasis added.
97 Joseph M. Proskauer, Memo to members of the American Jewish Committee, 7 October 1945, box 15, part 1, Celler Papers, Library of Congress.
98 "The United States and the Holocaust, 1942–45," United States Holocaust Memorial Museum, www.ushmm.org/wlc/en/article.php?ModuleId=10007094.
99 Sanua, *Let Us Prove Strong*, 51.
100 Ibid., 53.
101 Genizi, *America's Fair Share*, 35.
102 Proskauer, Memo to members of the American Jewish Committee, 7 October 1945, box 15, part 1, Celler Papers, Library of Congress.
103 "Drive is opened to admit 100,000 Jews into US."
104 Rep. Emanuel Celler to Joseph Proskauer, 18 October 1946, box 15, part 1, Celler Papers, Library of Congress.
105 "The Problem of Displaced Persons," 1947, box 2, series 26, War Relief Services Collection, Center for Migration Studies Archives.
106 Loescher and Scanlan, *Calculated Kindness*, 9.
107 AJC Immigration Committee Meeting Minutes, 25 October 1946, Immigration Committee, 1946, American Jewish Congress Digital Archives.
108 Ibid.
109 Genizi, *America's Fair Share*, 72.
110 Leonard Dinnerstein, qtd. in Genizi, *America's Fair Share*, 72.
111 Hyman, "Displaced Persons," 320.
112 United States Displaced Persons Commission, *Memo to America*.
113 The associated groups were as follows: Christian Committee for Refugees; American Friends of Service Committee; American Jewish Joint Distribution Committee; American ORT Federation; American Relief for Italy, Inc.; Central Location Index, Inc.; Hadassah; HIAS I-ICA Emigration Association; Intergovernmental Committee on Refugees; International Migration Services; International Rescue and Relief Committee; Italian Relief Workshop; Labor League for Human Rights (associated with the AFL); Russian Children's Welfare Society; Save the Children Foundation; Self-help for Émigrés from Central Europe; Tolstoy Foundation; Unitarian Service Committee; United States Committee for the Care of European

Children; and World Student Service Fund. See Tichenor, *Dividing Lines*, 163.
114 Charlotte Owen to Susan Petties, 22 September 1948, box 66, MC 655, American Council of Voluntary Agencies for Foreign Service, American Council of Voluntary Agencies for Foreign Service Papers, Rutgers University Archives.
115 Minutes from Joint Council on Resettlement, 22 June 1948, box 66, MC 655, American Council of Voluntary Agencies for Foreign Service, American Council of Voluntary Agencies for Foreign Service Papers, Rutgers University Archives.
116 Draft submission for the Displaced Persons Commission from the Joint Council on Resettlement, drafted by Joseph P. Chamberlain, 7 June 1948, box 66, MC 655, American Council of Voluntary Agencies for Foreign Service, American Council of Voluntary Agencies for Foreign Service Papers Collection, Rutgers University Archives.
117 United States Displaced Persons Commission, *Memo to America*, 274.
118 Kelley and Trebilcock, *The Making of the Mosaic*, 186–92.
119 Ibid., 187.
120 Ibid., 220.
121 Adelman, "Canadian Refugee Policy," 188.
122 Kelley and Trebilcock, *The Making of the Mosaic*, 312.
123 Dirks, *Canada's Refugee Policy*, 254.
124 Kelley and Trebilcock, *The Making of the Mosaic*, 312.
125 William Lyon Mackenzie King Diary entry, 29 March 1938, file 121, MG 26 J 14, King Diaries, Library and Archives Canada.
126 William Lyon Mackenzie King Diary entry, 23 November 1938, file 121, MG 26 J 14, King Diaries, Library and Archives Canada.
127 Knowles, *Strangers at Our Gates*, 117.
128 Gilmour, "'The Kind of People Canada Wants,'" 170.
129 Anderson, *Canadian Liberalism*, 136.
130 Abella and Troper, *None Is Too Many*, xx. According to Abella and Troper, Blair was recorded as saying: "Pressure on the part of Jewish people to get into Canada has never been greater than it is now, and I am glad to have been able to add, after 35 years [sic] experience here, that it was never so well controlled" (8).
131 Qtd. in Gilmour, "'The Kind of People Canada Wants,'" 166.
132 Ibid.
133 Abella and Troper, *None Is Too Many*, 7.
134 Basok and Simmons, "A Review of the Politics of Canadian Refugee Selection," 137.

135 Genizi, *The Holocaust, Israel, and Canadian Protestant Churches.*
136 Davies and Nefsky, *How Silent Were the Churches?*
137 Reverends Claris E. Silcox, E. Crossley Hunter, Ernest Marshall Howse, Stanley Russell, and James Bryce of the United Church, and Reverend Canon W.W. Judd of the Anglican Church.
138 Genizi, *The Holocaust*, 47.
139 WCC (in process of formation) Report from the Geneva Office of the Provisional Committee (July 1941–July 1942), 1 July 1942, file 103–1, vol. 103, MG 28 I 327, Canadian Council of Churches Collection, Library and Archives Canada.
140 Report of the Canadian Committee, World Council of Churches, 6 February 1942, file 103–1, vol. 103, MG 28 I 327, Canadian Council of Churches Collection, Library and Archives Canada.
141 Genizi, *The Holocaust*, 21.
142 Thompson, *In Defence of Principles*, 16.
143 Ibid.
144 Kelley and Trebilcock, *The Making of the Mosaic*, 326.
145 Canadian Council of Churches Memorandum for Rt. Hon. W.L. Mackenzie King, file 3–24–20, vol. 115, RG 26, Canadian Council of Churches Papers, Library and Archives Canada.
146 Thompson, *In Defence of Principles*, 17.
147 Kelley and Trebilcock, *The Making of the Mosaic*, 312.
148 Lacroix, "Immigration, Minority Rights, and Catholic Policy-Making in Post-War Canada," 186.
149 Now called the Canadian Conference of Catholic Bishops.
150 Fay, *A History of Canadian Catholics.*
151 Choquette, "The Archdiocese of Toronto and Its Metropolitan Influence in Ontario," 302.
152 Lacroix, "Immigration, Minority Rights, and Catholic Policy-Making in Post-War Canada," 202.
153 Ibid., 188.
154 Ibid., 190.
155 Ibid., 190.
156 Schmalz, "Former Enemies Come to Canada," 219.
157 Ibid.
158 Ibid.
159 Gilmour, "'The Kind of People Canada Wants,'" 171.
160 Ibid.
161 Knowles, *Strangers at the Gates*, 129.
162 Bumsted, *Canada's Diverse Peoples*, 206.
163 Abella and Troper, *None Is Too Many*, 216.

164 Sauer, "A Matter of Domestic Policy?" 239.
165 Ibid.
166 Schmalz, "Former Enemies Come to Canada."
167 Canadian Christian Council for Resettlement of Refugees to J.A. Glenn, minister of mines and resources, 24 October 1947, MG 28 V 120, Meetings – Minutes and Reports, 1947–48, 1951, CCCRR Files, Library and Archives Canada.
168 Dirks, *Canada's Refugee Policy*, 161.
169 Sauer, "A Matter of Domestic Policy?" 230.
170 Hawkins, *Canada and Immigration*, 72.
171 Ibid., 304.
172 Schmalz, "Former Enemies Come to Canada," 206–8.
173 Ibid., 213.
174 Ibid., 215.
175 Sauer, "A Matter of Domestic Policy?" 249.
176 Hawkins, *Canada and Immigration*, 304.
177 Joseph Kage, "JIAS Social Service for Immigrants," file 567–84, vol. 893, RG 76, Library and Archives Canada.
178 Abella and Troper, *None Is Too Many*, 11.
179 Ibid.
180 Ibid., 4.
181 Samuel Jacobs, Samuel Factor, and A.A. Heaps.
182 Abella and Troper, *None Is Too Many*, 40.
183 Ibid., 41.
184 Ibid.
185 "Beginning Anew: Bulletin of the Canadian National Committee on Refugees (Vol. 1)," January 1945, file 208, box 13, CJC ZA 1945, Canadian Jewish Congress Archives.
186 Brief submitted to the Senate Committee on Immigration by Saul Hayes, executive director of the Canadian Jewish Congress, 3 July 1946, file "1946," box 1, series G, Canadian Jewish Congress Archives.
187 Ibid.
188 Knowles, *Strangers at Our Gates*, 133.
189 Moses A. Levitt, JDC, to Saul Hayes, CJC, 23 July 1951, file "1951," CJC CA box 30, Canadian Jewish Congress Archives.
190 Hawkins, *Canada and Immigration*, 298.
191 Joseph Kage, "JIAS Social Services for Immigrants."
192 Caza, "Organizing Relief."
193 Brief submitted by the Canadian Jewish Congress to the Standing Committee on Immigration and Labour of the Senate of Canada, 7 May 1947, file 1947, box 1, CJC series G, Canadian Jewish Congress Archives.

194 Wald, Silverman, and Fridy, "Making Sense of Religion," 140.

CHAPTER TWO

1. Wyman, *DPs: Europe's Displaced Persons*; Cohen, *In War's Wake*.
2. For a critical discussion of the policy cycle, see Araral et al., *Routledge Handbook of Public Policy*. While public-policy theorists represent these phases as sequential, in practice the relationship between the phases is less systematic than this formulation suggests. As Sabatier notes, the policy process involves "multiple interacting cycles involving numerous policy proposals and statutes at multiple levels of government." Sabatier, *Theories of the Policy Process*, 7.
3. Araral et al., *Routledge Handbook of Public Policy*; Baumgartner and Jones, *Agendas and Instability*; McFarland, "Interest Group Theory"; Baumgartner and Leech, *Basic Interests*.
4. Kingdon, *Agendas*.
5. Tversky and Kahneman, "Rational Choice and the Framing of Decisions."
6. Simon, "Human Nature in Politics."
7. Sabatier, "Top-Down and Bottom-Up Approaches to Implementation Research"; deLeon and deLeon, "What Ever Happened to Policy Implementation?"
8. McFarland, *Neopluralism*, 166.
9. Ibid., 4.
10. Ibid.
11. Gibney, *The Ethics and Politics of Asylum*, 136.
12. Ibid.
13. Memorandum on Refugees and Displaced People, American Jewish Committee, 8 April 1946, Immigration Subject Files, 1946–48, American Jewish Committee Digital Archives.
14. Davidson Somers, War Department, to Louis Lipsky, chairman, AJC, 28 July 1945, box 15, part 1, Celler Papers, Library of Congress.
15. "New Directive on Immigrant Visas to the US."
16. Memorandum from Joseph M. Proskauer to members of the American Jewish Committee, 7 October 1946, box 15, part 1, Celler Papers, Library of Congress. Immigration to the United States was still limited by national origin, and low immigration over the preceding decades had left many quotas unfilled year after year.
17. Edwin Rosenberg to Monsignor Howard J. Carroll, National Refugee Service Interoffice Memo re: President Truman's Directive on Immigration, 26 December 1945, file 149, box 15, NCWC 23, Center for Migration Studies Archives.

18 Memorandum from Joseph M. Proskauer to members of the American Jewish Committee, 7 October 1946, box 15, part 1, Celler Papers, Library of Congress.
19 Loescher and Scanlan cite one particular attack on Jewish returnees to Kielce, Poland, where forty-one Jews were killed and seventy-five badly injured: "The Poles in Kielce – men, women, and children – beat Jews mercilessly, squeezed their genitals, crushed bones, broke legs, tore off limbs, and mutilated bodies in the most barbaric fashion." Loescher and Scanlan, *Calculated Kindness*, 8.
20 Memorandum from Joseph M. Proskauer to members of the American Jewish Committee, 7 October 1946, box 15, part 1, Celler Papers, Library of Congress.
21 "Drive Is Opened to Admit 100,000 Jews to the US."
22 President of the Federal Council of Churches to President Harry S. Truman, 27 December 1945, RG 18, box 31, file: Congress, National Council of Churches Collection, Presbyterian Historical Society.
23 Church World Service Resolution, 18 September 1946, RG 18, box 30, file: CCDP, National Council of Churches Collection, Presbyterian Historical Society.
24 "NCWC – Annual Report to the Board of Trustees – War Relief Services," 1 October 1945–30 September 1946, box 6, series 26, War Relief Services Collection, Center for Migration Studies Archives.
25 Genizi, "Interfaith Cooperation," 76.
26 AJC Immigration Committee Minutes, 25 October 1946.
27 Ibid.
28 Genizi, *America's Fair Share*, 70.
29 AJC Immigration Committee Minutes, 25 October 1946.
30 Loescher and Scanlan, *Calculated Kindness*, 10.
31 Genizi, "Interfaith Cooperation," 78.
32 Ibid.; AJC Memo from Nathan Weisman to All Immigration Committees, re: Immigration Project, 20 March 1947, Immigration Committee, 1947, American Jewish Committee Digital Archives.
33 Loescher and Scanlan, *Calculated Kindness*, 11.
34 Ibid., 10.
35 Ibid.
36 "Any person in Germany, Austria, or Italy at the time of the passage of this Act who (1) is outside of the country of former residence as a result of events subsequent to the outbreak of World War II; and (2) is unable or unwilling to return to the country of his nationality or former residence because of persecution of fear of persecution on account of race, religion, or political opinions."

37 Tichenor, *Dividing Lines*, 185.
38 NCWC Confidential Bulletin No. 42: Information on Legislation to Admit Displaced Persons to the United States, 22 January 1948, file 9, box 37, series 1, National Catholic Welfare Conference, Catholic University of America Archives.
39 Tichenor, *Dividing Lines*, 186.
40 Loescher and Scanlan, *Calculated Kindness*, 14–15.
41 Tichenor, *Dividing Lines*, 186.
42 Nichols, *The Uneasy Alliance*, 73–4.
43 Statement issued by a conference of representatives of the World Council of Churches, Church World Service, Lutheran World Federation, YMCA, and YWCA, 19 October 1947, file: Pres Committee, box 9, series NG 18, National Council of Churches Papers, Presbyterian Historical Society.
44 Minutes of the Meeting of the Board of Trustees – War Relief Services–NCWC, 11 November 1947, file 15, box 72, series 1, National Catholic Welfare Conference, Catholic University of America Archives.
45 NCWC Confidential Bulletin No. 42.
46 Ibid.
47 Nichols, *The Uneasy Alliance*, 74.
48 Circular letter from the Citizens Committee on Displaced People, 24 December 1947, file 9, box 37, series 1, National Catholic Welfare Conference, Catholic University of America Archives.
49 Minutes of the meeting of the National Catholic Resettlement Council, 12 December 1947, file 11, box 37, series 1, National Catholic Welfare Conference, Catholic University of America Archives.
50 CWS Press Release, 19 January 1948.
51 Ibid.
52 Genizi, "Interfaith Cooperation," 78.
53 Statement by the President upon Signing the Displaced Persons Act, 25 June 1948, Truman Library Digital Archives.
54 CCDP to cooperating organizations, local citizens' committees, and friends of the CCDP, 30 June 1948, file: CCDP, box 30, RG 18, National Council of Churches, Presbyterian Historical Society.
55 Meeting of representatives of three religious groups to discuss resettlement plans, 22 June 1948, box 66, MC 655, American Council of Voluntary Agencies Papers, Rutgers University Archives.
56 Ibid.
57 An assurance involved a guarantee of employment, housing, and transportation for a nominated and eligible displaced person.

58 Memo from Charlotte Owen to Susan Petties, 22 September 1948, box 66, MC 655, American Council of Voluntary Agencies for Foreign Service Papers, Rutgers University Archives.
59 A suggested Catholic program for the resettlement of displaced persons under Public Law 774–80th Congress, September 1948, file 9, box 37, series 1, NCWC, Catholic University of America Archives.
60 Ibid.
61 Ibid.
62 Working Paper on the Responsibility of the American Churches for Displaced Persons and Overseas Aid, November 1948, box 113, series RG 8, Church World Service Papers, Presbyterian Historical Society.
63 CWS: 3,574; NCWC: 30,353; USNA and HIAS: 22,000 (approximately). Minutes of the 28th Meeting of the Board of Directors, Church World Service, 13 September 1949, file: CWS, box 6, series RG 18, National Council of Churches Papers, Presbyterian Historical Society.
64 The U.S. government paid for transportation to the U.S. port of entry, and the groups wanted costs paid until refugees reached their final inland destination.
65 NCWC to Walter Van Kirk, Federal Council of Churches, 1 April 1949, file: Congress, box 3, series RG 18, National Council of Churches Papers, Presbyterian Historical Society.
66 Federal Council of Churches Press Release re: DPs, 23 February 1950, file: Congress, box 3, series RG 18, National Council of Churches Papers, Presbyterian Historical Society.
67 Tichenor, *Dividing Lines*, 188.
68 CCDP to cooperating organizations, local citizens committees, and friends of the CCDP, 18 April 1950, file: CCDP, box 30, series RG 18, National Council of Churches Papers, Presbyterian Historical Society.
69 Gibson, "The Displaced Placed," 78.
70 The security checks alone involved the following agencies and authorities: the Federal Bureau of Investigation, the Counter-Intelligence Corps of the United States Army, the Central Intelligence Agency, the provost-marshal-general of the U.S. Army in Germany, the Berlin Document Center, the Immigration and Naturalization Service of the Department of Justice, consular officers, and other special investigators in liaison with foreign-intelligence agencies. In addition, the Visa Division of the Department of State and the United States Public Health Services were also engaged.
71 Oral History Interview with Harry S. Rosenfield by James R. Fuchs, 23 July 1980, Truman Library Digital Archive.
72 Genizi, *America's Fair Share*, 117.

73 United States Displaced Persons Commission, *Memo to America*, 273.
74 Ibid.
75 The other groups were as follows: International Rescue Committee, Mennonite Central Committee, National Lutheran Council, National American Federation of International Institutes, and United Ukrainian Relief Committee.
76 United States Displaced Persons Commission, *Memo to America*, 273.
77 Ibid., 294.
78 Ibid.
79 Dirks, *Canada's Refugee Policy*, 150.
80 Canadian officials knew that the United States would make shipping available if Canada really were willing to resettle refugees from Europe, so this was not a problem that any attempt was made to remove.
81 Memo from the UJRA to the National Committee for Refugees, 12 April 1943, General Files, 1943, Canadian Jewish Congress Archives.
82 Memorandum from Saul Hayes, CJC, to Sam Factor, MP, 10 February 1944, file 231A, UJRA, Canadian Jewish Congress Archives.
83 The establishment of the Department of External Affairs in 1909 did not involve a separation of Canadian foreign policy from that of the United Kingdom. Canada gained more control over its foreign policy during and after the First World War; however, it was not until the passage of the Statute of Westminster in 1931 that Canada was granted full legal autonomy – including in the domain of foreign policy. The post-war period, therefore, presented Canada with the opportunity to establish an autonomous role in world affairs.
84 Dirks, *Canada's Refugee Policy*, 138.
85 Ibid.
86 Ibid.
87 Cairine Wilson to J.A. Glen, minister of mines and resources, 21 January 1946, file 34, box 3, ZA 1946, Canadian Jewish Congress Archives.
88 Kelley and Trebilcock, *The Making of the Mosaic*, 339.
89 Green, *Immigration and the Postwar Canadian Economy*, 30.
90 Abella and Troper, *None Is Too Many*, 242.
91 Ibid., 213.
92 Ibid., 214.
93 Prime Minister Mackenzie King to Senator Cairine Wilson, 6 May 1946, file 20, box 2, ZA 1946, Canadian Jewish Congress Archives.
94 Ibid.
95 Gilmour, "'The Kind of People Canada Wants,'" 170.

96 Cairine Wilson to J.A. Glen, minister of mines and resources, 21 January 1946.
97 Dirks, *Canada's Refugee Policy*, 123; Green, *Immigration*.
98 Dirks, *Canada's Refugee Policy*, 123.
99 Qtd. in Triadafilopoulos, *Becoming Multicultural*, 58.
100 Ibid.
101 Memo for Cabinet Committee on Immigration Policy from H.L. Keenleyside, 3 September 1948, file 3-18-1, vol. 100, RG 26, Library and Archives Canada.
102 Memo to Cabinet from H.L. Keenleyside, 4 June 1947, file 3-18-1, vol. 100, RG 26, Library and Archives Canada.
103 Annual Report of the Department of Mines and Resources for the fiscal year ending 31 March 1948.
104 Ibid.
105 Dirks, *Canada's Refugee Policy*, 156.
106 Stoessinger, *The Refugee*, 126.
107 Wyman, *DPs*, 193.
108 Ibid.
109 Knowles, *Strangers at Our Gates*, 133.
110 Dirks, *Canada's Refugee Policy*, 140.
111 Saul Hayes, executive director of the CJC, urged: "If ever there was a time for Canada to act quickly and generously in this matter now is the time ... The record of Canada in this case is not among the brightest and does not match the glory which the dominion has won for itself during the years of war." Brief submitted to the Senate Committee on Immigration by Saul Hayes, executive director of the Canadian Jewish Congress, 3 July 1946.
112 Dirks, *Canada's Refugee Policy*, 158.
113 Ibid., 161.
114 Letter from the CCCRR to J.A. Glenn, minister of mines and resources, 24 October 1947.
115 Dirks, *Canada's Refugee Policy*, 162.
116 Kelley and Trebilcock, *The Making of the Mosaic*, 343.
117 Dirks, *Canada's Refugee Policy*, 163.
118 Annual Report of the Department of Citizenship and Immigration for the fiscal year ending 31 March 1952.
119 When the CCCRR finally disbanded in 1955, it turned its operations over to the CCC.
120 Rev. Canon Judd, general secretary, to Dr H.L. Keenleyside, deputy minister, Ministry of Mines and Resources, re: Personal Sponsorship

121 of Displaced Persons and Other Immigrants, 27 September 1949, file 3-24-20, vol. 115, RG 26, Library and Archives Canada.
121 Memo from Laval Fortier, deputy minister, to the director of immigration, Department of Mines and Resources, 18 July 1951, file 3-24-20, vol. 115, RG 26, Library and Archives Canada.
122 Charles Jordan, JDC, to Saul Hayes, CJC, 23 July 1951, file 1951, box 30, series CA, Canadian Jewish Congress Archives.
123 W.J. Gallagher, general secretary of the Canadian Council of Churches, to Walter Harris, minister of citizenship and immigration, 15 May 1952, file 3-24-20, vol. 115, RG 26, Library and Archives Canada.
124 Directive no. 25 re: Sponsorship of Immigrants by the Canadian Council of Churches, 13 July 1952, file 3-24-20, vol. 115, RG 26, Library and Archives Canada.
125 Memorandum for file, re: Meeting between Col. Fortier and Dr. W.J. Gallagher and Alex Maclaren, CCC, 16 March 1953, file 3-24-20, vol. 115, RG 26, Library and Archives Canada.
126 Laval Fortier to T.F. Herzer, chairman, CCCRR, 8 April 1953, file 3-24-20, vol. 115, RG 26, Library and Archives Canada.
127 Hawkins, *Canada and Immigration*, 305.
128 Ibid.
129 Letter from a visa officer in Rome to the director of immigration, Department of Citizenship and Immigration, 14 January 1954, file 567-81, vol. 893, RG 76, Library and Archives Canada.
130 Report from Fred Poulton to the Committee on Immigration of Refugees, Canadian Council of Churches, 23 March 1954, file 120-5, vol. 120, I 327, MG 28, Library and Archives Canada.
131 Notes taken at a meeting of the four voluntary agencies (CCCRR, RSS, CCC, JIAS), called by Col. Laval Fortier, deputy minister, 14 October 1954, vol. 120, MG 28, Library and Archives Canada.
132 Memo to the deputy minister from the director of technical services re: meeting with the voluntary agencies, 19 October 1954, file 567-9, vol. 893, RG 76, Library and Archives Canada.
133 Notes from meeting recorded in a confidential memo to the Canadian Jewish Congress Executive Committee from Monroe Abbey and Saul Hayes, 22 October 1954, file 1954, box 30, series CA, Canadian Jewish Congress Archives.
134 Memo to Laval Fortier, deputy minister of Citizenship and Immigration, from the CCCRR, CJC, RSS, and CCC, 8 November 1954, file 3-24-20, vol. 115, RG 26, Library and Archives Canada.

135 Canadian Jewish Congress and Jewish Immigrant Aid Society to Minister Pickersgill, 15 March 1955, file "1955," box 1, series G, Canadian Jewish Congress.
136 Thelen, "Historical Institutionalism," 387.
137 Mahoney, "Path Dependence in Historical Sociology"; Pierson, "Increasing Returns"; Steinmo and Thelen, "Historical Institutionalism."
138 Kingdon, *Agendas*.
139 Hacker, Pierson, and Thelen, "Drift and Conversion," 187–8.
140 Ibid., 180.

CHAPTER THREE

1 Loescher, Betts, and Milner, UNHCR: *The Politics and Practice of Refugee Protection into the 21st Century*, 21.
2 Loescher and Scanlan, *Calculated Kindness*, 52; Dirks, *Canada's Refugee Policy*, 203. Other countries accepting Hungarian refugees for resettlement were as follows: Great Britain (21,000), West Germany (15,000), Switzerland (13,000), France (13,000), Australia (11,000), Sweden (7,000), Belgium (6,000), and Israel (2,000).
3 Price, *Rethinking Asylum*.
4 Arthur, "Competing Technologies"; Pierson, "Increasing Returns."
5 Pierson, "Power and Path Dependence."
6 Davis, "The Cold War, Refugees and U.S. Immigration Policy," 120. The remainder were supported by the secular International Rescue Committee and the United Ukrainian American Relief Committee.
7 Dirks, *Canada's Refugee Policy*; Thompson and Bangarth, "Transnational Christian Charity." The other 10 per cent arrived through different schemes in cooperation with industry and other sponsoring groups.
8 Gatrell, *Free World?*
9 Ibid., 79.
10 Ibid., 81. A UK Foreign Office official noted that "in the long run," the success of WRY would "save Her Majesty's Government a great deal of money."
11 The United States did not eliminate national-origins quotas until 1965, and Canada did not remove significant racial, religious, or ethnic barriers in immigration policy until 1962.
12 Madokoro, *Elusive Refuge*.
13 Mahoney and Thelen, *Explaining Institutional Change*, 16.
14 Nichols, *The Uneasy Alliance*, 86.

15 Bon Tempo, *Americans at the Gate*, 57.
16 American Jewish Committee, "Present Status of Operations under Refugee Relief Act," 8 March 1954, Refugees, 1950–54, American Jewish Committee Digital Archives.
17 Bon Tempo, *Americans at the Gate*, 59.
18 Meeting of the Advisory Committee on Voluntary Foreign Aid, State Department, 29 November 1956, boxes K and L, Voorhees Papers, Rutgers University Archives.
19 Ibid.
20 ACVA Report on the Hungarian Refugee Program, 6 August 1957, box 1, series 26, War Relief Services Collection, Center for Migration Studies Archives.
21 The Immigration and Nationality Act of 1952, 8 U.S.C. § 1182(d)(5) (1952).
22 Bockley, "A Historical Overview of Refugee Legislation," 267–8. Congressman Feighan, a member of the drafting committee for the statute, remarked that "it was intended to be used as a remedy for individual hardship cases, no more, no less."
23 Anker and Posner, "The Forty Year Crisis," 19. One of the motivating factors behind the overwhelming support in Congress for the Refugee Act was the desire to reassert congressional control over refugee admissions after the extensive use of parole authority to admit Indochinese refugees in the 1970s.
24 Herbert Hoover to Tracy Voorhees, 4 December 1956, boxes K and L, Voorhees Papers, Rutgers University Archives.
25 Eisenhower later wrote to Hoover to say that the decision to form the President's Committee had been taken based on his advice. Eisenhower to Herbert Hoover, 8 January 1957, boxes K and L, Voorhees Papers, Rutgers University Archives.
26 White House Press Release, 12 December 1956. Eisenhower wrote to Hoover before he formally announced the launch of the committee, informing him of the formation of the committee and thanking him for the help and advice he was providing to Voorhees. See Walch, *Herbert Hoover and Dwight D. Eisenhower*, 188–9.
27 White House Press Release, 12 December 1956, box 1, Records of the U.S. Foreign Assistance Agencies, 1948–61, RG 469, United States National Archives.
28 Memo for Loy W. Henderson, deputy under-secretary of state, Department of State, from Tracy Voorhees, re: Proposed Agreement between the State

Department and the Various Voluntary Agencies, 30 January 1957, box 1, Records of the U.S. Foreign Assistance Agencies, 1948–61, RG 469, United States National Archives.
29 Memo, "Highlights," February 1957, boxes K and L, Voorhees Papers, Rutgers University Archives.
30 Ibid. A few hundred were also resettled by the Tolstoy Foundation, the Ukrainian-American Relief Committee, and individuals.
31 Loescher and Scanlan, *Calculated Kindness*, 50–60.
32 Report of the Fact Finding Committee on the Hungarian Refugee Program, ACVA, 29 April 1958, box 82, MC 655, American Council of Voluntary Agencies, Rutgers University Archives.
33 Ibid., 91.
34 Catholic Relief Services Press Release, no. 123/44 re: Hungarian Refugee Work, 27 February 1957, folder 8, box 49, series 1, NCWC, Catholic University of America Archives.
35 Report of the Fact Finding Committee on the Hungarian Refugee Program, ACVA, 29 April 1958.
36 "90-Day Wonder," *Washington Post*, 10 March 1957, boxes K and L, Voorhees Papers, Rutgers University Archives.
37 Summary of Notes of a Meeting of the Committee on Migration and Refugee Problems, 16 May 1957, box 1, series 26, War Relief Services, Center for Migration Studies Archives.
38 Ibid.
39 Qtd. in a letter from Edward Swanstrom to Paul Tanner, 18 April 1958, folder 9, box 49, series 1, NCWC, Catholic University of America Archives.
40 Ibid.
41 Ibid.
42 Ibid.
43 Tichenor, *Dividing Lines*, 40.
44 Ibid., 204.
45 Ibid., 207.
46 Gatrell, *Free World?*
47 Ibid., 138.
48 NCWC Annual Report – Catholic Relief Services, 1 October 1958–30 September 1959, box 68, series 1, NCWC, Catholic University of America Archives.
49 Gatrell, *Free World?* 129.
50 Ibid., 124.
51 Ibid., 123.

52 Minutes of meeting of the Committee on Migration and Refugee Problems, 2 September 1959, box 70, MC 655, American Council of Voluntary Agencies for Foreign Service Papers, Rutgers University Archives.
53 Ibid.
54 AJC 52nd Annual Meeting – Statement on World Refugee Year, 19 April 1959, Refugees, 1957–59, American Jewish Committee Digital Archives.
55 Statement of Roland Elliott, Church World Service, to the Senate Subcommittee on Immigration, 20 May 1959, file: DPS Hungary, WRY, box 114, RG 8, Church World Service Papers, Presbyterian Historical Society.
56 Minutes of meeting of the Committee on Migration and Refugee Problems, 2 September 1959.
57 Statement of Legislative Recommendations before the House Subcommittee on Immigration, Migration and Refugee Committee of the American Council of Voluntary Agencies, 21 March 1960, box 70, MC 655, American Council of Voluntary Agencies for Foreign Service Papers, Rutgers University Archives.
58 NCWC Annual Report – Catholic Relief Services, 1 October 1960–30 September 1961, box 68, series 1, NCWC, Catholic University of America Archives.
59 Hawkins, *Canada and Immigration*, 114.
60 Ibid.
61 Molloy et al., *Running on Empty*.
62 Knowles, *Strangers at Our Gates*, 175.
63 Troper, "Canada and Hungarian Refugees," 188.
64 Memo to R. Alex Sim re: Hungarians in Toronto from A.E. Thompson, Department of Citizenship and Immigration, 2 November 1956, file 3–24–34–1, vol. 117, RG 26, Library and Archives Canada.
65 UNHCR deputy commissioner, James M. Read, to the secretary of state for external affairs for Canada, 6 November 1956, file 3–24–12–1, vol. 117, RG 26, Library and Archives Canada.
66 Memo to R. Alex Sim re: Hungarians in Toronto from A.E. Thompson, Department of Citizenship and Immigration, 2 November 1956, file 3–24–34–1, vol. 117, RG 26, Library and Archives Canada.
67 Excerpts from cabinet conclusions for meetings held on 14 November and 16 November 1956, file 3–24–12–1, vol. 117, RG 26, Library and Archives Canada.
68 Minutes of a meeting on immigration matters between the federal government and voluntary organizations, labour unions, and manufacturing groups, 19 March 1956, file: 1956, box 30, series CA, Canadian Jewish Congress Archives.

69 Ibid.
70 Dirks, *Canada's Refugee Policy*, 195.
71 Ibid.
72 Minutes of a meeting between Citizenship and Immigration officials and voluntary agencies, 19 November 1956, file 3-24-34-1, vol. 117, RG 26, Library and Archives Canada.
73 Ibid., 196.
74 Newspaper report of 14 November 1956, qtd. in Dirks, *Canada's Refugee Policy*, 195.
75 Molloy and Madokoro, "Effecting Change," 54.
76 Troper, "Canada and Hungarian Refugees," 190.
77 Ibid.
78 Memo from the director of immigration to the deputy minister, re: Hungarian Refugees, Department of Citizenship and Immigration, 22 November 1956, file 3-24-34-1, vol. 117, RG 26, Library and Archives Canada.
79 Ibid.
80 This meeting included the Canadian Conference of Catholic Bishops, the Rural Settlement Society, the Canadian Council of Churches, the Canadian Jewish Congress, the Red Cross, the Hungarian Federation, and the Canadian Christian Council for the Resettlement of Refugees.
81 Minutes from a meeting on Hungarian refugees, hosted by the Department of Citizenship and Immigration, 27 November 1956, file 3-24-12-1, vol. 111, RG 26, Library and Archives Canada.
82 Troper, "Canada and Hungarian Refugees," 183.
83 Memo re: Ottawa meeting on Hungarian refugees with Saul Hayes, 29 November 1956, file 11, box 1, ZA 1956, Canadian Jewish Congress Archives.
84 Keyserlingk, *Breaking Ground*, 8.
85 Troper, "Canada and Hungarian Refugees," 189.
86 Confidential Memorandum to all District Superintendents re: Hungarian Refugee Movement, 10 December 1956, file 3-24-34-1, vol. 117, RG 26, Library and Archives Canada.
87 Thompson and Bangarth, "Transnational Christian Charity," 190.
88 *House of Commons Debates*, vol. 100, no. 15, 5th session, 22nd Parliament.
89 Minutes of a meeting on immigration matters between the federal government and voluntary organizations, labour unions, and manufacturing groups, 19 March 1957, file: 1957, box 30, series CA, Canadian Jewish Congress Archives.

90 Memo from acting director of immigration to the deputy minister, Department of Citizenship and Immigration, 10 July 1957, file 3-24-12-1, vol. 111, RG 26, Library and Archives Canada.
91 Dirks, *Canada's Refugee Policy*, 211.
92 Ibid.
93 Ibid.
94 Ibid., 213.
95 Troper, "Canada and Hungarian Refugees," 191.
96 Memo from the acting director of immigration to the deputy minister, Department of Citizenship and Immigration, re: Hungarian Refugee Movement, 27 June 1957.
97 Memo to cabinet from the acting minister of citizenship and immigration, 10 July 1957, file 3-24-12-1, vol. 111, RG 26, Library and Archives Canada.
98 By 1960, only six Hungarian families were counted on the welfare rolls. See Dirks, *Canada's Refugee Policy*, 211.
99 Memo to cabinet from the acting minister of citizenship and immigration, 10 July 1957, file 3-24-12-1, vol. 111, RG 26, Library and Archives Canada.
100 Memo from the acting director of immigration to the deputy minister, Department of Citizenship and Immigration, re: Approved Church Program, 9 May 1957, file 3-24-20, vol. 115, RG 26, Library and Archives Canada.
101 Thompson and Bangarth, "Transnational Christian Charity," 307.
102 Minutes of Meeting respecting Immigration Policy, 6 August 1957, 1957, box 30, series CA, Canadian Jewish Congress Archives.
103 Memo for the acting minister from the deputy minister re: Approved Church Program, 7 May 1958, file 3-24-20, vol. 15, RG 26, Library and Archives Canada.
104 Ibid.
105 Ibid.
106 Ibid.
107 Minutes of a meeting to establish a Canadian Committee for World Refugee Year, 17 February 1959, vol. 112, RG 26, Library and Archives Canada.
108 Dirks, *Canada's Refugee Policy*, 217.
109 Under-Secretary of State Robertson to Deputy Minister Fortier re: Canadian Participation in World Refugee Year, 24 February 1959, vol. 112, RG 26, Library and Archives Canada.

110 Minutes from an interdepartmental meeting to discuss Canadian participation in World Refugee Year, 5 March 1959, vol. 112, RG 26, Library and Archives Canada.
111 Ibid.
112 Memo from the CCC, CCCRR, CCC, and Catholic Immigrant Service to Minister Fairclough, 28 January 1959, file 3–24–20, vol. 115, RG 26, Library and Archives Canada.
113 Memo for file from the director of immigration re: Meeting with Immigrant organizations (CCC, Catholic Immigrant Services, Canadian Jewish Congress, CCCRR), 12 May 1959, vol. 115, RG 26, Library and Archives Canada.
114 Memo from director of immigration to deputy minister re: Canada's Position with respect to World Refugee Year, 13 May 1959, vol. 112, RG 26, Library and Archives Canada.
115 Director of immigration to deputy minister, Department of Citizenship and Immigration, re: CCCRR submission re: Approved Church Program, 26 May 1959, file 3–24–20, vol. 115, RG 26, Library and Archives Canada.
116 Memo to the minister re: Approved Church Program, 3 June 1959, file 3–24–20, vol. 115, RG 26, Library and Archives Canada.
117 Laval Fortier to J.-B. Lanctôt, executive secretary, Catholic Immigrant Service, 3 July 1959, file 567–41, vol. 892, RG 76, Library and Archives Canada.
118 Fred Poulton, secretary, Department of Social Relations, Canadian Council of Churches, to Laval Fortier, deputy minister of citizenship and immigration, 20 August 1959, file 3–24–20, vol. 115, RG 26, Library and Archives Canada.
119 Canadian Christian Council for the Resettlement of Refugees, Canadian Council of Churches, Rural Settlement Society of Canada–Catholic Immigrant Service, Canadian Jewish Congress–Jewish Immigrant Aid Services.
120 Address by Ellen Fairclough at the Hamilton Council of Women, 6 November 1959, file 566–10–1, vol. 886, RG 76, Library and Archives Canada.
121 Dirks, *Canada's Refugee Policy*, 222.
122 World Refugee Year began on 28 June 1959.
123 Kelley and Trebilcock, *The Making of the Mosaic*, 348.
124 Ibid.
125 Knowles, *Strangers at Our Gates*, 186.

126 Madokoro, *Elusive Refuge*; Madokoro, "'Slotting' Chinese Families and Refugees."
127 Memo to the minister re: Approved Church Program, 3 June 1959.
128 Laval Fortier, deputy minister, to J.-B. Lanctôt, Catholic Immigrant Service, 3 July 1959.
129 Clifton L. Monk to Laval Fortier, Department of Citizenship and Immigration, 28 August 1959, file 3–24–20, vol. 115, RG 26, Library and Archives Canada.
130 Thompson and Bangarth, "Transnational Christian Charity," 296–7.
131 Beyer, "The Same or Not the Same," 4.
132 Somerville and Goodman, "The Role of Networks in the Development of UK Migration Policy."
133 Smith, *Pressure, Power, and Policy*, 10.
134 Nichols, *The Uneasy Alliance*, 97; McCleary, *Global Compassion*.
135 Smith, *Pressure, Power, and Policy*, 10.

CHAPTER FOUR

1 Triadafilopoulos, *Becoming Multicultural*; Triadafilopoulos, "Global Norms, Domestic Institutions and the Transformation of Immigration Policy in Canada and the US."
2 Tichenor, *Dividing Lines*, 221.
3 See Madokoro, "'Slotting' Chinese Families and Refugees," 50.
4 Dirks, *Canada's Refugee Policy*, 231.
5 Madokoro, "Good Material"; Dirks, *Canada's Refugee Policy*; Parai, "Canada's Immigration Policy."
6 Ptolemy, "Canadian Refugee Policies"; Ptolemy, "From Oppression to Promise"; Thompson, *In Defence of Principles*; Matthews, "The Christian Churches and Foreign Policy."
7 Diab, "Fear and (in)Security."
8 Anker, "U.S. Immigration and Asylum Policy," 78.
9 Loescher and Scanlan, *Calculated Kindness*, 63.
10 Ibid., 61.
11 Bon Tempo, *Americans at the Gate*, 109.
12 Murray, "Welcoming the Stranger," 127.
13 Baumgartner and Jones, *Agendas and Instability*.
14 Minutes of the meeting of the Migration and Refugee Affairs Committee, ACVA, with Tracy Voorhees, president's representative on Cuban refugees, 7 December 1960, box 71, MC 655, American Council of Voluntary Agencies for Foreign Service Papers, Rutgers University Archives.

15 Ibid.
16 Nichols, *The Uneasy Alliance*, 95.
17 Ibid.
18 Report to the President of the United States on the Cuban Refugee Problem, by Tracy Voorhees, 18 January 1961, box 495, part 2, Celler Papers, Library of Congress.
19 Bon Tempo, *Americans at the Gate*, 121.
20 Fey, *Cooperation in Compassion*, 125.
21 Church World Service Report to the U.S. Senate Subcommittee on Refugees and Escapees, 19 June 1970, file: DPs Hungary, World Refugee Year, box 114, RG 8, Church World Service Archives, Presbyterian Historical Society.
22 Murray, "Welcoming the Stranger," 125–46.
23 Ibid.
24 Ibid.
25 Ibid., 145.
26 John McCarthy, NCWC, to diocesan resettlement directors re: Cuban Refugee Program, 1 April 1966, box 28, collection 141, Mohler Papers, Catholic University of America.
27 Ibid.
28 Bon Tempo, *Americans at the Gate*, 129.
29 The United States and the Refugee, 5 December 1961, box 74, MC 655, American Council of Voluntary Agencies for Foreign Service Papers, Rutgers University Archives.
30 News Release: Celler Introduces Immigration Legislation to Eliminate National Origins Quota System, 21 February 1963, box 495, Part 2, Celler Papers, Library of Congress.
31 Testimony of Emanuel Celler before the House Judiciary Subcommittee on Immigration and Nationality, 11 June 1963, box 495, part 2, Celler Papers, Library of Congress.
32 Ibid. Emphasis in original.
33 Tichenor, *Dividing Lines*.
34 National Council of Churches Resolution on the Churches and United States Immigration Policy, 24 February 1965, file: DPs Hungary, World Refugee Year, box 114, RG 8, Church World Service Archives, Presbyterian Historical Society.
35 Statement by John E. McCarthy, NCWC, before the Immigration and Nationality Subcommittee of the House Judiciary Committee, 18 May 1965, box 48, series 23, NCWC Papers, Center for Migration Studies.
36 Hubert Humphrey, qtd. in Tichenor, *Dividing Lines*, 215.

37 Tichenor, *Dividing Lines*, 217.
38 Tichenor, "The Historical Presidency."
39 Ibid., 695.
40 Ibid., 700.
41 Bon Tempo, *Americans at the Gate*, 90.
42 Davis, *The Cold War*, 271–2.
43 Ibid., 280.
44 Ibid., 287.
45 Bon Tempo, *Americans at the Gate*, 97.
46 Davis, *The Cold War*, 276.
47 "Ex-Rep. Michael A. Feighan, 98; Architect of '65 Immigration Law," *New York Times*, 20 March 1992.
48 The American Legion testified in favour of the legislation, making this argument. See House Hearings, 20 May 1965, qtd. in Davis, *The Cold War*, 305.
49 Qtd. in Loescher and Scanlan, *Calculated Kindness*, 74.
50 Tichenor, *Dividing Lines*, 222.
51 Davis, *The Cold War*, 319.
52 Loescher and Scanlan, *Calculated Kindness*, 86.
53 Ibid., 89.
54 Anker and Posner, "The Forty Year Crisis," 21–30.
55 Ibid., 21.
56 Freeman and Betts, "The Politics of Interests and Immigration Policymaking in Australia and the United States," 82.
57 Loescher and Scanlan, *Calculated Kindness*, 87.
58 Moyn, *The Last Utopia*; Moyn, *Christian Human Rights*; Barnett, *The Star and the Stripes*.
59 Hoffmann, *Human Rights in the Twentieth Century*; Bon Tempo, *Americans at the Gate*.
60 Eckl and Moyn, *The Breakthrough*.
61 Bon Tempo, *Americans at the Gate*, 140; Barnett, *The Star and the Stripes*, 173.
62 Loescher and Scanlan, *Calculated Kindness*, 94–5.
63 Qtd. in Barnett, *The Star and the Stripes*, 180.
64 Ibid., 174. In August 1972 the Soviets instituted a "diploma tax" requiring Soviet Jews who applied for emigration to "repay" the cost of their public education.
65 Loescher and Scanlan, *Calculated Kindness*, 86; Barnett, *The Star and the Stripes*, 180.
66 Barnett, *The Star and the Stripes*, 176.

67 Religious News Service, "Solidarity with Soviet Jewry Pledged by Christian Leaders," 24 April 1972, 1972, Soviet Jewry, American Jewish Committee Digital Archives.
68 Press Release: "Senator Kennedy Comments on Emigration of Jews and Others from Soviet Union – Charges Administration with Broken Promises," 6 May 1973, box 77, MC 655, American Council of Voluntary Agencies Papers, Rutgers University Archives.
69 Ibid.
70 Loescher and Scanlan, *Calculated Kindness*, 90.
71 Anker and Posner, "The Forty Year Crisis," 25.
72 Nichols, *The Uneasy Alliance*, 109.
73 Loescher and Scanlan, *Calculated Kindness*, 92.
74 Nichols, *The Uneasy Alliance*, 111.
75 Bon Tempo, *Americans at the Gate*, 9, 138.
76 Statement by Senator Kennedy before a congressional hearing on refugee and humanitarian problems in Chile, 28 September 1973, box 77, MC 655, American Council of Voluntary Agencies Papers, Rutgers University Archives.
77 John W. Schauer, Church World Service, to Francis Kellogg, special assistant to the secretary of state for refugee and migration affairs, cc: House and Senate Judiciary Committee, members, 11 September 1974, box 77, MC 655, American Council of Voluntary Agencies Papers, Rutgers University Archives.
78 Response to Senator Kennedy on Provision of Asylum and Resettlement Opportunities to a Reasonable Number of Political Refugees from Chile, 24 October 1973, box 77, MC 655, American Council of Voluntary Agencies Papers, Rutgers University Archives.
79 Statement of Louis Wiesner, director, Office of Refugee and Migration Affairs, Department of State, to the Subcommittee on Immigration, Citizenship, and International Law, House Committee on the Judiciary, October 1974, box 77, MC 655, American Council of Voluntary Agencies Papers, Rutgers University Archives.
80 Bon Tempo, *Americans at the Gate*, 143.
81 Ibid.
82 Hawkins, *Canada and Immigration*, 137.
83 Laval Fortier to Saul Hayes, Canadian Jewish Congress, 14 June 1961, file 300, box 31, series CA, Canadian Jewish Congress Archives.
84 Admission of European Refugees to Canada and the Private Sponsorship Programmes, Department of Citizenship and Immigration, 1 November 1962, file 300, box 32, series CA, Canadian Jewish Congress Archives.

85 Soon after these new procedures were put in place, the director of immigration reported to the deputy minister: "While we continue to receive applications from sponsors for distant relatives or friends, cases involving private organization sponsorship are falling off." Acting director of immigration to the deputy minister, Department of Citizenship and Immigration, re: 1963 Refugee Program, 1 October 1962, file 566–10–1, vol. 886, RG 76, Library and Archives Canada.
86 Hawkins, *Canada and Immigration*, 307.
87 Ibid.
88 Madokoro, *Elusive Refuge*, 143.
89 Annual Report of the Department of Citizenship and Immigration, 1965–66.
90 Madokoro, *Elusive Refuge*, 143; Madokoro, "'Slotting' Chinese Families and Refugees," 50.
91 Dirks, *Canada's Refugee Policy*, 226.
92 Madokoro, "'Slotting' Chinese Families and Refugees," 51.
93 Kelley and Trebilcock, *The Making of the Mosaic*, 352.
94 Exceptions were the larger movements of Czechoslovakians in 1968 (~11,000), Asian Ugandans in 1972 (~7,000), and Chileans in 1973 (~7,000).
95 Hawkins, *Canada and Immigration*, 150.
96 Ibid., 152–3.
97 Ibid., 153–4.
98 Memorandum to cabinet from minister of citizenship and immigration re: Immigration White Paper – New Policy on Refugees, April 1965, vol. 724, RG 76, Library and Archives Canada. The memo still notes that "although our selection of refugees should not be racially biased, it would be folly to extend our 'unlimited' European refugee polices on a global scale," referring to concern about large admissions of Asian immigrants.
99 Immigration White Paper Study no. 15: Participation of the Canadian Public in Immigration, 14 May 1965, vols. 778 and 725, RG 76, Library and Archives Canada.
100 Ibid.
101 Ibid.
102 Qtd. in Dirks, *Canada's Refugee Policy*, 229.
103 Qtd. in Labman, *Crossing Law's Border*, 83.
104 Memo to the minister re: Approved Church Program, 3 June 1959.
105 Janzen, "The 1979 MCC Canada Master Agreement."
106 Department of Manpower and Immigration Annual Report, 1970–71.
107 Dirks, *Canada's Refugee Policy*, 231.

108 Ibid., 230.
109 Dirks, *Canada's Refugee Policy*, 233.
110 Troper, "Canada's Immigration Policy since 1945," 271.
111 Madokoro, "Good Material," 168.
112 Ibid., 166.
113 Ibid.
114 Dirks, *Canada's Refugee Policy*, 239.
115 Molloy and Madokoro, "Effecting Change," 56.
116 *Globe and Mail*, 26 August 1972.
117 Ibid.
118 Dirks, *Canada's Refugee Policy*, 243.
119 Kelley and Trebilcock, *The Making of the Mosaic*, 367.
120 Molloy and Madokoro, "Effecting Change"; Madokoro, "Good Material."
121 Ptolemy, "From Oppression to Promise," 145.
122 Canadian Groups Request the Canadian Government to Aid Refugees from Chile, 15 September 1973, vol. 8, B 58, MG 32, Library and Archives Canada.
123 Reftel from Santiago (Ambassador Ross) to Ottawa, 14 September 1973, vol. 9409, RG 25, Library and Archives Canada.
124 The leadership of the committee included Frances Arbour (United Church), George Cram (Anglican Church), John Foster (United Church), Ted Draimin (Jesuit Centre for Social Faith and Justice), and Fred Franklin (Society of Friends in Toronto).
125 Lind and Mihevc, *Coalitions for Justice*, 203–18.
126 Urtel from Ottawa to Santiago, 25 October 1973, vol. 9337, RG 25, Library and Archives Canada.
127 Telegram from Geoffrey Pearson re: Situation in Chile – Refugees, Immigrants, Asylees, 28 November 1973, vol. 9409, RG 25, Library and Archives Canada.
128 Ptolemy, "From Oppression to Promise," 145.
129 "Chilean Refugees: Canada's Reluctant Response," United Church of Canada, March 1974, vol. 190, I 327, MG 28, Library and Archives Canada.
130 Floyd Honey, Canadian Council of Churches, to Prime Minister Pierre Elliott Trudeau, 11 July 1974, vol. 185, I 327, MG 28, Library and Archives Canada.
131 Diab, "Fear and (in)Security."
132 Molloy and Madokoro, "Effecting Change," 56.
133 Floyd Honey, Canadian Council of Churches, to Robert Andras, minister of manpower and immigration, 5 December 1974, vol. 185, I 327, MG 28, Library and Archives Canada.

134 Molloy et al., *Running on Empty*, 69–70.
135 Memo from W.K. Bell to J. Cross, Department of Citizenship and Immigration, 14 September 1978, file 8620–8, vol. 1815, RG 76, Library and Archives Canada.
136 McFarland, *Neopluralism*, 155.
137 Molloy et al., *Running on Empty*, 70.

CHAPTER FIVE

1 Bon Tempo, *Americans at the Gate*, 167.
2 Adelman, "Causes of the Indochinese Refugee Exodus and Resettlement." As will be discussed below, the *Hai Hong* was a large boat transporting refugees which Malaysia refused to accept – forcing it to idle at sea until an international agreement could be reached.
3 Janzen, "The 1979 MCC Canada Master Agreement."
4 Molloy et al., *Running on Empty*, 104–52.
5 Anker and Posner, "The Forty Year Crisis," 30.
6 Leibowitz, "The Refugee Act of 1980," 164.
7 Tichenor, *Dividing Lines*, 246–8.
8 Anker and Posner, "The Forty Year Crisis," 64.
9 The United States and the Refugee, 5 December 1961, box 74, MC 655, American Council of Voluntary Agencies for Foreign Service Papers, Rutgers University Archives.
10 President's Advisory Committee on Refugees, Background Papers, Inter-Agency Task Force, 19 May 1975, box 19(2), John Marsh Files, Ford Library.
11 Bon Tempo, *Americans at the Gate*, 171–2.
12 Ibid.
13 Zolberg, *A Nation by Design*, 346.
14 Loescher and Scanlan, *Calculated Kindness*, 104.
15 Memo from Henry Kissinger to President Ford re: National Committee for Vietnamese and Cambodian Refugees, May 1975, box 19(1), John Marsh Files, Ford Library.
16 President's Advisory Committee on Refugees, Background Papers, Inter-Agency Task Force, 19 May 1975.
17 Ibid.
18 White House Press Release: Status Report: Refugees from Indochina, 24 December 1975, box 19, White House Press Releases, Ford Library.
19 Loescher and Scanlan, *Calculated Kindness*, 114.
20 Ibid.

21 North, Lewin, and Wagner, *Kaleidoscope*, 25.
22 Ibid.
23 Ibid.
24 Indochina Evacuation and Refugee Problems, a report prepared for the use of the Subcommittee on Refugees of the Senate Judiciary Committee, 94th Congress, First Session, 9 June 1975, box 2, Inter-Agency Task Force on Indochinese Refugees, RG 220, National Archives.
25 Telegram from U.S. secretary of state to civil coordinators, Refugee Resettlement re: Support for Voluntary Agencies, 2 July 1975, box 3, Inter-Agency Task Force on Indochinese Refugees, RG 220, National Archives.
26 The Role of the Voluntary Agencies in the Indo-China Refugee Resettlement Program – 1975, 14 January 1977, box 74, MC 655, American Council of Voluntary Agencies Papers, Rutgers University Archives.
27 Ibid.
28 Loescher and Scanlan, *Calculated Kindness*, 122.
29 Ibid., 129.
30 Smith, *Rescuing the World*, 177.
31 Loescher and Scanlan, *Calculated Kindness*, 130.
32 Ibid., 133.
33 Ibid.
34 Bon Tempo, *Americans at the Gate*, 152.
35 Loescher and Scanlan, *Calculated Kindness*, 133.
36 Smith, *Rescuing the World*, 121.
37 Minutes of a meeting of the Migration and Refugee Affairs Committee, American Council of Voluntary Agencies, with Dr Jessica Tuchman, director of the Office of Global Issues, National Security Council, 22 February 1978, entry P 483, box 20, RG 59, National Archives.
38 Ibid.
39 Loescher and Scanlan, *Calculated Kindness*, 135.
40 Ibid.
41 Ibid., 137.
42 Ibid., 141.
43 "Non-refoulement" is a principle of international law that prevents states from returning refugees or asylum seekers to countries where they will face persecution.
44 Ibid., 145.
45 Memo from Brzezinski to secretary of state, attorney general, and secretary of health, education, and welfare on refugee policy, 6 April 1978, entry P 483, box 16, RG 59, National Archives.

46 Ibid.
47 Cyrus Vance, secretary of state, to Griffin Bell, attorney general, 8 April 1978, entry P 483, box 16, RG 59, National Archives.
48 Tichenor, *Dividing Lines*, 246.
49 Press Release: "Senator Kennedy Introduces Bill to Overhaul US Refugee Policy," 15 March 1978, box 77, MC 655, American Council of Voluntary Agencies Papers, Rutgers University Archives.
50 USCC interoffice memo from John E. McCarthy to members of the Administrative Committee, re: Migration and Refugee Services, 8 January 1979, box 125, Migration and Refugee Services, Catholic University of America Archives.
51 Statement of Edward Swanstrom before the Committee on the Judiciary of the U.S. Senate, 14 March 1979, box 125, Migration and Refugee Services, Catholic University of America Archives.
52 Gimpel and Edwards, Jr, *The Congressional Politics of Immigration Reform*, 125.
53 Jerry M. Tinker, counsel for immigration and refugee affairs, Senate Committee of the Judiciary, to Ingrid Walter, chairman, ACVA, 5 April 1979, box 81, MG 655, American Council of Voluntary Agencies Papers, Rutgers University Archives.
54 Ingrid Walter to Senator Edward Kennedy, 12 July 1979, box 77, MC 655, American Council of Voluntary Agencies Papers, Rutgers University Archives.
55 Congressional Record, Senate, 18 July 1979, box 36, series "Judiciary Committee, 96th Congress," RG 46, National Archives.
56 Ingrid Walter to senators on behalf of the main voluntary groups, 31 August 1979, box 125, Migration and Refugee Services, Catholic University of America Archives.
57 Archbishop John Quinn, president of the United States Catholic Conference, to Senator Ted Kennedy, 12 June 1979, box 125, Migration and Refugee Services, Catholic University of America Archives.
58 Wells C. Klein, on behalf of the American Council of Voluntary Agencies, to Arthur Andres, House Subcommittee on Immigration, Refugees, and International Law, Committee of the Judiciary, 6 August 1979, box 81, MC 655, American Council of Voluntary Agencies Papers, Rutgers University Archives.
59 Gimpel and Edwards, Jr, *Congressional Politics*, 133.
60 Ibid., 144.
61 Tichenor, *Dividing Lines*, 234.
62 Bon Tempo, *Americans at the Gate*, 169.

63 Zolberg, *A Nation by Design*, 348.
64 Press Release: "Senator Kennedy Hails Final Congressional Action on the Refugee Act of 1980," 4 March 1980, box 36, series "Judiciary Committee, 96th Congress," RG 46, National Archives.
65 Tichenor, *Dividing Lines*, 219–88.
66 Meissner, "Political Asylum, Sanctuary, and Humanitarian Policy," 124.
67 Kelley and Trebilcock, *The Making of the Mosaic*, 374.
68 Andras, "A Historical Sketch of Canadian Immigration and Refugee Policy."
69 Girard, "The Evolution of Immigration Selection Policy."
70 Andras, "A Historical Sketch," 7.
71 Triadafilopoulos, *Becoming Multicultural*, 111.
72 Dirks, "The Green Paper and Canadian Refugee Policy."
73 Triadafilopoulos, *Becoming Multicultural*, 110–11. The paper argued that the introduction of "new racial groups into the population outstripped the ability of societies to adapt to ... changes harmoniously" and expressed concern over "consequences for national identity that might follow any significant change in the composition of the population."
74 Kelley and Trebilcock, *The Making of the Mosaic*; Hawkins, "Canada's Green Paper on Immigration Policy"; Dirks, "The Green Paper."
75 Triadafilopoulos, *Becoming Multicultural*, 110.
76 Knowles, *Strangers at Our Gates*, 207.
77 Janzen, "The 1979 MCC Canada Master Agreement," 216.
78 Kelley and Trebilcock, *The Making of the Mosaic*, 379.
79 Qtd. in Labman, *Crossing Law's Border*, 83.
80 Special Joint Committee of the Senate and the House of Commons on Immigration Policy: Report to Parliament, December 11, 1975 (Queen's Printer for Canada).
81 Ibid.
82 Hawkins, "Canada's Green Paper," 239. The others were non-discrimination in selection, selection according to labour-market needs, and an emphasis on family reunion.
83 Kelley and Trebilcock, *The Making of the Mosaic*, 378.
84 Knowles, *Strangers at Our Gates*, 208.
85 Triadafilopoulos, *Becoming Multicultural*, 116–17.
86 Wood, "East Indians and Canada's New Immigration Policy"; Triadafilopoulos, *Becoming Multicultural*, 117.
87 Kelley and Trebilcock, *The Making of the Mosaic*, 379.
88 "Gallup Report: Most Canadians Unwilling to Admit Refugees," 12 March 1977, vol. 7, box 58, MG 32, Library and Archives Canada.

"Canadians were asked if they felt Canada should relax its requirements for entry [so as to increase] significantly the number of refugees coming here. Nationally, 24% felt that we should, while 62% believe we should not."
89 See "Canada: Immigration Act, 1976–77, c. 52, s. 1," Refworld, www.refworld.org/docid/3ae6b5c60.html.
90 Labman, *Crossing Law's Border*, 83–4.
91 Ibid., 217.
92 Molloy et al., *Running on Empty*, 70.
93 Ibid., 71.
94 Ibid., 72.
95 Ibid., 74–5.
96 Ibid., 75.
97 Employment and Immigration Canada, *The Indochinese Refugees*, 8.
98 Memorandum to the minister of employment and immigration from J.L. Manion (deputy minister), 10 November 1977, file 8700–15, vol. 1838, RG 76, Library and Archives Canada.
99 Employment and Immigration Canada, *The Indochinese Refugees*, 8.
100 Memorandum to the minister of employment and immigration from J.L. Manion (deputy minister), 10 November 1977.
101 "Gallup Report: Canada Plans to Admit Too Many Indo-China Refugees," 21 March 1979, vol. 7, box 58, MG 32, Library and Archives Canada.
102 Employment and Immigration Canada, *The Indochinese Refugees*, 8.
103 Adelman, "Causes of the Indochinese Refugee Exodus," 4.
104 Letter from Minister of Foreign Affairs Don Jamieson to Minister of Employment and Immigration Bud Cullen, 20 December 1977, file 8700–15, vol. 2838, RG 76, Library and Archives Canada.
105 Circular memorandum on the resettlement of refugees and displaced persons, by R.G. Tait, 13 January 1978, file 8700–15, vol. 1838, RG 76, Library and Archives Canada.
106 Circular to regional directors of immigration from J.C. Best re: Refugee Sponsorship System, 22 August 1978, file 8630–1, vol. 1831, RG 76, Library and Archives Canada.
107 Molloy et al., *Running on Empty*, 95–8.
108 Ibid., 99.
109 Ibid.
110 "Asian Refugees Must Be Helped."
111 Confidential Circular Memorandum re: Indochina Refugees: Large Boat Escapees, from R.L. Bell to Canadian missions, November 1978, file 8700–15 V 2, vol. 1839, RG 76, Library and Archives Canada.
112 Employment and Immigration Canada, *The Indochinese Refugees*, 8

113 Molloy et al., *Running on Empty*, 118.
114 Information Strategy: Indochinese Refugee Movement, 30 July 1979, file 8700-12-1, vol. 1836, RG 76, Library and Archives Canada.
115 Molloy et al., *Running on Empty*, 119.
116 Ibid., 120.
117 "Notes for a Speech by the Secretary of State for External Affairs, Flora MacDonald, to the United Nations Conference on Refugees, Geneva," 20 July 1979. Qtd. in Molloy et al., *Running on Empty*, 506.
118 Molloy et al., *Running on Empty*, 122.
119 Knowles, *Strangers at Our Gates*, 175.
120 *Montreal Gazette*, 22 June 1979; "It's up to Us," *Globe and Mail*, 28 June 1979.
121 Adelman, "The Grassroots Response Then and Now."
122 Molloy et al., *Running on Empty*, 118.
123 Ibid., 119.
124 Janzen, "The 1979 MCC Canada Master Agreement," 211.
125 Molloy et al., *Running on Empty*, 75–6.
126 Master Agreements signed included the following: Mennonite Central Committee (5 March 1979); Presbyterian Church of Canada (9 March 1979); Council of Canadian Reformed Churches of Canada (5 April 1979); Canadian Lutheran World Relief (11 May 1979); World Vision of Canada (6 July 1979); United Church of Canada (23 July 1979); Baptist Convention of Ontario and Quebec (27 July 1979); National Council of YMCAs of Canada (1 August 1979); twenty-one Roman Catholic dioceses and five Anglican dioceses (August 1979); Baptist Union of Western Canada (10 August 1979); Ukrainian Canadian Committee (20 September 1979); Ontario Conference of Seventh Day Adventist Church (24 September 1979); United Baptist Convention Council of the Atlantic Provinces (25 September 1979); Seventh Day Adventist Church of Canada (26 October 1979); Christian and Missionary Alliance (31 October 1979). See "Refugee and Humanitarian Programs," 5 December 1979, file 8620-1, vol. 1811, RG 76, Library and Archives Canada.
127 Ibid.
128 Memo to Minister Ron Atkey from Deputy Minister J.D. Love, re: Indochinese Refugees: Consultation with Voluntary Agencies, 10 December 1979, file 8700, vol. 1838, RG 76, Library and Archives Canada.
129 Memorandum from Chief, Refugee Policy Division, re: Minister's Announcement on Indochinese Sponsorship Program, Summary of Breakfast Meeting (5 December 1979), 14 December 1979, file 8703-1, vol. 1839, RG 76, Library and Archives Canada.

130 Memo to Minister Atkey re: Committee of Organizations Concerned for Refugees, Annual Meeting, 12 December 1979, file 8700-12-1, vol. 1837, RG 76, Library and Archives Canada.
131 Indochinese Refugee Program, 1979-1980, Discussion Paper, Refugee Policy Division, 11 February 1980, file 8700, vol. 1836, RG 76, Library and Archives Canada.
132 Glen Cedar Conference on Refugees to minister of employment and immigration, re: Proposal for a Government Refugee Policy for South East Asia in 1980, 10 March 1980, file 8700-1, vol. 1836, RG 76, Library and Archives Canada.
133 Employment and Immigration Canada, *The Indochinese Refugees*.
134 Ibid., 20.
135 Ibid., 6.
136 "The Experiences of Sponsors of Indochinese Refugees: A Statistical Analysis," Immigration Program Division, 8 December 1981, file 8703-1, vol. 1839, RG 76, Library and Archives Canada.
137 Molloy and Madokoro, "Effecting Change," 58.
138 Canada's 1981 Refugee Resettlement Programs and the Prospects for 1982, 20 May 1981, file 8620-8, vol. 1815, RG 76, Library and Archives Canada. "A further, welcome result of the active partnership between government and the voluntary sector which characterized the special Indochinese program, has been the broadening of the consultation process leading to the preparation of the Annual Refugee Plan. For example, in the spring and summer of 1980, extensive consultations concerning 1981 programs took place, both through face to face discussions and written exchanges, with the leadership of all the major voluntary groups who wished to do so ... This process of consultation on a wide range of refugee issues is being continued and further developed in 1981 to reflect those factors identified by the groups concerned."
139 Molloy and Madokoro, "Effecting Change," 60. The latter quotation is from Kirk Bell.
140 Ibid.

CONCLUSION

1 Collier and Collier, *Shaping the Political Arena*, 29.
2 Capoccia and Kelemen, *The Study of Critical Junctures*, 355-6.
3 Price, *Rethinking Asylum*.
4 Madokoro, "Good Material."
5 Labman, "Private Sponsorship: Complementary or Conflicting Interests?"

6. Government of Canada, "Notice – Supplementary Information 2019–2021 Immigration Levels Plans."
7. Lenard, "How Should We Think about Private Sponsorship of Refugees?"
8. Cameron, "Reluctant Partnership."
9. Environics Institute, "Canada's World Survey 2018."
10. Markusoff, "Canada Now Brings in More Refugees than the U.S."
11. Amos, "For Refugees and Advocates, Trump Immigration Order Stay Leads to Disarray."
12. Kerwin, "The US Refugee Resettlement Program – a Return to First Principles."
13. Zucker and Zucker, *The Guarded Gate*, 103.
14. Ibid., 121–2.
15. Lutheran Immigration and Refugee Service, *The Real Cost of Welcome*.
16. Libal and Harding, "'Doing Something to Fight Injustice.'"
17. Kerwin, "The US Refugee Resettlement Program – a Return to First Principles."
18. See Hansen, "The Comprehensive Refugee Response Framework."
19. Stamatov, *The Origins of Global Humanitarianism*.

Bibliography

PRIMARY SOURCES

American Council of Voluntary Agencies Papers, MC 655, Rutgers University Archives, New Brunswick, NJ.
American Jewish Committee Digital Archives.
Bruce M. Mohler Papers, Collection 141, Catholic University of America, Washington, DC.
Canadian Council of Churches Papers, MG 28, Library and Archives Canada, Ottawa.
Canadian Jewish Congress Collection, Alex Dworkin Canadian Jewish Archives, Montreal.
Church World Service Archives, RG 8, Presbyterian Historical Society, Philadelphia.
Department of External Affairs Documents, RG 25, Library and Archives Canada, Ottawa.
Department of State Central Files, RG 59, National Archives and Records Administration, College Park, MD.
Emmanuel Celler Papers, Library of Congress, Washington, DC.
Inter-Agency Task Force on Indochinese Refugees, RG 220, National Archives and Records Administration, College Park, MD.
Jake Epp Papers, MG 32 B 58, Library and Archives Canada, Ottawa.
John Marsh Files, Gerald R. Ford Presidential Library, Ann Arbor, MI.
Migration and Refugee Services Collection, Catholic University of America Archives, Washington, DC.
National Catholic Welfare Conference Collection, Catholic University of America Archives, Washington, DC.

National Catholic Welfare Conference Files, Center for Migration Studies Archives, New York.
National Council of Churches Archives, RG 18, Presbyterian Historical Society, Philadelphia.
President Harry S. Truman Library Digital Archives, www.trumanlibrary.gov/library/online-collections.
Records of Citizenship and Immigration, RG 26, Library and Archives Canada, Ottawa.
Records of the Department of Employment and Immigration, RG 118, Library and Archives Canada, Ottawa.
Records of the Department of External Affairs, RG 25, Library and Archives Canada, Ottawa.
Records of the Immigration Branch, RG 76, Library and Archives Canada, Ottawa.
Records of the U.S. Foreign Assistance Agencies, 1948–1961, RG 469, National Archives and Records Administration, College Park, MD.
Records of the United States Senate, RG 46, National Archives and Records Administration, Washington, DC.
Tracy Voorhees Papers, Rutgers University Archives, New Brunswick, NJ.
War Relief Services Collection, Center for Migration Studies Archives, New York.
William Lyon Mackenzie King Papers, MG 26, Library and Archives Canada, Ottawa.
World Council of Churches Papers, Burke Library, Columbia University, New York.

SECONDARY SOURCES

Abella, Irving, and Harold Troper. *None Is Too Many: Canada and the Jews of Europe, 1933–1948*. New York: Random House 1983.
Adelman, Howard. "Canadian Refugee Policy in the Postwar Period: An Analysis." In Howard Adelman, ed., *Refugee Policy Canada and the United States*, 172–223. Staten Island, NY: Center for Migration Studies 1991.
– "Causes of the Indochinese Refugee Exodus and Resettlement." Unpublished manuscript (28 July 2015): 1–23.
– "The Grassroots Response Then and Now." Unpublished manuscript (28 July 2015): 1–30.
Allison, Graham T. *Essence of Decision: Explaining the Cuban Missile Crisis*. Boston: Little Brown 1971.

Bibliography

Amos, Deborah. "For Refugees and Advocates, Trump Immigration Order Stay Leads to Disarray." *National Public Radio*, 13 February 2017, www.npr.org/sections/parallels/2017/02/13/514966051/for-refugees-and-advocates-trump-immigration-order-stay-leads-to-disarray.

Anderson, Christopher G. *Canadian Liberalism and the Politics of Border Control, 1867–1967*. Vancouver: University of British Columbia Press 2012.

Andras, Robert. "A Historical Sketch of Canadian Immigration and Refugee Policy." In Howard Adelman, ed., *The Indochinese Refugee Movement the Canadian Experience*, 3–9. Toronto: Operation Lifeline 1980.

Anker, Deborah E. "U.S. Immigration and Asylum Policy: A Brief Historical Perspective." *In Defense of the Alien* 13 (1 January 1990): 74–85.

Anker, Deborah E., and Michael H. Posner. "The Forty Year Crisis: A Legislative History of the Refugee Act of 1980." *San Diego Law Review* 19, no. 9 (1982): 1–83.

Araral, Eduardo, et al., eds. *Routledge Handbook of Public Policy*. London: Routledge 2012.

Arendt, Hannah. *The Origins of Totalitarianism*. New York: Houghton Mifflin Harcourt 1951.

Arthur, W. Brian. "Competing Technologies, Increasing Returns, and Lock-in by Historical Events." *Economic Journal* 99, no. 394 (5 October 2007): 116–31.

"Asian Refugees Must Be Helped." *Toronto Star*, 15 November 1978.

Atkinson, David. *The Burden of White Supremacy: Containing Asian Migration in the British Empire and the United States*. Chapel Hill: University of North Carolina Press 2016.

Barnett, Michael. *Empire of Humanity: A History of Humanitarianism*. Ithaca, NY: Cornell University Press 2011.

– *The Star and the Stripes: A History of the Foreign Policies of American Jews*. Princeton, NJ: Princeton University Press 2016.

Basok, Tanya, and Alan Simmons. "A Review of the Politics of Canadian Refugee Selection." In Vaughan Robinson, ed., *The International Refugee Crisis: British and Canadian Responses*, 132–57. London: Refugee Studies Programme 1993.

Baumgartner, Frank R., and Bryan D. Jones. *Agendas and Instability in American Politics*, 2nd ed. Chicago: University of Chicago Press 1993.

Baumgartner, Frank R., and B.L. Leech. *Basic Interests: The Importance of Groups in Politics and in Political Science*. Princeton, NJ: Princeton University Press 1998.

Bennett, John C. "Breakthrough in Ecumenical Social Ethics: The Legacy of the Oxford Conference on Church, Community, and State (1937)." *Ecumenical Review* 40, no. 2 (1 April 1988): 132–46.
Berger, Peter. *The Sacred Canopy: Elements of a Sociological Theory of Religion*. New York: Random House 1967.
Betts, Alexander. "Institutional Proliferation and the Global Refugee Regime." *Perspectives on Politics* 7, no. 1 (12 February 2009): 53–8.
– "North-South Cooperation in the Refugee Regime: The Role of Linkages." *Global Governance* 14, no. 2 (1 April 2008): 157–78.
– "Public Goods Theory and the Provision of Refugee Protection: The Role of the Joint-Product Model in Burden-Sharing Theory." *Journal of Refugee Studies* 16, no. 3 (1 September 2003): 274–96.
Betts, Alexander, and Gil Loescher. "Introduction: Continuity and Change in Global Refugee Policy." *Refugee Survey Quarterly* 33, no. 1 (March 2014): 1–7.
Beyer, Jürgen. "The Same or Not the Same: On the Variety of Mechanisms of Path Dependence." *International Journal of Social Sciences* 5, no. 1 (2010): 1–11.
Beyer, Peter. "Deprivileging Religion in a Post-Westphalian State." In Winnifred Sullivan and Lori Beaman, eds., *Varieties of Religious Establishment*, 75–92. New York: Routledge 2013.
Bockley, Kathryn M. "A Historical Overview of Refugee Legislation: The Deception of Foreign Policy in the Land of Promise." *North Carolina Journal of International Law and Commercial Regulation* 21 (1995): 253–91.
Bon Tempo, Carl J. *Americans at the Gate: The United States and Refugees during the Cold War*. Princeton, NJ: Princeton University Press 2008.
Brown, Anastasia, and Todd Scribner. "Unfulfilled Promises, Future Possibilities: The Refugee Resettlement System in the United States." *Journal on Migration and Human Security* 2, no. 2 (2014): 101–20.
Bumsted, John M. *Canada's Diverse Peoples: A Reference Sourcebook*. Oxford: ABC CLIO 2003.
Cameron, Geoffrey. "Reluctant Partnership: A Political History of Private Sponsorship in Canada (1947–1980)." In Shauna Labman and Geoffrey Cameron, eds., *Strangers to Neighbours: Refugee Sponsorship in Context*, 19–41. Montreal and Kingston: McGill-Queen's University Press 2020.
Cameron, Geoffrey, and Shauna Labman. "Private Refugee Sponsorship: An Evolving Framework for Refugee Resettlement." In Shauna Labman and Geoffrey Cameron, eds., *Strangers to Neighbours: Refugee*

Sponsorship in Context, 3–15. Montreal and Kingston: McGill-Queen's University Press 2020.

"Canada: Immigration Act, 1976–77, c. 52, s. 1." Refworld, www.refworld.org/docid/3ae6b5c60.html.

Capoccia, Giovanni, and R. Daniel Kelemen. "The Study of Critical Junctures: Theory, Narrative, and Counterfactuals in Historical Institutionalism." *World Politics* 59, no. 3 (2007): 341–69.

Casanova, José. *Public Religions in the Modern World*. Chicago: University of Chicago Press 1994.

Caza, Melissa. "Organizing Relief: A Review of the Records of the United Jewish Relief Agencies of Toronto, 1938–1953." *Canadian Jewish Studies* 24 (2016): 176–81.

Chamedes, Giuliana. *A Twentieth-Century Crusade: The Vatican's Battle to Remake Christian Europe*. Cambridge, MA: Harvard University Press 2019.

Chiba, Hiromi. "The Role of the Protestant Church in the US Refugee Resettlement Program during the Early Cold War Era: The Methodist Case." *Exchange* 43 (2014): 9–28.

Choquette, Robert. "The Archdiocese of Toronto and Its Metropolitan Influence in Ontario." In Mark McGowan and Brian P. Clarke, eds., *Catholics at the Gathering Place: Historical Essays on the Archdiocese of Toronto, 1841–1991*, 297–31. Toronto: Dundurn Press 1993.

Clark, Peter B., and James Q. Wilson. "Incentive Systems: A Theory of Organizations." *Administrative Sciences Quarterly* 6, no. 2 (September 1961): 129–66.

Cohen, Gerard Daniel. *In War's Wake: Europe's Displaced Persons in the Postwar Order*. Oxford: Oxford University Press 2011.

Collier, Ruth Berins, and David Collier. *Shaping the Political Arena: Critical Junctures, the Labor Movement, and Regime Dynamics in Latin America*. Notre Dame, IN: University of Notre Dame Press 1991.

Couldrey Marion, and Maurice Herson, eds. "Resettlement." *Forced Migration Review* 54 (February 2017).

Culpepper, Pepper D. *Quiet Politics and Business Power: Corporate Control in Europe and Japan*. Cambridge: Cambridge University Press 2012.

Curtis, Heather D. *Holy Humanitarians: American Evangelicals and Global Aid*. Cambridge, MA: Harvard University Press 2018.

Dauvergne, Catherine. *Making People Illegal: What Globalization Means for Migration and Law*. Cambridge: Cambridge University Press 2008.

Davies, Alan, and Marilyn F. Nefsky. *How Silent Were the Churches?: Canadian Protestantism and the Jewish Plight during the Nazi Era.* Waterloo, ON: Wilfrid Laurier University Press 1998.

Davis, Michael Gill. "The Cold War, Refugees and U.S. Immigration Policy, 1952–1965." PhD diss., Vanderbilt University, 1996.

deLeon, Peter, and Linda deLeon. "What Ever Happened to Policy Implementation?: An Alternative Approach." *Journal of Public Administration Research and Theory* 12, no. 4 (2002): 467–92.

Diab, Suha. "Fear and (in)Security: The Canadian Government's Response to the Chilean Refugees." *Refuge* 31, no. 2 (28 November 2015): 51–62.

Dirks, Gerald E. *Canada's Refugee Policy: Indifference or Opportunism?* Montreal and Kingston: McGill-Queen's University Press 1977.

– "The Green Paper and Canadian Refugee Policy." *Canadian Ethnic Studies* 7, no. 1 (1 January 1975): 61–5.

Dowding, Keith. "Model or Metaphor?: A Critical Review of the Network Approach." *Political Studies* 43, no. 1 (1995): 136–58.

"Drive Is Opened to Admit 100,000 Jews into US." *Herald Tribune*, 10 October 1946.

Duranti, Marco. *The Conservative Human Rights Revolution: European Identity, Transnational Politics, and the Origins of the European Convention.* New York: Oxford University Press 2017.

Eckl, Jan, and Samuel Moyn, eds. *The Breakthrough: Human Rights in the 1970s.* Philadelphia: University of Pennsylvania Press 2014.

Egan, Eileen. *Catholic Relief Services, the Beginning Years: For the Life of the World.* New York: Catholic Relief Services 1988.

Employment and Immigration Canada. *The Indochinese Refugees: The Canadian Response, 1979 and 1980.* Ottawa: Minister of Supply and Services Canada 1980.

Environics Institute. "Canada's World Survey 2018." Accessed 18 August 2019. www.environicsinstitute.org/projects/project-details/canada%27s-world-2017-survey.

"Ex-Rep. Michael A. Feighan, 98; Architect of '65 Immigration Law." *New York Times*, 20 March 1992.

"Exsul Familia Nazarethana: Apostolic Constitution of Pius XII, dated August 1, 1952." Papal Encyclicals Online. Accessed 21 January 2016. www.papalencyclicals.net/Pius12/p12exsul.htm.

Fay, Terence J. *A History of Canadian Catholics: Gallicanism, Romanism, and Canadianism.* Montreal and Kingston: McGill-Queen's University Press 2002.

Fey, Harold Edward. *Cooperation in Compassion: The Story of the Church World Service*. New York: Friendship Press 1966.

Freeman, Gary P., and Katharine Betts. "The Politics of Interests and Immigration Policymaking in Australia and the United States." In Gary P. Freeman and James Jupp, eds., *Nations of Immigrants Australia, the United States, and International Migration*, 72–88. Oxford: Oxford University Press 1992.

Garnier, Adele, Liliana Lyra Jubilut, and Kristin Bergtora Sandvik, eds. *Refugee Resettlement: Power, Politics, and Humanitarian Governance*. Oxford: Berghahn Books 2018.

Gatrell, Peter. *Free World?: The Campaign to Save the World's Refugees, 1956–1963*. Cambridge: Cambridge University Press 2011.

Genizi, Haim. *American Apathy: The Plight of Christian Refugees from Nazism*. Israel: Bar-Ilan University Pres 1983.

– *America's Fair Share: The Admission and Resettlement of Displaced Persons, 1945–1952*. Detroit, MI: Wayne State University Press 1994.

– *The Holocaust, Israel, and Canadian Protestant Churches*. Montreal and Kingston: McGill-Queen's University Press 2002.

Gibney, Matthew J. *The Ethics and Politics of Asylum: Liberal Democracy and the Response to Refugees*. Cambridge: Cambridge University Press 2009.

Gibney, Matthew J., and Randall Hansen. "Asylum Policy in the West: Past Trends, Future Possibilities." In George J. Borjas and Jeff Crisp, eds., *Poverty, International Migration and Asylum*, 70–96. Hampshire, UK: Palgrave 2005.

Gibson, John W. "The Displaced Placed." *Journal of International Affairs* 7, no. 1 (1953): 75–81.

Gilmour, Julie. "'The Kind of People Canada Wants': Canada and the Displaced Persons, 1943–1953." PhD diss., University of Toronto, 2009.

Gimpel, James G., and James R. Edwards, Jr. *The Congressional Politics of Immigration Reform*. New York: Longman 1998.

Girard, Raphael. "The Evolution of Immigration Selection Policy: Diversity in the Canadian Population." Lecture, the Balsillie School of International Affairs, Waterloo, ON, 25 January 2017.

Goodall, Christine. "Shouting towards the Sky: The Role of Individuals, Communities, Organizations and Institutions in Support for Refugees and Asylum Seekers." *UNHCR Policy Development and Evaluation Service*, 4 May 2015. www.unhcr.org/research/working/554764b49/shouting-towards-sky-role-religious-individuals-communities-organisations.html.

Government of Canada. "Notice – Supplementary Information 2019–2021 Immigration Levels Plan." Accessed 18 August 2019. www.canada.ca/en/immigration-refugees-citizenship/news/notices/supplementary-immigration-levels-2019.html.

Green, Alan G. *Immigration and the Postwar Canadian Economy*. Toronto: Macmillan 1976.

Greif, Mark. *The Age of the Crisis of Man: Thought and Fiction in America, 1933–1973*. Princeton, NJ: Princeton University Press 2016.

Grzymala-Busse, Anna. *Nations under God: How Churches Use Moral Authority to Influence Policy*. Princeton, NJ: Princeton University Press 2015.

– "Weapons of the Meek: How Churches Influence Public Policy." *World Politics* 68, no. 1 (2 November 2015): 1–36.

Gurowitz, Amy. "Mobilizing International Norms: Domestic Actors, Immigrants, and the Japanese State." *World Politics* 51, no. 3 (1 April 1999): 413–45.

Hacker, Jacob S., Paul Pierson, and Kathleen Thelen. "Drift and Conversion: Hidden Faces of Institutional Change." In James Mahoney and Kathleen Thelen, eds., *Advances in Comparative-Historical Analysis*, 180–210. New York: Cambridge University Press 2015.

Hampshire, James. *The Politics of Immigration: Contradictions of the Liberal State*. Cambridge: Polity 2013.

Handlin, Oscar. *A Continuing Task: The American Jewish Joint Distribution Committee, 1914–1964*. New York: Random House 1964.

Hansen, Randall. *Citizenship and Immigration in Post-War Britain: The Institutional Origins of a Multicultural Nation*. Oxford: Oxford University Press 2000.

– "The Comprehensive Refugee Response Framework: A Commentary," *Journal of Refugee Studies* 31, no. 2 (June 2018): 131–51.

Hansen, Randall, and Desmond King. "Eugenic Ideas, Political Interests, and Policy Variance: Immigration and Sterilization Policy in Britain and the US." *World Politics* 53, no. 2 (2001): 237–63.

Hashimoto, Naoko. "Refugee Resettlement as an Alternative to Asylum." *Refugee Survey Quarterly* 37, no. 2 (2018): 162–86.

Hathaway, James C., and R. Alexander Neve, "Making International Refugee Law Relevant Again: A Proposal for Collectivized and Solution-Oriented Protection." *Harvard Human Rights Journal* 10 (1997): 115–211.

Hawkins, Freda. *Canada and Immigration: Public Policy and Public Concern*. Montreal and Kingston: McGill-Queen's University Press 1988.

- "Canada's Green Paper on Immigration Policy." *International Migration Review* 9, no. 2 (summer 1975): 237–49.
- *Critical Years in Immigration: Canada and Australia Compared*, 2nd ed. Montreal and Kingston: McGill-Queen's University Press 1991.

Heclo, Hugh. "Issue Networks and the Executive Establishment." In Anthony King, ed., *The New American Political System*, 87–107, 115–24. Washington, DC: Aei Press 1978.

Hertzke, Allen D. 2012. www.pewforum.org/2011/11/21/lobbying-for-the-faithful-exec/.

- "Religious Interest Groups in American Politics." In James L. Guth, Lyman A. Kellstedt, and Corwin E. Smidt, eds., *The Oxford Handbook of Religion and American Politics*, 299–329. Oxford: Oxford University Press 2009. Oxford Handbooks Online.

Hildreth, Anne. "The Importance of Purposes in 'Purposive' Groups: Incentives and Participation in the Sanctuary Movement." *American Journal of Political Science* 38, no. 2 (1994): 447–63.

Hoffmann, Stefan-Ludwig, ed. *Human Rights in the Twentieth Century*. New York: Cambridge University Press 2010.

Hollinger, David. *Protestants Abroad: How Missionaries Tried to Change the World but Changed America*. Princeton, NJ: Princeton University Press 2017.

House of Commons Debates, vol. 100, no. 15, 5th session, 22nd Parliament.

Hyman, Abraham S. "Displaced Persons." *American Jewish Year Book* 51, no. 1950 (1950): 315–24.

Hyndman, Jennifer, William Payne, and Shauna Jimenez. "Private Refugee Sponsorship in Canada." *Forced Migration Review* 54 (2017): 56–9.

Inboden, William. *Religion and American Foreign Policy: 1945–1960; The Soul of Containment*. Cambridge: Cambridge University Press 2010.

"It's up to Us." *Globe and Mail*, 28 June 1979.

Jacobs, Alan. *The Year of Our Lord 1943: Christian Humanism in an Age of Crisis*. Oxford: Oxford University Press 2018.

Jacobson, David. *Rights across Borders: Immigration and the Decline of Citizenship*. Baltimore, MD: John Hopkins University Press 1996.

Janzen, William. "The 1979 MCC Canada Master Agreement for the Sponsorship of Refugees in Historical Perspective." *Journal of Mennonite Studies* 24 (2006): 211–22.

John, Peter. *Analyzing Public Policy*, 2nd ed. London: Routledge 2012.

Jones, Bryan D., and Frank Baumgartner. "A Model of Choice for Public Policy." *Journal of Public Administration Research and Theory* 15, no. 3 (2005): 325–51.

Jordan, Grant. "Sub-Governments, Policy Communities and Networks: Refilling Old Bottles?" *Journal of Theoretical Politics* 2, no. 3 (1990): 1–20.

Kelley, Ninette, and Michael Trebilcock. *The Making of the Mosaic: A History of Canadian Immigration Policy*. Toronto: University of Toronto Press 2010.

Kenis, Patrick, and Volker Schneider. "Policy Networks and Policy Analysis: Scrutinizing a New Analytical Toolbox." In Bernd Marin and Renate Mayntz, eds., *Policy Networks: Empirical Evidence and Theoretical Considerations*, 25–59. Boulder, CO: Policy Networks 1991.

Kerwin, Donald. "The US Refugee Resettlement Program – a Return to First Principles: How Refugees Help to Define, Strengthen, and Revitalize the United States." *Journal on Migration and Human Security* 6, no. 3 (2018): 205–25.

Keyserlingk, Robert H. *Breaking Ground: The 1956 Hungarian Refugee Movement to Canada*. Toronto: York Lanes Press 1993.

King, David. *God's Internationalists: World Vision and the Age of Evangelical Humanitarianism*. Philadelphia: University of Pennsylvania Press 2019.

Kingdon, John. *Agendas, Alternatives, and Public Policies*. Boston: Little Brown 1984.

Knowles, Valerie. *Strangers at Our Gates: Canadian Immigration and Immigration Policy, 1540–2006*, rev. ed. Toronto: Dundurn Press 2007.

Labman, Shauna. *Crossing Law's Border: Canada's Refugee Resettlement Program*. Vancouver: University of British Columbia Press 2019.

– "At Law's Border: Unsettling Refugee Resettlement." PhD diss., University of British Columbia, 2012.

– "Private Sponsorship: Complementary or Conflicting Interests?" *Refuge: Canada's Journal on Refugees* 32, no. 2 (2016): 67–80.

Lacroix, Patrick. "Immigration, Minority Rights, and Catholic Policy-Making in Post-War Canada." *Social History* 47, no. 93 (16 May 2014): 183–203.

Leech, Beth L., et al. "Drawing Lobbyists to Washington: Government Activity and the Demand for Advocacy." *Political Research Quarterly* 58, no. 1 (March 2005): 19–30.

Leibowitz, Arnold H. "The Refugee Act of 1980: Problems and Congressional Concerns." *Annals of the American Academy of Political and Social Science* 467, no. 1 (1 May 1983): 163–71.

Lenard, Patti Tamara. "How *Should* We Think about Private Sponsorship of Refugees?" In Shauna Labman and Geoffrey Cameron, eds.,

Strangers to Neighbours: Refugee Sponsorship in Context, 61–73. Montreal and Kingston: McGill-Queen's University Press 2020.

Levi, Margaret. "A Model, a Method, and a Map: Rational Choice in Comparative and Historical Analysis." In Mark Irving Lichbach and Alan S. Zuckerman, eds., *Comparative Politics Rationality, Culture, and Structure*, 19–41. Cambridge: Cambridge University Press 1997.

Levine, Daniel H. "Review: Religion and Politics in Comparative and Historical Perspective." *Comparative Politics* 19, no. 1 (1 October 1986): 95–122.

Libal, Kathryn, and Scott Harding. "'Doing Something to Fight Injustice': Voluntarism and Refugee Resettlement as Political Engagement in the United States." In Shauna Labman and Geoffrey Cameron, eds., *Strangers to Neighbours: Refugee Sponsorship in Context*, 247–63. Montreal and Kingston: McGill-Queen's University Press 2020.

Lind, Christopher, and Joseph Mihevc, eds. *Coalitions for Justice: The Story of Canada's Interchurch Coalitions*. Ottawa: Novalis Press 1994.

Lipset, Seymour Martin. *Continental Divide: The Values and Institutions of the United States and Canada*. London: Routledge 1990.

Loescher, Gil, Alexander Betts, and James Milner. *The United Nations High Commissioner for Refugees (UNHCR): The Politics and Practice of Refugee Protection into the Twenty-First Century*, 1st ed. London: Routledge 2008.

Loescher, Gil, and John A. Scanlan. *Calculated Kindness: Refugees and America's Half-Open Door, 1945–Present*. New York: Simon and Schuster 1998.

Lutheran Immigration and Refugee Service. *The Real Cost of Welcome: A Financial Analysis of Local Refugee Reception*. Baltimore, MD: LIRS 2009.

Macklin, Audrey, et al. "A Preliminary Investigation into Private Refugee Sponsors." *Canadian Ethnic Studies* 50, no. 2 (2018): 35–57.

Madokoro, Laura. *Elusive Refuge: Chinese Migrants in the Cold War*. Cambridge, MA: Harvard University Press 2016.

– "Good Material: Canada and the Prague Spring Refugees." *Refuge: Canada's Journal on Refugees* 26, no. 1 (8 October 2010): 161–71.

– "'Slotting' Chinese Families and Refugees, 1947–1967." *Canadian Historical Review* 93, no. 1 (2011): 25–56.

Mahoney, James. "Path Dependence in Historical Sociology." *Theory and Society* 29, no. 4 (2000): 507–48.

Mahoney, James, and Kathleen Thelen. *Explaining Institutional Change: Ambiguity, Agency, and Power.* Cambridge: Cambridge University Press 2009.

Mahoney, James, and Kathleen Thelen, eds. *Advances in Comparative-Historical Analysis.* New York: Cambridge University Press 2015.

Markusoff, Jason. "Canada Now Brings in More Refugees than the U.S." *Maclean's,* 23 January 2019, www.macleans.ca/news/canada/refugee-resettlement-canada/.

Marsh, David, and R.A.W. Rhodes, *Policy Networks in British Government.* Oxford: Clarendon Press 1992.

Matthews, Robert O. "The Christian Churches and Foreign Policy: An Assessment." In Bonnie Greene, ed., *Canadian Churches and Foreign Policy,* 161–79. Toronto: James Lorimer and Company 1990.

Mavelli, Luca, and Erin K. Wilson, eds. *The Refugee Crisis and Religion: Secularism, Security and Hospitality in Question.* London: Rowman and Littlefield 2017.

McCleary, Rachel M. *Global Compassion: Private Voluntary Organizations and U.S. Foreign Policy since 1939.* Oxford: Oxford University Press 2009.

McFarland, Andrew S. "Interest Group Theory." In L. Sandy Maisel and Jeffrey M. Berry, eds., *The Oxford Handbook of American Political Parties and Interest Groups,* 37–56. Oxford: Oxford University Press 2010.

– *Neopluralism: The Evolution of Political Process Theory.* Lawrence: University Press of Kansas 2004.

Meissner, Doris M. "Political Asylum, Sanctuary, and Humanitarian Policy." In Bruce J. Nichols and Gil Loescher, eds., *The Moral Nation Humanitarianism and US Foreign Policy Today,* 123–43. South Bend, IA: University of Notre Dame Press 1989.

Miller, Sarah Deardoff. "Global Refugee Policy: Varying Perspectives, Unanswered Questions." Oxford: Refugee Studies Centre 2012. www.rsc.ox.ac.uk/files/files-1/dp-global-refugee-policy-conference.pdf.

Milner, James. "Introduction: Understanding Global Refugee Policy." *Journal of Refugee Studies* 27, no. 4 (2014): 477–94.

Molloy, Michael J., et al. *Running on Empty: Canada and the Indochinese Refugees, 1975–1980.* Montreal and Kingston: McGill-Queen's University Press 2017.

Molloy, Michael J., and Laura Madokoro. "Effecting Change: Civil Servants and Refugee Policy in 1970s Canada." *Refuge: Canada's Journal on Refugees* 33, no. 1 (2017): 52–61.

Moyn, Samuel. *Christian Human Rights*. Philadelphia: University of Pennsylvania Press 2015.
- *The Last Utopia: Human Rights in History*. Cambridge, MA: Harvard University Press 2012.
- "Personalism, Community, and the Origins of Human Rights." In Stefan-Ludwig Hoffmanm, ed., *Human Rights in the Twentieth Century*, 85–104. New York: Cambridge University Press 2010.
Murray, George V. "Welcoming the Stranger: the American Catholic Church and Refugee Newcomers, 1936–1980." PhD diss., George Washington University, 1995.
Nawyn, William E. *American Protestantism's Response to Germany's Jews and Refugees, 1933–1941*. Ann Arbor, MI: UMI Research Press 1981.
"New Directive on Immigrant Visas to the US." United States Holocaust Memorial Museum. www.ushmm.org/learn/timeline-of-events/1942-1945/truman-directive-on-immigrant-visas.
Nichols, J. Bruce. *The Uneasy Alliance: Religion, Refugee Work, and U.S. Foreign Policy*. New York: Oxford University Press 1988.
Norris, James J. "The International Catholic Migration Commission." *Catholic Lawyer* 4, no. 118 (1 January 1958): 118–22.
North, David S., Lawrence S. Lewin, and Jennifer R. Wagner. *Kaleidoscope: The Resettlement of Refugees in the United States by the Voluntary Agencies*. New TransCentury Foundation 1982.
Nurser, Canon John. "The 'Ecumenical Movement' Churches, 'Global Order,' and Human Rights: 1938–1948." *Human Rights Quarterly* 25, no. 4 (1 November 2003): 841–81.
Oldham, J.H. "The Function of the Church in Society," prepared for the Universal Christian Council for Life and World Research Department, January 1937. File 2, box 4, series 1, WCC Papers, Burke Library, Columbia University.
Olson, Mancur. *The Logic of Collective Action: Public Goods and the Theory of Groups*. Cambridge, MA: Harvard University Press 1965.
Parai, Louis. "Canada's Immigration Policy, 1962–1974." *International Migration Review* 9, no. 4 (1975): 449–77.
Penkower, Monty N. "Jewish Organizations and the Creation of the U.S. War Refugee Board." *Annals of the American Academy of Political and Social Science* 450, no. 1 (1980): 122–39.
Philpott, Daniel. "Has the Study of Global Politics Found Religion?" *Annual Review of Political Science* 12 (2009): 183–202.
Pierson, Paul. "Increasing Returns, Path Dependence, and the Study of Politics." *American Political Science Review* 94, no. 2 (2000): 251–67.

- "Power and Path Dependence." In James Mahoney and Kathleen Thelen, eds., *Advances in Comparative-Historical Analysis*, 123–46. Cambridge: Cambridge University Press, 2015.
Price, Matthew E. *Rethinking Asylum, History, Purpose, and Limits.* Cambridge: Cambridge University Press 2009.
Ptolemy, Kathleen. "Canadian Refugee Policies." *International Review of Mission* 71, no. 283 (1982): 362–67.
- "From Oppression to Promise: Journeying Together with the Refugee." In Bonnie Greene, ed., *Canadian Churches and Foreign Policy*, 143–60. Toronto: James Lorimer and Company 1990.
Putnam, Robert D., and David E. Campbell. *American Grace: How Religion Divides and Unites Us.* New York: Simon and Schuster 2012.
Riera, José, and Marie-Claude Poirier. "'Welcoming the Stranger' and UNHCR's Cooperation with Faith-Based Organisations." *Forced Migration Review* 48 (18 November 2014): 64–8.
Roof, Tracy. "Interest Groups." In Daniel Béland, Kimberly J. Morgan, and Christopher Howard, eds., *The Oxford Handbook of U.S. Social Policy*, 83–7. Oxford: Oxford University Press 2014.
Rudolph, Susanne Hoeber, and James Piscatori, eds. *Transnational Religion and Fading States.* Boulder, CO: Westview Press 1997.
Sabatier, Paul. "Top-Down and Bottom-Up Approaches to Implementation Research: A Critical Analysis and Suggested Synthesis." *Journal of Public Policy* 6, no. 1 (1986): 21–48.
Sabatier, Paul, and Daniel Mazmanian. "The Implementation of Public Policy: A Framework of Analysis." *Policy Studies Journal* 8, no. 4 (January 1980): 538–60.
Sabatier, Paul, and Hank Jenkins-Smith. *Policy Change and Learning: An Advocacy Coalition Approach.* Boulder, CO: Westview Press 1993.
Salehyan, Idean. *The Strategic Case for Refugee Resettlement.* Washington, DC: Niskanen Center 2018.
Salisbury, R.H. "An Exchange Theory of Interest Groups." *Midwest Journal of Political Science* 1 (1969): 1–32.
Sanua, Marianne R. *Let Us Prove Strong: The American Jewish Committee, 1945–2006.* Lebanon, NH: Brandeis University Press 2007.
Sauer, Angelika E. "A Matter of Domestic Policy?: Canadian Immigration Policy and the Admission of Germans, 1945–50." *Canadian Historical Review* 74, no. 2 (June 1993): 226–63.
Schattschneider, E.E. *The Semi-Sovereign People: A Realist's View of Democracy in America.* New York: Holt, Reinhart and Winston 1960.

Schmalz, Ronald E. "Former Enemies Come to Canada: Ottawa and the Postwar German Immigration Boom, 1951–57." PhD diss., University of Ottawa, 2000.

Schmitter, Philippe C. "Still the Century of Corporatism?" *Review of Politics* 36, no. 1 (January 1974): 85–131.

Scribner, Todd. "'Pilgrims of the Night': The American Catholic Church Responds to the Post-World War II Displaced Persons Crisis." *American Catholic Studies* 124, no. 3 (2013): 1–20.

Shah, Timothy Samuel. *Faith on Fire: The Global Expansion of Political Religion*. Stanford, CA: Hoover Institution Press 2011.

Shaw, Caroline. *Britannia's Embrace: Modern Humanitarianism and the Imperial Origins of Refugee Relief*. Oxford: Oxford University Press 2015.

Shuck, Peter. "Refugee Burden-Sharing: A Modest Proposal." *Yale Journal of International Law* 22, no. 243 (1997): 243–97.

Skogstad, Grace. "Policy Networks and Policy Communities: Conceptualizing State-Societal Relationships in the Policy Process." In Linda White et al., eds., *The Comparative Turn in Canadian Political Science*, 205–20. Vancouver: University of British Columbia Press 2008.

Skran, Claudena M. *Refugees in Inter-War Europe: The Emergence of a Regime*. Oxford: Oxford University Press 1995.

Simon, Herbert. "Human Nature in Politics: The Dialogue of Psychology with Political Science." *American Political Science Review* 79, no. 2 (1985): 293–304.

Smith, Andrew F. *Rescuing the World: The Life and Times of Leo Cherne*. New York: SUNY Press 2012.

Smith, Martin J. *Pressure, Power, and Policy: State Autonomy and States*. Edinburgh: Edinburgh University Press 2007.

Somerville, Will, and Sara Wallace Goodman. "The Role of Networks in the Development of UK Migration Policy." *Political Studies* 58, no. 5 (4 November 2010): 951–70.

Soysal, Yasemin Nuhoglu. *Limits of Citizenship: Migrants and Postnational Membership in Europe*. Chicago: University of Chicago Press 1994.

Special Joint Committee of the Senate and the House of Commons on Immigration Policy: Report to Parliament, 11 December 1975. Ottawa: Queen's Printer for Canada.

Stamatov, Peter. *The Origins of Global Humanitarianism: Religion, Empires, and Advocacy*. New York: Cambridge University Press 2013.

Steinmo, Sven, Kathleen Thelen, and Frank Longstreth, eds. *Structuring Politics: Historical Institutionalism in Comparative Analysis*. Cambridge: Cambridge University Press 1992.

Stenning, Ronald E. *Church World Service: Fifty Years of Help and Hope*. New York: Friendship Press 1996.

Stoessinger, John George. *The Refugee and the World Community*. Minneapolis: University of Minnesota Press 1956.

Suhrke, Astri. "Burden-Sharing during Refugee Emergencies: The Logic of Collective Versus National Action." *Journal of Refugee Studies* 11, no. 4 (1998): 396–415.

Teitelbaum, Michael S. "Immigration, Refugees, and Foreign Policy." *International Organization* 38, no. 3 (1984): 429–50.

Thelen, Kathleen. "Historical Institutionalism in Comparative Politics." *Annual Review of Political Science* 2 (1999): 369–404.

– *How Institutions Evolve: The Political Economy of Skills in Germany, Britain, the United States, and Japan*. Cambridge: Cambridge University Press 2004.

Thelen, Kathleen, and Sven Steinmo. "Historical Institutionalism in Comparative Politics." In Sven Steinmo, Kathleen Thelen, and Frank Longstreth, eds., *Structuring Politics: Historical Institutionalism in Comparative Analysis*, 1–31. Cambridge: Cambridge University Press 1992.

Thielemann, Eiko, and Nadine El-Enany, "Refugee Protection as a Collective Action Problem: Is the EU Shirking Its Responsibilities?" *European Security* 19, no. 2 (June 2010): 209–29.

Thompson, Andrew S. *In Defence of Principles: NGOs and Human Rights in Canada*. Vancouver: University of British Columbia Press 2010.

Thompson, Andrew S., and Stephanie Bangarth. "Transnational Christian Charity: The Canadian Council of Churches, the World Council of Churches, and the Hungarian Refugee Crisis, 1956–1957." *American Review of Canadian Studies* 38, no. 3 (October 2008): 295–316.

Thompson, Michael G. *For God and Globe: Christian Internationalism in the United States between the Great War and the Cold War*. Ithaca, NY: Cornell University Press 2015.

Tichenor, Daniel J. *Dividing Lines: The Politics of Immigration Control in America*. Princeton, NJ: Princeton University Press 2002.

– "The Historical Presidency: Lyndon Johnson's Ambivalent Reform: The Immigration and Nationality Act of 1965." *Presidential Studies Quarterly* 46, no. 3 (September 2016): 691–705.

Treviranus, Barbara, and Michael Casasola. "Canada's Private Sponsorship of Refugees Program: A Practitioners Perspective of Its Past and

Future." *Journal of International Migration and Integration / Revue de l'Integration et de la Migration Internationale* 4, no. 2 (2003): 177–202.

Triadafilopoulos, Triadafilos. *Becoming Multicultural: Immigration and the Politics of Membership in Canada and Germany*. Vancouver: University of British Columbia Press 2012.

– "Global Norms, Domestic Institutions and the Transformation of Immigration Policy in Canada and the US." *Review of International Studies* 36, no. 1 (January 1, 2010): 169–93.

Troper, Harold. "Canada and Hungarian Refugees: The Historical Context." In Christopher Adam et al., ed., *The 1956 Hungarian Revolution: Hungarian and Canadian Perspectives*, 176–93. Ottawa: University of Ottawa Press 2010.

– "Canada's Immigration Policy since 1945." *International Journal* 48, no. 2 (1993): 255–81.

Truman, David Bicknell. *The Governmental Process: Political Interests and Public Opinion*. New York: Knopf 1951.

Truman, Harry S. "Statement and Directive by the President on Immigration to the United States of Certain Displaced Persons and Refugees in Europe." 22 December 1945. Accessed 19 December 2016. www.presidency.ucsb.edu/ws/index.php?pid=12253.

Tversky, Amos, and Daniel Kahneman. "Rational Choice and the Framing of Decisions," *Journal of Business* 59, no. 4 (1986): 251–78.

United States Displaced Persons Commission, *Memo to America: The DP Story, the Final Report of the United States Displaced Persons Commission*. Washington, DC: Government Printing Office 1952.

"The United States and the Holocaust, 1942–45, United States Holocaust Memorial Museum, www.ushmm.org/wlc/en/article.php?ModuleId=10007094.

Walch, Timothy, ed. *Herbert Hoover and Dwight D. Eisenhower: A Documentary History*. New York: Palgrave Macmillan 2013.

Wald, Kenneth D., Adam L. Silverman, and Kevin S. Fridy. "Making Sense of Religion in Political Life." *Annual Review of Political Science* 8, no. 1 (15 June 2005): 121–43.

Wilson, James Q. *Political Organizations*, rev. ed. Princeton, NJ: Princeton University Press 1995.

Wimmer, Andreas, and Nina Glick Schiller. "Methodological Nationalism and Beyond: Nation-State Building, Migration and the Social Sciences." *Global Networks* 2, no. 4 (2002): 301–34.

Wood, John. "East Indians and Canada's New Immigration Policy." *Canadian Public Policy* 4, no. 4 (autumn 1978): 547–67.

Wyman, David S. *The Abandonment of the Jews: America and the Holocaust, 1941–1945*. New York: Pantheon Books 1984.
– *Barring the Gates to America*. New York: Garland Science 1990.
– *DPs: Europe's Displaced Persons, 1945–51*. Ithaca, NY: Cornell University Press 1998.
Zolberg, Aristide R. *A Nation by Design: Immigration Policy in the Fashioning of America*. Cambridge, MA: Harvard University Press 2009.
– "The Roots of American Refugee Policy." *Social Research* 55, no. 4 (1 December 1988): 649–78.
Zubovich, Gene. "For Human Rights Abroad, against Jim Crow at Home: The Political Mobilization of American Ecumenical Protestants in the World War II Era." *Journal of American History* 105, no. 2 (1 September 2018): 267–90.
Zucker, Norman L. "Refugee Resettlement in the United States: Policy and Problems." *Annals of the American Academy of Political and Social Science* 467 (1 May 1983): 172–86.
Zucker, Norman L., and Naomi Flink Zucker. *The Guarded Gate: The Reality of American Refugee Policy*. New York: Harcourt 1987.

Index

Abella, Irving, 53, 74
absorptive capacity, 75
Adelman, Howard, 13, 153
Allende, Salvador, 124, 131
American Christian Committee for German Refugees (ACCR), 33–5
American Committee of the World Council of Churches, 35
American Council of Voluntary Agencies for Foreign Service, 32, 43, 60, 164; creation of the Citizens Committee on Displaced Persons, 62; implementing the 1948 Displaced Persons Act, 68–70; Joint Council on Resettlement, 43, 69; lobbying for immigration reform, 117, 139, 145; Migration and Refugee Affairs Committee, 115, 143; policy community, 110, 115; resettlement of Hungarian refugees, 92; role in the Citizens Commission on Indochinese Refugees, 143; World Refugee Year, 97
American Federation of Labor, 95
American Jewish Committee, 32, 40; appointment of special liaisons with the U.S. Army, 60; Immigration Committee, 42, 62; lobbying to admit displaced persons, 41–2, 60–1; relationship to World Refugee Year, 97; role in the Citizens Commission on Indochinese Refugees, 143; role in the Citizens Committee on Displaced Persons, 42, 62
Amin, Idi, 130
Amnesty International, 124
Andras, Robert, 148–50
Anglican Church, 48, 127, 131, 159
Anker, Deborah, 139
anti-Communism, 86; influence on refugee policy, 94; role in selection of refugees, 89
Anti-Defamation League: role in the Citizens Commission on Indochinese Refugees, 143
antisemitism: among bureaucrats, 13, 77, 101; in Congress, 18, 57, 60, 64, 66; public opinion, 29,

54, 58; among religious groups, 39, 96; in the U.S. State Department, 30
Approved Church Program, 53, 82–3, 87, 98, 99, 162, 164; attempt to reinstate the program, 105–8; discontinuation of the program, 103–4, 113, 126
Arendt, Hannah, 26
Atkey, Ron, 156, 158
Axworthy, Lloyd, 159–60

B'nai Brith, 152
Bahá'ís, 16
Baptist World Alliance, 53
Barnett, Gordon, 157
Barnett, Michael, 123
Basok, Tanya, 46
Baumgartner, Frank, 20
Beaverbrae, 79
Berger, Peter, 22
Betts, Alexander, 12
Betts, Katherine, 122
Beyer, Jürgen, 109
Blair, Frederick, 46
Bloom, Sol, 41
Bon Tempo, Carl, 9, 120, 125
Brown, Anastasia, 9
Brzezinski, Zbigniew, 144
Bumsted, J.M., 51
burden sharing, 11–13, 20
bureaucracy: cooperation with groups, 19, 59; inter-bureau politics, 19; in Westminster system, 19

Cambodian refugees. *See* Indochinese refugees
Canadian Catholic Conference, 50; Migration Commission, 152

Canadian Christian Council for Resettlement of Refugees, 47, 52–3, 57, 79; Hungarian refugee program, 101; proposal of a church-sponsorship program, 80; role in the Close Relatives Program, 79–81
Canadian Committee for World Refugee Year, 104–5, 107
Canadian Council of Churches, 47–9; attempt to reinstate the Approved Church Program, 106, 108; commentary on the Green Paper, 150; embrace of refugee resettlement, 49–50; Hungarian resettlement program, 88, 100–1; initiation of a refugee-sponsorship program, 80–1; Inter-Church Committee on Human Rights in Latin America, 132–3; lobbying to admit Chilean refugees, 133, 137; lobbying to admit Chinese refugees, 126; lobbying to admit Indochinese refugees, 159; membership in the Committee for the Repeal of the Chinese Immigration Act, 49; memo to Prime Minister William Lyon Mackenzie King, 49–50
Canadian Jewish Congress, 47, 53–4; advocacy for refugees, 56, 72, 126; correspondence with the American Jewish Congress, 40–1; involvement in the Canadian National Committee for Refugees, 55; lobbying William Lyon Mackenzie King, 45, 54; sponsorship of refugees, 80–1, 137

Canadian League of Nations Society, 55
Canadian Lutheran World Relief, 47, 51; membership in the Canadian Christian Council for Resettlement of Refugees, 53, 79; relationship with Lutheran World Relief, 53
Canadian Mennonite Board of Colonization, 47, 51, 79
Canadian National Committee on Refugees, 47, 48, 55, 73; advocacy for refugees, 72–4
Capoccia, Giovanni, 165
Carroll, Coleman Bishop, 114
Carter, Jimmy, 147; use of parole authority, 143–5
Carter administration, 142
Carusi, Ugo, 71
Casanova, José, 22
Catholic Action, 36
Catholic Committee for Refugees, 32, 37–8. *See also* National Catholic Welfare Conference
Catholic Conference (United States), 32, 142, 145, 146
Catholic Immigrant Aid Society, 47, 51; advocacy for Hungarian refugees, 100; membership in the Canadian Christian Council for Resettlement of Refugees, 79
Catholic Immigration Commission (Holy See), 50–1
Catholic Immigration Service, 47, 50
Catholic Relief Services, 32; resettlement of displaced persons, 66; resettlement of Cuban refugees, 115–16; USEP contracts, 89; World Refugee Year, 88, 97

Catholic Worker, 36
Cavert, Samuel McCrea, 34
Celler, Emanuel, 3, 41, 95–6, 117
Chamberlain, Joseph P., 43
Cherne, Leo, 142–3
Chilean refugees, 113, 131–4, 152
Chile coup, 113, 123, 131, 148, 152
Chinese immigrants: exclusion of, 11, 88; from Hong Kong, 113, 126, 127
Chinese Immigration Act (1885), 44
Choquette, Robert, 50
Church Sponsorship Plan, 80–1
Christian Century, 143
Christian Social Council of Canada. *See* Canadian Council of Churches
Church World Service, 32, 35, 36, 97, 142; accreditation to the Displaced Persons Commission, 71; cooperation with American Christian Committee for German Refugees, 35; formation of the Joint Council on Resettlement, 69; government subsidies, 110; immigration reform, 119, 140; implementation of the Displaced Persons Act, 68, 70; lobbying to admit Chilean refugees, 125; planning to resettle displaced persons, 67; resettlement of Cuban refugees, 115–16; resettlement of Hungarian refugees, 92; USEP contracts, 89; World Refugee Year, 97
Citizens Commission on Indochinese Refugees, 143
Citizens Committee on Displaced Persons, 32, 42, 62–3, 164; criticism of the Displaced Persons

Act (1948), 68, 70; framing of the refugee issue, 62, 63; influence on Displaced Persons Act of 1948, 63, 165; model for the Citizens Commission on Indochinese Refugees, 143; planning to resettle refugees, 67; position on the Stratton Bill, 67
Clark, Joe, 155–6, 159
Collier, David, 163
Collier, Ruth, 163
Committee of Industrial Organization, 95
Committee of Organizations Concerned for Refugees, 158
Committee for the Repeal of the Chinese Immigration Act, 49
Commonweal, 36
corporate affidavit, 31, 61. *See also* Truman Directive
corporatism, 6, 17, 20
counterfactuals, 165–6
critical juncture, 17, 84, 163, 165; and path dependency, 17, 163; after Second World War, 6
Cuban Refugee Committee, 114
Cuban Refugee Emergency Center, 115
Cuban refugees, 113, 135; admission under presidential parole authority, 114, 121; Cuban Refugee Program, 115–16, 164; Mariel boatlift, 148
Cuban Status Adjustment Act, 117. *See also* parole authority
Cullen, Bud, 155
Czechoslovakian refugees, 113, 121–2, 129–30, 134, 136, 166

Department of Citizenship and Immigration (1950–66), 83; attempt to reinstate the Approved Church Program, 105–8; discontinuation of the Approved Church Program, 103–4, 136; role in the Hungarian refugee policy process, 99, 101; World Refugee Year, 104–5
Department of Employment and Immigration (1977–91): development of the private refugee sponsorship program, 152–3; Indochinese refugee program, 153–61
Department of External Affairs, 11; tensions with the Immigration Branch, 45–6, 73, 105; World Refugee Year, 105
Department of Manpower and Immigration (1966–77), 127–8; drafting of the White Paper on Immigration, 128; hearings on the Green Paper, 150; refugee programs, 129, 137
Department of Mines and Resources (1936–50), 11, 46; Immigration-Labour Committee, 76. *See also* Immigration Branch
Diefenbaker, John, 103, 126
Dirks, Gerald, 45, 103
displaced persons: lobbying by the American Jewish Committee, 41, 61; lobbying by the Canadian Council of Churches, 49–50; lobbying by Church World Service, 36; lobbying by the National Catholic Welfare Conference, 62; repatriation, 10; resettlement, 4,

36, 43, 58, 80; response by Pope Pius XII, 37, 38
Displaced Persons Act (1948), 36, 42, 44, 68–9, 89, 165; Ferguson-Graham-Kilgore amendments, 70; lobbying by the Citizens Committee on Displaced Persons, 42, 63, 68, 70; role of Christian groups, 69, 84
Displaced Persons Commission, 44, 69, 71
Duplessis, Maurice, 45

Eckl, Jan, 123
ecumenical movement, 33–6, 48–9, 96; Ecumenical Secretariat for Refugees, 34; Oxford Conference, 34; role in supporting Church World Service, 36. *See also* World Council of Churches
Eisenhower, Dwight: appointment of Tracy S. Voorhees, 89–90, 114–15; proclamation in support of World Refugee Year, 97; resettlement of Cuban refugees, 114–16; resettlement of Hungarian refugees, 90; use of parole authority, 90–1, 114, 117
Electoral Franchise Act (1885), 44
Elliott, Roland, 97
Évian conference, 29

Fairclough, Ellen, 104, 105–7, 125, 127
Fair Share Act (1960), 12, 97, 120
Federal Council of Churches, 32, 36, 42, 62; correspondence with President Truman, 62; creation of Church World Service, 34–5;

meeting with President Roosevelt, 30. *See also* National Council of Churches
Federation of Polish Jews, 56
feedback effects, 17, 25, 59, 85, 109, 161, 163; increasing returns, 87; learning and coordinating effects, 87
Feighan, Michael A., 120
Fellows, Frank, 65, 67
Ford, Gerald, 141
Foreign Missions Conference, 35
Fortier, Laval, 82
Fortune magazine, 29
Freeman, Gary, 122
Fulton, E.D, 103–4

Gallagher, Rev. W.J., 49
Geneva Convention. *See* United Nations Convention Relating to the Status of Refugees
Genizi, Haim, 38, 42, 62
German Baptist Immigration and Colonization Society, 47, 51, 79
Gibney, Matthew, 11, 59
Gibson, John W., 71
Gilmour, Julie, 13
Globe and Mail, 130, 156
Gotlieb, Allan, 148–9
Green, Alan, 74
Green Paper, 127, 133, 149–51
Greif, Mark, 26

Hacker, Jacob, 85
Harrison, Earl, 41, 42, 62
Hart-Celler Act (1965). *See* Immigration Reform Act (1965)
Hathaway, James, 13
Hawkins, Freda, 9, 56, 99, 126

Hayes, Saul, 100. *See also* Canadian Jewish Congress
Health, Education and Welfare, Department of
Hebrew Immigrant Aid Society (HIAS), 32, 40, 142; accreditation to the Displaced Persons Commission, 71; comment on decline of refugee resettlement, 168; formation of the Joint Council on Resettlement, 69; immigration reform, 119, 140; implementation of the Displaced Persons Act, 68–70; lobbying for resettlement of Soviet Jews, 123–4; resettlement of Cuban refugees, 115; resettlement of Hungarian refugees, 92; World Refugee Year, 97
Herzer, T.O.F., 78
Howe, C.D., 74, 75
human rights: genealogy, 26, 39; and refugee policy, 14–15, 111, 122–5, 134–6
Human Rights Watch, 123
Hungarian Federation, 99
Hungarian refugees: resettlement in Canada, 102–3, 156; resettlement in the United States, 92, 135, 164
Hungary: refugee crisis, 86–7; Soviet invasion, 86

Intergovernmental Committee for European Migration, 126
International Catholic Migration Commission, 37
Immigration Act (1906), 44
Immigration Act (1910), 44
Immigration Act (1976), 7, 9, 151, 157, 160, 162, 164
Immigration Branch (Canada): role in policymaking, 45, 53, 72–4; tension with the Department of External Affairs, 46, 73
Immigration and Nationality Act (1952), 97, 139, 144; parole-authority statute, 90. *See also* parole authority
Immigration Reform Act (1965), 113, 119–21; seventh preference, 121
Indochina Inter-Agency Task Force, 141
Indochina Migration and Refugee Assistance Act (1975), 141
Indochinese refugees, 140; Hai Hong, 138, 154–5; resettlement in Canada, 138, 153–61; resettlement in the United States, 138, 141–5, 147
Inter-Church Committee on Human Rights in Latin America. *See* Canadian Council of Churches
International Refugee Organization, 10, 52, 64, 75, 78
International Rescue Committee, 43, 142, 143; resettlement of Cuban refugees, 115; resettlement of Hungarian refugees, 92; World Refugee Year, 97
issue framing, 60, 74
issue network, 17–18; breakdown of issue network in Canada, 113–14, 126, 136; creation of issue network in Canada, 107–8, 110–11; re-establishment of

issue network in Canada, 133–4, 137, 160

Jacobsen, David, 14
Janzen, William, 152, 157
Jewish Immigrant Aid Services (JIAS), 47, 53–4, 57, 107, 129; Green Paper process, 150; Hungarian resettlement program, 88, 100–1; private refugee sponsorship, 152; resettlement of refugees, 56; USEP contracts, 89
Jewish Joint Distribution Committee, 32, 40; assistance to Jewish community of Canada, 56, 81; collaboration with the War Refugee Board, 31; meeting with President Roosevelt, 30; support for the American Christian Committee for German Refugees, 33; USEP contracts, 89
Jewish Peoples' Relief Committee, 56
John XXIII, Pope, 96; encyclical *Pacem in Terris*, 118
Johnson, Lyndon: immigration reform, 118–19, 121; parole of Cuban refugees, 121
Joint Committee for Evangelization of Canadian Life. *See* Canadian Council of Churches
Joint Council on Resettlement. *See* American Council of Voluntary Agencies for Foreign Service
Jones, Bryan, 20
Jordan, Grant, 18
Judd, Rev. Canon, 80
Judiciary Committee (U.S. House of Representatives), 3, 42, 118, 122

Judiciary Committee (U.S. Senate), 67, 121–2, 142, 145

Kage, Joseph, 128
Keenleyside, H.L., 76, 80
Kelemen, R.D., 165
Kelley, Ninette, 9, 45
Kennedy, John F., 115–16, 118, 119
Kennedy, Ted, 124, 139, 142, 145–7
Kerwin, Donald, 168
Kilmer, Camp, 92–3
King, William Lyon Mackenzie: meeting with Canadian Jewish Congress, 54; resistance to admitting refugees, 45, 75; speech to the House of Commons, 75
Kingdon, John, 58
Kissinger, Henry, 122, 123, 135, 141
Knowles, Valerie, 99, 156

Labman, Shauna, 9
Lacroix, Patrick, 50
LaGuardia, Fiorello, 63
League of Nations, 5
League of Nations Society, 73
Leibowitz, Arnold, 139
Levi, Margaret, 17
Life Magazine, 3, 63
Lipset, Seymour, 6
Loescher, Gil, 59, 64, 121, 122, 144
Lutheran Immigration and Refugee Service, 168
Lutheran World Federation, 35; resettlement of Hungarian refugees, 92; World Refugee Year, 97
Lutheran World Relief, 53

MacDonald, Flora, 155–6, 158
Madokoro, Laura, 11, 130, 131, 161
Manion, Jack, 152
Marshall, George, 63, 64
McCarran, Pat, 68, 94
McDonald, James G., 33
Meissner, Doris M., 148
Mennonite Central Committee, 53
Mennonite Central Committee of Canada, 7, 157–8, 164; relationship with the Mennonite Central Committee, 53
Michener, James, 93
Migration and Refugee Assistance Act (1962), 114
Mitchell, John, 122
Molloy, Michael, 131, 152, 156, 161
Montreal Gazette, 156
Morganthau, Jr, Henry, 30
Moyn, Samuel, 26, 123
Murray, George, 36, 116

Nagy, Imre, 86, 89
National Catholic Resettlement Council, 39–40, 67
National Catholic Welfare Conference, 32, 61; accreditation to the Displaced Persons Commission, 71; advocacy to raise immigration quotas, 62; establishment of the Catholic Committee for Refugees, 37; formation of the Joint Council on Resettlement, 69; immigration reform, 118–19, 140; implementation of the Displaced Persons Act, 68; resettlement of Hungarian refugees, 92; support for the Fellows Bill, 67

National Council of Churches, 32, 35; immigration reform, 118; publication of "Improve our Immigration Law," 94–5. *See also* Federal Council of Churches
National Council of Jewish Women, 143
National Interfaith Immigration Committee, 129, 137
National Lutheran Council, 32, 71
national-origins quota system, 65, 89, 91, 95; removal of quota system, 119; support for abolition, 95, 117–18
National Refugee Service, 43, 61. *See also* United Service for New Americans
National Security Council, 143
Neve, Alexander, 13
New York Times, 63, 143
Nixon, Richard: use of parole authority, 121–2, 124–5; foreign policy, 123, 135

O'Connor, Edward M., 71
Office of Migration (Holy See), 37
Oldham, J.H., 34
Operation Lifeline, 156, 159
Oppressed Minority policy, 133, 151
orders-in-council: PC 695 (1931), 44–5; PC 2071 (1946), 51–2, 77–81; PC 2180 (1947), 76. *See also* Bulk Labour Program; Close Relatives Program

parole authority: consultation between executive and Congress, 122; Fair Share Act, 97; Immigration and Nationality Act

(1952), 119–21; use to admit Cuban refugees, 114, 117, 121; use to resettle Czechoslovakian refugees, 122; use to resettle Hungarian refugees, 90–1, 94; use to resettle Indochinese refugees, 138, 143–5
path dependence, 17, 87, 109
Patterson, Robert, 63
Pearson, Lester B., 99, 127, 128
personalism, 26, 34, 39, 65, 123
Pickersgill, J.W., 83, 99, 100–2
Pierson, Paul, 85
Pinochet, Augusto, 123, 124, 131
Pius XII, Pope, 37
pluralism, 16–17
policy community, 17–18; effects on path dependence, 87, 113; insider status, 109–10, 136; shared view of the refugee, 114–15; status quo bias, 20
policy conversion, 85
policy cycle, 58; agenda setting, 58, 59–63, 72–4; decision making, 58, 65–70, 76–8; policy implementation, 58–9, 70–2, 78–84; policy formulation, 58, 63–5, 74–6
policy image, 18
political opportunity structures, 22, 27, 28, 46–7, 57
Pontifical Commission for Relief, 37
Posner, Michael, 139
Presidential Advisory Committee on Refugees (Indochinese), 141
President's Committee for Hungarian Refugee Relief Refugee Relief Act (1953), 91–4
Price, Matthew, 10
private refugee sponsorship, 5, 7, 19–20; development of program after 1976 Immigration Act, 138–9, 152–3, 156–8; early models, 56–7, 78–82, 87, 102–9, 111, 113–14, 136–7, 152; establishment in the 1976 Immigration Act, 7, 151–3; family migration, 85, 166; Green Paper discussions, 133–4; Hungarian program, 102–4, 111; Master Agreements, 158, 160; proposal by JIAS, 150; role of the Chilean refugee crisis, 133–4; role in the Indochinese refugee crisis, 139, 156–62; World Refugee Year, 106–8, 111, 125–6. *See also* Approved Church Program
public goods, 11–12

quiet politics, 40, 42
Quinn, Archbishop John, 146
Quota Law (1924), 61

race thinking, 11, 108
Refugee Act (1980), 7, 91, 122, 136, 139, 145–8, 162, 164, 167
Refugee Relief Act (1953), 89–90
religious groups: characteristics, 27–9; declining resources, 167; distinction from interest groups, 23, 27, 28; historical role in humanitarianism and relief, 4, 16, 21, 37; as political variable, 23–4
Revercomb, Chapman, 67
Robinson, Leland Rex, 34
Rodino, Peter, 122
Roosevelt, Eleanor, 63
Roosevelt, Franklin Delano, 29–30

Rosenberg, Edwin, 61
Rosenfield, Harry N., 71
Rural Settlement Society, 47, 51;
    Hungarian refugee program, 101

Saint Laurent, Louis, 103
St Louis, 45
Samson, Hugh, 96
Sauer, Angelika, 53
Save the Children, 43
Scanlan, John, 59, 64, 121, 122, 144
Schmitter, Philippe, 17
Schwartz, Abba, 119, 120
Scribner, Todd, 9
secularization, 22, 34
Shah, T.S., 22
Shaw, Caroline, 4
Shuck, Peter, 13
Silcox, Rev. Claris, 48
Simmons, Alan, 46
Skran, Claudena, 31
Smith, Martin, 110
social movement theory, 27–9
Soviet Jewish refugees: emigration, 123; resettlement, 123–4, 152
Soysal, Yasemin Nuhoglu, 14
Special Joint Committee of the Senate and House of Commons, 150–1
State Department: dependence on voluntary groups, 142; influence of restrictionists, 30; subsidization of Hungarian refugee program, 92; support of presidential parole, 144
Stratton, William, 63; Stratton Bill, 63–4, 65, 67, 69, 70
Suhrke, Astri, 12

Swanstrom, Edward, 66, 88, 120, 145

Teitelbaum, Michael, 10
Thelen, Kathleen, 85
Thompson, Andrew, 4, 49
de Tocqueville, Alexis, 169
Toronto Star, 154
Treasury Department, U.S.; 1944 report on Jewish refugees, 30
Trebilcock, Michael, 9, 45
Tremblay, René, 127
Triadafilopoulos, Triadafilos, 15, 16, 151
Troper, Harold, 53, 103, 130
Trudeau, Pierre Elliott, 150, 153, 154, 155
Truman, Harry S., 64, 70, 165
Truman Directive (1945), 31, 33, 35, 37, 38, 40, 41, 46, 61, 64, 69: assurances, 89; influence on Canada, 73
Tuchman, Jessica, 143

Ugandan refugees, 130–1, 166
United Church of Canada, 48, 127, 131, 159
United Jewish Appeal, 33
United Jewish Relief Agencies, 47, 55
United Nations Convention Relating to the Status of Refugees, 15, 63, 128, 129, 151; 1967 Protocol, 15, 129
United Nations High Commissioner for Refugees (UNHCR), 126, 127; Hungarian refugee program, 99; refugee-status determination, 15; role in

the Comprehensive Plans of Action, 12
United Service for New Americans, 32, 43; accreditation to the Displaced Persons Commission, 71; involvement in implementing the 1948 Displaced Persons Act, 70
United States Escapee Program (USEP) (1952), 89

Vance, Cyrus, 144
Vatican Information Service, 37
Vietnamese refugees. *See* Indochinese refugees
Voorhees, Tracy S., 91–3; appointment as president's coordinator for Hungarian refugee and relief work, 89–90; appointment as president's representative for Cuban refugees, 114–15

Wall Street Journal, 143
Walter, Francis, 97, 119
Walter, Ingrid, 145
War Refugee Board, 30–1
War Relief Control Board, 38
War Relief Services, 32, 38–9. *See also* National Catholic Welfare Conference
Washington Post, 63, 64, 93

White Paper on Immigration, 127–9, 149
Wiley, Alexander, 67
Wilson, Senator Cairine, 55, 75
Wood, John, 151
World Council of Churches, 32, 34–5; collaboration with Church World Service, 35; Department of Inter-Church Aid and Service to Refugees, 34; involvement in World Refugee Year, 88, 96; networks in Chile, 133; relationship with the Canadian Christian Council for Resettlement of Refugees, 53; relationship with the Canadian Council of Churches, 48–9, 80, 132–3
World Refugee Year, 88, 96–7, 104–5, 112, 135, 139; private-sponsorship program, 106–8, 125–6
Wyman, David, 77

YMCA, 43

Zolberg, Aristide, 10
Zucker, Naomi, 158
Zucker, Norman, 9, 168